Social Advertising and Youth

Social Advertising and Youth

Dr. G.Y. Shitole
Dr. Bangeshree P.B.B.

ADHYAYAN

ADHYAYAN PUBLISHERS & DISTRIBUTORS
NEW DELHI (INDIA)

Published by

ADHYAYAN PUBLISHERS & DISTRIBUTORS

4378/4B, 105, J.M.D. House, Murari Lal Street
Ansari Road Darya Ganj, New Delhi - 110002
Ph.: 011-23263018, 011-23277156, Fax: 011-23280028
Email: adhyayanpublishers@yahoo.com

Social Advertising and Youth

Edition 2011
ISBN 978-81-8435-265-8

Printed in India

Published by Harish Chandra Yadav for Adhyayan Publishers & Distributors, Laser Typeseting at A.V. Rao and Printed at Tarun Offset Printers, Delhi

FOREWORD

AMITABH BACHCHAN

"Advertising" ministers to the spiritual side of trade. It is 'great power' that has been entrusted to your keeping, which charges you with the high responsibility of inspiring and ennobling the commercial world. It is all part of the greater work of the regeneration and redemption of mankind.

At most times rational arguments are not enough to change behaviour or attitudes. Social advertisements use the wide range of emotions to influence one's behaviour. It can arouse feelings of fear, love, pleasure, vanity, anger or, make one laugh.

Social advertising invites us to help others and warn us against dangerous behaviour or prod us to change behaviour for our own good. First and foremost an advertisement has to catch your attention. One way in which it does this is by appealing to your emotions.

Changing behaviour is not an easy task. It requires strategic work, engagement and understanding of human motivations. People do not exist in a vacuum. Advertising alone, will never change or shape human behaviour and attitudes. All gimmicks are allowed to catch people's attention, but they are not enouhg. Getting people to laugh and cry does not guarantee they will take action

The primary aim of 'social marketing' is 'social good', while in 'commercial marketing' the aim is primarily 'financial'. This does not mean that commercial marketers can not or not contribute to achievement of social good.

Bageshree's research has led her to the conclusion that celebrities has an impact on youth and they must be used in social advertising. All celebrities who are asked to shoulder this responsibility should bear in mind how poweful their influence is on young budding intellect. May they always use this power for the development and progress of our future citizens. "Jai Hind"

Amitabh Bachchan

Amb:pd:jaisa

PRATIKSHA JUHU MUMBAI 400 049

PREFACE

Advertising is a fascinating and provocative phenomenon. At the outset it is used by many advertisers for many purposes with many different possible effects. In this book the authors have concentrated on the social side of advertising, where in the intents of such advertising ranges from altering behaviour to affecting the way people think about a particular social or economic position. The book *Social Advertising and Youth* is a full length research based volume highlighting on the holistic side of advertising, purely aimed at general welfare often tagged as Social Advertising.

In the recent times, the Indian media is flooded with social advertising waged by Government, NGOs, Corporate and Media houses. Host of social issues such as Polio, H1N1 Flu, AIDS, need for immunization and cleanliness awareness are commonly flaunted on various media. Many popular faces belonging to films, sports and television are regularly seen pleading to the populace for adopting or changing to socially desirable behaviour. In spite of using mass media and familiar faces the social advertising in India barring a few fail to make any mark. After careful observation several reasons can be attributed for the failure of these social advertisements.

The authors through this book have made an attempt in identifying the factors that could aid in making social advertisements effective and capable enough to change or alter the audience's behaviour. Accordingly five such factors viz. celebrity, fear appeals, clutter, medium and repetition were extensively studied for their impact. Youth constitute an important segment of our society and social advertising can be an entertaining and educative tool for addressing their issues. The authors have therefore laid their focus on the urban youth and made an attempt to study it through different dimensions.

The fascinating revelation of social advertising shall elicit interest among students, teachers and academicians.The advertisers, media planners, advertising agencies and media owners involved in the process of advertising can find valuable facets of social advertising which can be utilized to make their social advertising more fruitful. This book shall be a useful aid as a reference material to researchers in similar or allied fields as well.

Dr. G.Y. Shitole

Dr. Bageshree P.B.B

LIST OF TABLES

LIST OF GRAPHS

LIST OF CHARTS

ABBREVIATIONS

ADAG .... Anil Dhirubhai Ambani Group
AIDS .... Acquired Immune Deficiency Syndrome
AIR .... All India Radio
A M .... Amplitude Modulation
AME .... Advertising and Marketing Effectiveness
AV .... Audio and Visual
BBC .... British Broadcasting Corporation
BBCWST ...... British Broadcasting Corporation World Service
.... Trust
CBA .... Commercial Broadcasting Association
CBS .... Commercial Broadcasting Service
CEO .... Chief Executive Officer
CPAA .... Cancer Patients Aid Association
CSR .... Corporate Social Responsibility
DANIDA .... Danish International Development Agency
DAR .... Day After Recall
DAVP .... Directorate of Audio Visual Publicity
DCD .... Development Communication Division
DD .... Doordarshan
DFP .... Directorate of Field Publicity
DNA .... Daily Newspaper and Analysis
DOTS .... Directly Observed Treatment, Short-course
DTH .... Direct-To-Home
ENIL .... Entertainment Network India Limited
FM .... Frequency Modulation

GMAI .... Global Media AIDS Initiative
GNP .... Gross National Product
HIV .... Human Immunodeficiency Virus
IOCL .... Indian Oil Corporation Limited
IPRA .... International Public Relations Association
IRDA .... Insurance Regulatory Development Authority of India
ITC .... Indian Tobacco Company
ITPO .... India Trade Promotion Organisation
LCD .... Liquid Crystal Display
MCGM .... Municipal Corporation of Greater Mumbai
MoRD .... Ministry of Rural Development
NACO .... National AIDS Control Organisation
NDA .... National Democratic Alliance
NGO .... Non Government Organisation
NIE .... Newspaper in Education
NORAD .... Norwegian Agency for International Development
NTPC .... National Thermal Power Corporation
O & M .... Ogilvy and Mather
ONGC .... Oil and Natural Gas Corporation
PETA .... People for Ethical Treatment of Animals
PSA .... Public Service Advertising
PIMS .... Profit Impact of Marketing Strategy
PSI .... Public Service International
RAPA .... Radio and Television Practitioner's and Advertiser
.... Association
SEBI .... Securities and Exchange Board of India

SET .... Sony Entertainment Television
TCS .... Tata Consultancy Services
UN .... United Nations
UNFPA .... United Nations Fund for Population Activities
UNICEF .... United Nations International Children's Fund
UPA .... United Progressive Alliance
USAID .... United States Agency for International
.... Development
WHO .... World Health Organisation
WWF .... World Wildlife Fund

CONTENTS

1
Introduction to Social Advertising

1.1 Advertising for a Social Cause?

"Why can't you sell brotherhood like you sell soap?"[1]

In 1952, Wiebe raised this question which implied the art of selling soap or other commodities may have some bearing on the art of selling social causes or what is commonly referred as "Social Cause Advertising". Considering advertising has a role in society, the question pertinent here is, can advertising be used for bringing about a positive social change? Can advertising principles and strategies which have been extensively used for commercial purposes, foster a social cause?

Well the answer is yes, advertising can indeed be a catalyst for social change. The same promotional techniques with which it sells the products and services can be effectively employed to deliver social welfare messages too. Well crafted advertisements delivered with a blend of persuasion and appropriate appeal, backed with ample exposures shall not only make audience sit up and notice social issues but also command positive attitudinal change.

---

[1] G. D.Weibe, "Merchandising Commodities and Citizenship on Television," *Public Opinion Quarterly*, Vol. 1b, Oxford University Press, USA, (Winter, 1951-52), p. 679.

Social messages such as urging people to quit smoking or pleading public to practice safer sex are frequently heard on radio or seen on hoardings vying for attention along with commercial advertisements. Indian media today is flooded with host of social messages. Many popular faces belonging to films, sports and television are regularly seen persuading the populace to adopt socially desirable behaviour.

There are multiple social issues regularly being addressed on Indian media, yet barring a few social advertisements majority of them fail to make any mark. After careful observation several reasons can be attributed for the failure of these social advertisements. Firstly content wise social advertisements seem to be too bland. Social advertisements have limitations in terms of creativity and lack the charm to captivate audience's interest. Secondly the choice of celebrities to endorse social issues seldom coincides with the need of the social cause under question. Celebrities are often selected arbitrarily without considering the celebrity's credibility, popularity among the target audience and expertise in the respective area. As a result, the celebrity's charisma either overshadows the social issue or his/her limited popularity fails to seek required attention. Several flaws are noticed even in the conduct of social advertisements. Social advertisements and commercial advertisements are run in the same space or slot. Compared to commercial advertisements, social advertisements have fewer repetitions. As a result social advertisements fail to make any mark amidst the clutter with limited recurrence leading to poor recall of such advertisements. Again audio-video medium like television is often used sparingly for social advertising compared to print or outdoor media. The wasteful and inappropriate decisions ultimately lead to ineffective social advertisements. There is no doubt about the potentials of social advertising but considering the way they are promoted in India definitely genuine efforts seem to be missing.

From a research point of view too, social advertising has received significantly less theoretical and applied research. The study of social advertising scene in India revealed that social advertising is quite an ignored area in spite of its worthy cause. There could be several reasons for this secondary treatment it gets. Firstly it does not bring any material benefit to anybody who is involved in it. From the advertisers point of view specially in case of private companies it is just a philanthropic exercise. Many companies in India boast of their corporate social responsibility through various media. For such companies maintaining an altruistic image among its public is just a profit oriented pursuit in the long run. Many companies run social advertisements along with their regular commercial product advertisements nonetheless their insincerity is obvious from the extravagant media exposure of commercial advertisements in comparison to meager existence of social advertising amidst the clutter. The advertiser's concern and keenness in all aspects pertaining to analyzing impact and response for their products and services advertising is found to be missing when it comes to analyzing the impact of social advertising.

Advertisers like government or its ministries and non-governmental organizations are often seen assigning inadequate funds for social advertising that could produce only mediocre social advertisements which fail to seek even attention. Further their paucity also forces them to solicit assistance for creativity and media space from advertising agencies and media respectively. As a result what reaches to audience is a result of the media or advertising agency's generosity and as such made and promoted out of their convenience where advertisers hardly have any control. It is often observed that media organizations donate the space and time for social advertising but such advertisements are ordinarily relegated to status behind regular paidup advertising and often appear only as space and time becomes available. This is the reason most of the social advertisements on television appear during lesser watched day parts which ruins its purpose of reaching the appropriate audience.

In India many advertising agencies also promote social advertising. For many of these agencies advertisements with social bent are nothing but one of the means to secure a nomination for national or international advertising awards. For many years this has been a common practice in Indian advertising where social advertisements are only created for awards and they make entry to the various national and international advertising competitions without even being aired or published. Occasionally such advertisements are aired / published, but that's only for the sake of providing evidence or meeting the eligibility criteria, which rarely serves any purpose.

In short neither the advertisers, nor the media and not even the advertising agencies are earnestly interested in acquiring any feedback on the reach and impact of social advertisements. Obviously any consequential research is genuinely missing from the parties directly involved with social advertising. However, from academician's point of view one cannot sideline the educational role of social advertising. Considering the impact advertising has on its public in general one can definitely assume if done effectively social advertising can lead to positive influence on its audience. In fact, it can play a dual role; it can be entertaining and simultaneously can educate its audience. Social advertisements can reach their communication goals and bring the desired change provided the factors that make social advertising more meaningful are correctly identified and appropriately used.

1.2 Introduction to Advertising

Advertising has a long and fascinating history and has been believed to have considerable impact both good and bad on the society. Advertising has entertained, moved and motivated its audience for more than a century. Unfortunately though, its role had been under scanner for wrong reasons and its contributions have been underplayed.

Advertising is defined as any paid form of non-personal communication about an organisation, product, service or idea by an identified sponsor.[2] The paid aspect relates to the fact that the space or time for an advertising message has to be bought. The non-personal component means that advertising involves mass media like television, radio, newspaper and magazines that can transmit a message to large group of individuals at a time. This also means that there is no opportunity for any sort of immediate feedback from the recipient.[3]

Advertising is one of the elements along with others like sales promotion, salesmanship and public relation that compose promotion. Promotion is one of the four controllable elements of the marketing mix. The others being product, price and place. The basic task of marketing is combining these four elements into a marketing programme to facilitate the potential for exchange of goods and services with consumers in then marketing place.

From a service provider at a local level to a multinational in global markets, the application of advertising has been universal. Varying degrees of advertising are used by small and big advertisers. Advertising's contribution is indispensable in the marketers' promotional mixes. Companies targeting their products at mass consumer markets consider advertising as a cost effective method of communication. The consumers too rely on advertising for appropriate purchase decisions. The role of advertising in marketing over the years has undergone many changes. This has happened due to the dynamic nature of the environment in which it operates. Industrialisation, innovations in media and technological advancements have revolutionalised advertising in its conduct and spectrum as well. Since the last century there has been upsurge in

---

[2] G.Belch and M.Belch, *Advertising and Promotion: An Integrated Marketing Communications Perspective,* 6th edu., Tata McGraw-Hill Publishing Company Limited, New Delhi, 2003, p. 16.

[3] Ibid.

advertising's role in marketing strategies beyond the periphery of promotion. In the era of globalisation marketers look up to advertising integrated along with other marketing communication tools to play a more complex role of creating distinct brand images and symbolic appeals. In the highly vibrant competitive marketing situations it holds a strategic position for achieving differentiation across other elements in the marketing mix.

Advertising is not merely a marketing function but also an important economic force in society. It performs economic function for an advertiser, affects economic decisions of the audience and is an integral part of the whole economic system. Advertiser is benefited as advertising creates demand, motivates consumption, maintains and enhances brand equity and brings economies of scale. Advertising provides information utility to consumers that helps them make better economic decisions than they would otherwise. Advertising fosters economic growth by facilitating new entrants and promoting competition. Competitive forces lead to real product innovation, efficient distribution of goods and absence of inflated prices. The development of new products and improvement of existing products can mean an expanding economy with more jobs and investment opportunities and a product selection that is continually improving in breadth and quality.

In spite of its contribution, advertising has been apprehensively examined with regards to its economic effects. There is criticism that advertising is a detrimental force and that has a negative effect on competition, product costs and consumer price. It is believed that marketers use advertising to change the customer's tastes, lower their sensitivity to price and build brand loyalty among buyers of advertised brands. This results in higher profits, reduced competition and market power for larger advertisers and higher prices and fewer choices for consumers.[4]

1.2.1 Society and Advertising

Advertising is an institution within the social, ethical, economic and legal environment due to its definitive role that helps in shaping the reality it depicts. Advertising's position as an institution in society can be compared with other institutions such as marriage, family or school. Like these institutions it is influential on individuals in different ways. The institution of advertising is used to inform and persuade people about products just like schools function as institution. Advertising establishes the role of the consumer helping him or her to make judgments as to which brands to buy or use just as marriage puts people in to familial role.[5]

Advertising's supporters maintain that the message it conveys merely reflects the values of society as whole and in that manner advertising just mirrors society. Proponents of advertising say advertising reflects popular culture, depicting in advertisements such scenes or people with which the audience can relate. This also gives the audience a sense of belongingness to a larger society. It also reflects the values of the society as a whole such as the materialism or value consciousness.

In contrast according to critics of the institution, advertising is a force that is able to mold the society. The criticism of advertising concerns the specific techniques and methods used as well as its effect on societal values, tastes and lifestyles and behaviour. In fact, its ability to persuade and its presence in mass media have led to criticisms that it plays a major role in influencing and transmitting social values. It promotes materialism and in a way exerts social control over consumers without any sense of social responsibility. By promoting certain items as desirable, advertising creates unnecessary demand among people who may not need them. Advertising is even believed to be working at subliminal or

---

[4] Ibid.

[5] B. G. Bergh V. and H. Katz, *Advertising Principles*, NTC Business Books, Lincolnwood, Illinois, USA, 1999, pp. 62-63.

subconscious level, especially to persuade consumers to purchase goods that they otherwise would not buy, though of course there is no scientific evidence to this.

By depicting individuals in certain ways in the advertisements, advertising provides behavioural norms for how society should act. The impact of advertising on special audiences like children, women and youth indicates the power that institution can have on society. Advertising can shape society's beliefs by using stereotypes which reduce people or objects into classes such as race, gender, age and socio-economic status among others, based on inferences that are made from an individual or social context.

The debate on advertising's contributions and in effects on the society has been around almost as long as the field itself and it is unlikely that it would ever disappear. Critics focus more on its social role which is more than that of a mirror that reflects society but that of a social force which shapes society. On the contrary, the proponents present an economic argument that advertising benefits the society directly and indirectly, by providing employment and financing the media. The pervasiveness of advertising though makes it impossible to be but immune from its impact, either harmful or beneficial.

1.2.2 Introduction to Social Advertising

Advertising is undeniably an influential force, irrespective of whether it is believed to be a mirror of a society or a shaper of that society (or some of both). And perhaps because of that its use has been extensively noticed even in non-commercial areas beyond purely economical or marketing periphery. Social advertising is a form of advertising that is designed to educate or motivate people to undertake socially desirable actions. Advertisements meant for the general welfare on Polio eradication or AIDS awareness are commonly found along with commercial advertising on mass media. This type of advertising is generally made by government and non government organisations (NGOs) who primarily shoulder the responsibility of society's well-being, though this is not necessarily a pre-condition for social advertising. Several private companies in India are seen promoting social advertising as a part of their corporate social responsibility. Some companies undertake such social issues that are directly connected to their product or service while many others promote independent issues not connected to their line of business. The primary objective in social advertising is however social and not private gain. The only obvious benefit the advertisers enjoy is in terms of goodwill since their name appears in the advertisement as a sponsor. Contributions to social advertising are made by advertising agencies in the form of creative services which are provided at no or subsidised cost. The media contributes by way of free space or airtime.

An essential attribute of social advertising is use of emotions. Emotions in social advertising influence perception, memory and recall. They have the ability to bring about changes in attitudes and behaviour. Emotions also help people to remember the situations and messages in which they appeared. Emotions reduce criticism and rational thinking abilities and evoke physiological changes as well as changes of perception. Those changes have a strong impact on people and can motivate them to act, follow the suggestions expressed in advertising and deliver the promise of satisfaction. Social advertising covers serious and fundamental human problems like human suffering and moral choices. However, existence of social cause and emotions are not enough to ensure the desired change. Getting people to cry or laugh is not enough. The emotions need to reach the mind and for this a sustained effort for a considerable time is required to build ways to conscience and subconscious. Social advertising needs to have a longterm strategy and deep understanding of human motivations in order to achieve its goal – change in behaviour or/and attitudes. It requires both serious and genuine solutions. Social advertising has to get people thinking, talking and acting on the social problems. Effective social advertising needs to be able to ignite a social debate and provide solution for general welfare.

Social advertising is promoted for varied objectives and directed at different target audiences by various advertisers. According to the International Survey of Social Advertising there is no consensus on the terms that are used to explain advertising, which is not to promote any commercial information but to plead for a cause. The diversified objectives of different advertisers in reaching their target audience makes it all the more difficult to use one term, which satisfactorily conveys the meaning of this type of advertising. At various times, it is referred to as "Public Service", "Institutional", "Idea", "Non-product", "Social", "Advocacy" and "Public Relations" advertising. It is also referred to as Public-interest Advertising, Public Awareness Advertising, Public Service Announcements, Non-profit Advertising, Social Service Advertising, Opinion Advertising, Adversary Advertising and Cause-and-issue Advertising.[6]

Kotler[7] classifies non profit advertising into five subgroups: political advertising, social cause advertising, philanthropic organisation advertising, government organisation advertising and private non-profit organisation advertising. Though political advertising does not directly come into the purview of social advertising discussed here, all the other four forms of non-profit organisations are directly concerned with social advertising. Social cause advertising has been aided by work of the Advertising Council, started during second World War as a means of securing public support for such causes as the purchase of war

---

[6] Watson S. Dunn and Arnold M. Barban, *Advertising its Role in Modern Marketing*, 5th ed., Holt Saunders International Editions, Japan, 1982, p. 647.

[7] Philips Kotler, *Marketing for Non-Profit Organisation*, 2nd edu., Prentice Hall of India Private Ltd., New Delhi, India, 1985, pp. 356-57.

bonds, donation of blood and the enlistment of women into the armed services. Social cause advertising is primarily propagandistic in intent; it aims to persuade the public to adopt a particular point of view. Philanthropic or charitable advertising focuses on raising donations for worthwhile causes on an urgent or regular basis. The government organisation advertising relates to various state governments' and municipality's advertisements to attract tourists and new industries to their areas.[8] Advertising by units of local government, such as park commissions and police departments about recreational opportunities, local events and safety tips to the residents of the community all fall under this category. Then there are advertisements by universities, colleges, museums, symphonies, hospitals and religious organisations for various purposes. These are termed as private non-profit organisation advertising.[9]

Public relation advertising involves the use of non personal, media communication by an identified sponsor to accomplish objectives that are not related directly to products or commercial services.[10] The objectives of public relation advertising falls under two categories: image building and action inducing. Accordingly there are four types of public relations advertising and public service advertising is one of them. The rest three being institutional, advocacy and political advertising. Public service advertising is a type of public relations advertising which has a nonproduct or nonservice perspective. Its distinguishing feature is that the focus of the advertising is on some matter of importance to public welfare. The social, economic or cultural issues dealt within the advertising are worthy of public attention and often public

---

[8] J. S.Wright, W. L.Winter and S. K. Jr. Zeigler, *Advertising*, 5th edu., Tata McGraw Hill Publishing, New Delhi, 1983, pp. 497-498.

[9] Kotler Philips, op. cit.

[10] Watson S.Dunn and Arnold M.Barban, op. cit.

[11] C. H.Sandage, Vernon Fryburger and Kim Rotzoll, *Advertising Theory and Practice*, All India Traveller Book Seller, Delhi, 1987, pp. 73-75.

action. Sometimes the organisation may feel strongly about an issue and would wish to express its concern to such a cause and therefore promote issue related messages. This way it manages to generate a positive image in the minds of its audience too.

In 1980s USA witnessed a splurge in advertising which was for other than selling the product. Sandage terms such advertising as "Issue or Cause advertising" that includes three principal subspecies: public service advertising, advertorials and political advertising.[11] The advertisements primarily conducted by US based private non-profit organisation, The Advertising Council were termed as public service advertising. This organisation was responsible for conducting advertisements on worthy causes largely through the volunteer services of media and advertising organisations, advertising agencies, and thousands of individual magazines, newspaper radio station and television channels that offered their time or space to transmit the advertisements. Basically the causes it dealt in were non controversial by nature. Advertorial as explained by Sandage is another non product / service approach which is basically an expression of a position by an individual group or organisation, on a topic of some controversy through the medium of advertising. The third variety being the political advertising, this is conducted by political parties for promoting candidates and issues during elections in particular or whenever need arises.

Sandage has identified several reasons for the growth in these types of advertising in America. According to Sandage there was a philosophical climate favouring individual decision-making considering that the individual is 'sovereign' and is capable of making reasonable decisions that affect their lives when provided with full range of views on any given subject. Advertising's attempts of persuasion were considered permissible and even expected as ultimately people were capable of decision making and acting rationally. Secondly the use of advertising on behalf of the war effort during second World War was crucial to the development of advertising in non-product forms. War time experience showed that advertising was more than a sales tool. A new perception emerged: Advertising as a communications system adaptable to many needs. From that premise, there was room for experimentation. If it was useful to government and public service organisation, it could also be useful to those who were looking for new ways to communicate ideas.[12] Lastly and perhaps most importantly advertising became one of the many conduits of expression in an increasingly complex society apparently demanding interdependency of governmental-social-group-individual units. Considering the various public issues that adversely affect the people in the society from all corners, nonproduct advertising became a familiar form of expression.

1.2.2.1 Definitions of Social Advertising

Two definitions, one by Philip Kotler and other by Garbett highlight the essence of social advertising:

According to Philip Kotler 'Social Change Campaign' is an organised effort conducted by one group (the change agent), which intends to persuade others (the target adopters) to accept, modify or abandon certain ideas, attitudes, practices and behaviour.[13]

In the words of Garbett, Social / Public Service advertising is "that kind of advertising, either government or association sponsored, which promotes causes and activities generally accepted as desirable. By its nature, public service advertising is usually non-controversial. It may, then, be paid or presented by the media

---

[12] "Advertising Increasing in 'Non Commercial' uses", Advertising Age, 30 April ,1998,p.104

[13] Philip Kotler and Roberto Eduardo, *Social Marketing, Strategies for Changing Public Behaviour*, The Free Press, New York, 1989, p. 6.

[14] Thomas Garbett F., *Corporate Advertising*, McGraw-Hill, New York, 1981, p. 12.

without charge. Most importantly, it is associated with "good works" about which there is consensus".[14]

From the above definitions certain characteristics of social advertising can be deduced:

- Social / Public service advertising is a type of public relations advertising and as such has a non-product, non-service, non-profit perspective.
- The main focus of this advertising is on an issue which is socially desirable and generally non-controversial in nature.
- The social issues dealt in this advertising are targeted at a definite audience and often, calls for public action to accept, modify or abandon certain ideas, attitudes, practices and behaviour.
- The media and advertising agency make contributions by offering time/space and creative services respectively, either free or at subsidised rates. In case the media is paid for, someone other than the sponsor pays for it.
- This kind of advertising is an organised effort of the 'change agents' like government, voluntary organisations, media, advertising agencies and business houses, who intend to bring about a change in the society.
- The motive behind such advertising is non-profit irrespective of who conducts it. Social welfare could be the sole purpose for governments and social organisations to conduct such advertising. Business houses and media may undertake social advertising to discharge their social responsibility by doing it for free.

1.2.2.2 Social Advertising vis-à-vis Commercial Advertising

A brief assessment of social advertising in comparison to the general advertising of products or services for commercial reasons can facilitate better understanding of the concept.

Table 1.1
Advertising vis-à-vis Social Advertising

Advertising	Social Advertising
Advertising is always one of the many activities conducted under marketing. The advertising objectives reflect and are necessarily a part of the marketing objectives.	Social advertising is not necessarily a part of social marketing, though in some cases it may be just one of the many aspects of social marketing. Many sponsors may conduct social advertising out of genuine concern about an issue. But apart from social advertising they may not take up any other responsibility of the issue they are advertising. For e.g. an organisation with a concern for environment may carry social advertisements on reducing the use of plastic bags but not actually provide alternatives for plastic bags.
The benefit to the advertiser is in the form of personal gain or profit that he aims to earn in case the advertisement is successful in creating sales.	The benefit is neither personal nor is it in any material form and the sponsor is likely to gain only goodwill for his concern for the society.
The objective is usually sale of the product, though advertising is also conducted for other objectives like countering the competition, creating a positive image or indicating the change in the brand name.	The objective in social advertising is general welfare.
Advertising at large is aimed at selling a product or service of the advertiser and sometimes while attempting this they may need to sell an idea also. For e.g. an airlines company trying to sell their services might initially start with selling an idea of air travel being quick and hassle-free compared to road or rail travel.	Social advertising aims at bringing about an attitudinal or behavioural change in the audience. The anti tobacco advertisements attempt to bring behavioural change in the smokers by motivating them to give up smoking while advertisements creating awareness about 'no discrimination against AIDS patients' aims at bringing about an attitudinal change among the general audience towards these patients.
Popular celebrities charge exorbitantly for endorsing various brands.	Celebrities may lend support for social advertising for free also.
Advertising agencies and media earn substantial revenue by creating and promoting advertising respectively.	Social advertising is an opportunity for advertising agencies and media to exhibit their concern for the society and therefore they either do not charge at all or charge at subsidised rates for creating and promoting social advertising respectively.
On certain occasions advertisers have used themes or ideas in advertising which were derogative or detrimental to society at large or for certain sections. Advertisers adopt such strategies to incite a controversy or spur up a debate and thereby enjoy a good recall amidst the clutter.	The ideas promoted in social advertising are generally non argumentative and non-controversial. Though some times certain groups may object to the idea put across but the cause behind social advertising is by and large noble.
The impact of commercial advertising can be measured to some extent in terms of sales generated by the advertising.	The impact of social advertising is very difficult to gauge, especially in cases where it expects to bring changes in the attitudes and deep-rooted behaviour patterns of people.

1.2.2.3 History of Social Advertising

Campaigns for social change are not a new phenomenon. They have been waged from time immemorial. In Ancient Greece and Rome campaigns were launched to free the slaves. In England during the Industrial Revolution, campaigns were mounted to abolish debtor prisons, grant voting rights to women and abolish child labour. Colonial America was also the scene of numerous campaigns. In 1721, Cotton Mather sought to convince the citizens of Boston, in what was then the Massachusetts Bay Colony, to accept inoculations to ward off a small pox epidemic. James Madison, Alexander Hamilton and others published the Federalist Papers after the 1787 Constitutional Convention to win public acceptance of the new US constitution. American social campaigns in nineteenth century included the abolition movement; the temperance and prohibition movements and a movement to have the federal government regulate the quality of food and drugs.[15] Though these are social change campaigns and strictly not social advertising campaigns, use of certain degree of social advertising is inevitable in bringing about the desired change.

In India too the socio-religious reform movements in different parts of our country during the nineteenth century to overcome the outdated practices of dowry, sati and devdasi, prevention of female infanticide and awareness about education to women are all examples of campaigns with social motives. Various social reformers like Raja Rammohan Roy, Dayanand Saraswati, Swami Vivekanand and their institutions have used such campaigns to create a social awakening. Lokmanya Tilak, Lala Lajpat Rai, Bipin Chandra Pal and many other extremist leaders of the nationalist movement launched their revolt against the British reign in the twentieth Century through tools of social advertising like newspapers, periodicals and public gatherings. Social advertising is aimed at creating awareness among the masses, inform and

[15] Philip Kotler and Eduardo Roberto, op. cit., p. 5.

educate them about socially relevant issues and in that sense even *satyagraha* and public meetings through which Mahatma Gandhi addressed the nation were the early forms of social advertising.

In recent times, social change campaigns have focused on health reforms (antismoking, prevention of drug abuse, nutrition and physical fitness), environmental reforms (safe water, clean air, preservation of national parks and forests and protection of wildlife), educational reforms (to increase adult literacy, to improve public schools and to provide scholarships for needy students) and economic reforms (to revitalise older industrial cities; boost job skills and training and attract foreign investors). Other countries, such as Sweden, Canada and Australia, have launched vigorous campaigns to reduce smoking and alcoholic consumption, encourage safe driving and protect the environment. In some cases, these countries have been more effective in their social change campaigns than United States. Developing countries, such as the Philippines, Indonesia and China, conduct forceful social campaigns to inoculate children against viruses; to make widespread the use of oral rehydration therapies; and to promote family planning, literacy and healthful diets.[16]

Thus, it can be concluded that though it is difficult to pinpoint exact date of origin of social advertising, it has existed since time immemorial.

1.2.2.4 Social Advertising as an Element of Social Marketing

Just as advertising is a component of marketing, social advertising too remains a component of social marketing. The term Social marketing was first conceived as phenomena in 1971 with an article in *Journal of Marketing* by Kotler and Zaltman.[17] They

---

[16] Ibid., pp. 6-7.

[17] Philip Kotler and Gerald Zaltman, "Social Marketing: An Approach to Planned Social Change", *Journal of Marketing*, July 1971, vol. 35, pp. 3-12.

defined social marketing then as "the design, implementation, and control of programmes calculated to influence the acceptability of social ideas and involving considerations of product planning, pricing, communications and marketing research". They discussed the use of commercial marketing methods for social issues. They brought out some important similarities between commercial marketing and social marketing such as customer orientation, exchange theory, marketing research, segmentation, the use of the marketing mix and the focus on monitoring and evaluation but also substantial differences when it comes to the product, gain / profit, the behavioural change and the type of competitive environment. The main components of social marketing are marketing research, segmentation, product, price, place, promotion, monitoring and evaluation. Further the authors discuss the meaning, power, and limitations of social marketing as an approach to planned social change. The authors define the instruments of social marketing, followed by a systems view of the application of marketing logic to social objectives. Kotler[18] then after the initial attempt tried to modify the concepts of marketing as applied to social causes. However, he coined the term 'marketing for non-profit organization' in the year 1975.

Subsequently, in 1980, Fox and Kotler[19] reviewed the development of marketing social causes for the past decade. While analysing the evolution of social marketing, they identified the relationship of the major approaches producing a social change, such as legal, technological, technical and informational approaches. The authors illustrated this with the case of reducing cigarette smoking. The earlier social marketing was mostly informational approach in the form of social advertising. It subsequently was broadened to evolve itself to social communication which included

---

[18] Philip Kotler, *Marketing for Nonprofit Organisations*, Prentice Hall Inc., New Jersey, U.S.A., 1975.

[19] Karen F. A.Fox and Kotler Philip, "The Marketing of Social Causes: The First 10 years", Journal of Marketing, 1980, vol. 44, pp. 24-33.

personal selling like family planning campaigns. Subsequently, it resulted in social marketing "as a larger paradigm for effecting social change". In this the marketing research element became a part of the social marketing. They identified few elements in development of social marketing. These were: marketing research, product development, use of incentives and facilitation. With this the authors tried to integrate the 4 Ps – Product, Place, Price and Promotion as part of social marketing. This was illustrated with the cases of family planning, heart disease prevention, etc.

In 1990, Kotler and Roberto[20] described in several social campaigns the change in the public behaviour through the marketing approach. In addition to 4 Ps, they suggested three additional Ps which require an understanding of social marketing. They were Personnel, Presentation and Process. The Personnel include all those who sell and deliver the social product to the target adopters. The Presentation is visible sensory elements and the Process refers to the steps that target adopters undertake to acquire social product. These seven elements played a major role in successful social campaign of American Cancer Society, Amnesty International, contraception through condom usage in Philippines and drug abuse in Canada. They emphasised the critical component of offering a superior product solution in solving a social problem. This could be done by first identifying a social problem, need and want. This is followed by designing a new social product as a superior solution.

Andearson[21] defines social marketing as "the adaptation of commercial marketing techniques to the analysis, planning, execution, and evaluation of programmes designed to influence the voluntary behaviour in order to improve their personal welfare and that of the society to which they are a part."

---

[20] Philip Kotler and Eduardo Roberts L., *Social Marketing: Strategies for Changing Public Behaviour*, The Free Press, Collier Macmillan Publisher, London, 1990.

Philip Kotler, Ned Roberto and Nancy Lee[22] defined social marketing as "Social marketing is the use of marketing principles and techniques to influence a target audience to voluntarily accept, modify, or abandon behaviour for the benefit of individuals, groups or society as a whole."

Weibe[23] too felt that it is possible to combine marketing and sociology. According to him marketers of soaps or any commodity for that matter were effective while marketers of social causes usually were inept. He based his conclusion on his research of several social campaigns in which he determined the reason for their success or failure. He found social campaigns that used elements of business marketing were more successful than those that disregarded those techniques. In order to facilitate understanding of social marketing, Weibe analysed four social campaigns such as Kate Smith to sell bonds during Second World War, the campaign to recruit civil defence volunteers, campaign on juvenile delinquency and Kefauver Committee to set their house in order. Analysing these four campaigns, Weibe used five factors which will determine the effectiveness of the campaign. They are:

The force: intensity of person's motivation toward the goal

The direction: knowledge of how and where to consummate his motivation

Mechanism: existence of an agency

Adequacy and compatibility: ability and effectiveness of the agency

Distance: the target groups energy and task required to consummate the motivation

---

[21] Alan R. Andearson, *Marketing Social Change: Changing Behaviour to Promote Health, Social Development, and the Environment*, San Francisco, Jossey-Bass, 1995.

[22] Philip Kotler, Ned Roberto and Nancy Lee, *Social Marketing, Improving the Quality of Life*, Sage Publications, California, 2002.

[23] G. B. Weibe, as quoted in Wasem George, *Marketing in Non-profit Organisation*, ed. Patrick Montana, Amacom a Division of American Marketing Associations, 1978, p. 31.

However, there are some differences between social marketing and commercial or business marketing .[24] Commercial or business marketing is an exchange of money for goods or services whereas social marketing aims to influence the behaviour of individuals and community using marketing concepts directed to provide social benefits rather than commercial profits. Social marketers usually persuade audience to change their practices or behaviour in return for something of value. The core challenge of any social marketing programme is to establish exchange which is likely to satisfy both the marketeers' needs and the target audience's wants while simultaneously contributing towards an overall social benefit. Its offerings include physical products, services and intangible ideas. Social marketers rely primarily on voluntary exchange with focus on social uplift. Social marketing mix elements have four traditional Ps of business marketing, viz., product, price, place and promotion, and has four additional Ps that are public, partnership, policy and purse strings for effective implementation.

Social Marketing Mix Elements

Product : A continuum of products involves product ranging from tangible physical products (condoms) to services (medical checkups), practices (breast feeding, eating healthy diet) and finally more intangible ideas (environment conservation).

Price : Social marketing programs are supported by revenue contributions received as grants / donations / subsidies.

Place : The customer access may be facilitated through doctors' chambers, shopping malls, mass circulation media, or in-home demonstrations.

Promotion : In social marketing the promotion objective is to determine the widest reach at an affordable cost.

---

[24] Pradip Kumar Deb, "Marketing Social Change and Community Development", *Advertising Express*, October 2008, The ICFAI University Press, pp. 25-27.

Additional social marketing Ps

Public : It refers to both the external and internal groups which social marketers have to address. The external groups refers to people responsible for framing policy and gatekeepers and internal publics refers to people directly associated with final shaping and implementation of social marketing programmes.

Partnership : Social marketing calls for close collaborations with other organizations in order to be effective.

Policy : To bring about the necessary change there is need for supportive policy environment and media advocacy.

Purse strings: Social marketing programmes are mostly implemented by NGOs through funds provided by sources such as foundations / federal grants and donations.

It is widely accepted that social marketing applies the principles and practices of commercial marketing yet there are some basic differences between the two[25] as indicated in the Table 1.2 below:

Table 1.2

Difference between Social Marketing and Commercial Marketing

Social Marketing	Commercial Marketing
To do good	To make profits
Financed by donations and taxes	Leverages investments
Accountable to the public	Accountable privately
Sells behaviour	Sells product/ services
High risk target audience	Low risk audience
Hard to measure effectiveness	Market share / profits indicates the effectiveness

1.1.2.5 Classification of Social Advertising

Social advertisements have become a mainstay of advertising scene and all media carry multiple social advertisements. Social advertising can be differentiated on the basis of the issues they focus on, the media on which they are run and the languages in which they are conducted. Apart from these typical differences the authors have identified several bases on which social advertisements particularly in India can be categorised, that are as follows:

[1] *Sponsor*

One of the most common ways of classifying social advertising is on the basis of the advertiser. In India often government and its various ministries run social advertising at national level to address issues such as awareness against disasters, promotion of Indian tourism and payment of Income Tax. In fact, government had been the leading advertiser in terms of volume for the years 2006 and 2007.[26] Local units of state governments such as Mumbai Police uses advertising for alerting citizens against terrorism, while Municipal Corporation of Greater Mumbai (MCGM) urges people through advertising to keep the city clean. Nonprofit organisations such as Cancer Patients Aid Association (CPAA) run advertising for early detection and prevention of cancer. Media is the advertiser when television channel, Aaj Tak seeks public support for issues such as eve-teasing and second hand smoke. Advertising agency is an advertiser when Percept advertises to fight against film piracy. Companies are regular advertisers; Maruti Udyog had launched advertisements for inculcating safe driving practices among people.

- - - - - - - - - - - - - - - -

[25] S. Jaya Krishna and R. Padmaja, "Marketing Social Change", *Marketing Mastermind*, Vol. VIII, Issue 10, October 2008, pp. 45-49.

[26] Priyanka Mehra, "Riding on Discounted Rates, Govt Ads Rule TV", www.livemint.com, 21 August, 2008.

[2] *Objectives of the advertising campaign*

On the basis of the objectives that social advertising intends to achieve it can be classified into awareness oriented and action oriented campaigns. Some social advertisements are aimed at just informing the audience about a matter such as government informing the audience about a new power plant it has set up for facilitating power supply through social advertisements in media. While social advertising by NGO working for orphans would expect a concrete action from the audience such as sponsoring a child's education.

[3] *Nature of change expected by social advertising*

Social advertising may be classified on the basis of the change or the difference that they want to bring about. The changes can be in attitude, behaviour and sometimes even both. These changes could vary on the basis of time they take; some could be achieved on immediate basis while others may take time to ensue. Further, these changes may be obvious and easily visible and sometimes they may actually take place but may not be visible. Social advertising waged against discrimination suffered by AIDS patients at work aim to bring attitudinal changes among the general people. Here the purpose of advertisement is to create awareness about the issue and the change expected is in the attitude of the audience. Moreover the expected attitudinal change may take considerable time to sink in and even if the change takes place it may not be visible at all. On the other hand, there is social advertising aimed at bringing about changes in the audience's behaviour. Social advertising appealing audience to use seat belts while driving is a visible change that can be brought about in a short time, especially if the system involves penalising the offenders.

[4] *Time frame*

On the basis of time frame social advertising can be classified into time bound social advertising and social advertising without any specific time frame. The popular Pulse Polio drive is conducted on specific dates and as such appeals parents to bring their children for the oral polio vaccinations on the prescribed dates. The advertisements by tax authorities for paying service or income tax want their audience to file their tax returns before the deadlines. While social advertisements for donating eyes or organs do not have any time frame. In case the audience is convinced with the idea of donating they can complete the formalities for donation as per their wish.

[5] *Relevance in terms of duration or event*

In certain cases social advertising are relevant only for a particular duration or event and later it seems meaningless. Social advertisements based on fund raising for earthquake victims in a particular village will have relevance only for few days or months after the earthquake. Social advertisements on long distance trains introduced by railway ministry during festive seasons will not hold any relevance after the season is over. Whereas, appeal to plant more trees or save water will perhaps never cease its relevance as it is not connected to any event.

[6] *Target audience*

Social advertising can be classified on the basis of the target audience they are meant for. There are social advertisements that are targeted towards a specific segment of the society such as anti tobacco advertisements that are specifically targeted towards smokers. Whereas some social advertisements are pervasive in their appeal and do not target any specific audience like fostering brotherhood.

[7] *Geographic area covered*

On the basis of the geographical area social advertising can be classified into local, regional, national and international. Some social advertisements are limited in their scope and their applicability is limited to a particular locality. A hospital organising health camp for people from specific locality will restrict its advertisement to the locality only. A state government advertises about employment schemes for people only belonging to its state. The health ministry of India promoting social advertisements against consumption of tobacco products in public places are applicable nation wide. The United Nations promoting advertisement against terrorism has an international appeal.

[8] *Independent social advertising versus social advertising as a part of social marketing*

Social advertising can be a part of social marketing and in such case is expected to function as per the role assigned to it in under social marketing. In India to tackle the AIDS epidemic social marketing adopts various approaches, such as distributing free condoms, providing treatment to the patients at subsidised rates and conducting lectures on sex education for youth. Along with all these, AIDS related social advertising is also promoted in keeping with the need of the entire social marketing effort aimed at fighting AIDS. On the other hand there are social advertisements conducted on issues independently like eve-teasing and domestic violence just to create awareness that may not be part of social marketing.

[9] *Relation of social advertising to the advertiser's line of product or service*

This classification is applicable to social advertising campaigns that are run by business organisations such as manufacturers or service providers apart from government and nongovernmental organisations. The contribution to the cause is the cost of obtaining objectives of goodwill, high employee morale and enhanced corporate and brand image, though in certain cases the organisations also seem to make higher sales and increase their market share by taking advantage of social cause advertising. The social advertising conducted by such advertisers basically falls in two categories, issues connected in some way to the line of product or service they manufacture/provide and the issues not connected in any way to their line of business. Car manufacturers promoting use of seatbelts and liquor manufacturers creating awareness about drunken driving are social advertisements associated with the advertisers businesses. In some cases the advertisers adopt a social cause not associated with their line of business, either out of genuine concern or out of profit motive. For example a manufacturing organisation conducting social advertising to raise awareness on female feticide or child abuse will be benefited by way of goodwill only without any material gain. But an organisation appealing to audience to buy the company's brands because the profit from sales will be used for a noble cause is actually trying to use the social cause as a peg to motivate the socially aware customer to buy the brand and show their support. The organisation in such cases stands to gain a positive image amongst its audience as well as make monetary benefits by riding on the social issue.

[10] *Paid versus free social advertising*

On the basis of the money involved in running social advertisements, social advertising can be categorised in free or paidup advertisements. Some social advertising because of their noble cause may enjoy contributions from different quarters, like advertising agency providing creative service for free and media allotting free space or slots. In some cases social advertisements can be conducted by paying for the services undertaken exactly in the same manner in which commercial advertisements are run. The professional advertising agency is hired to create advertisements and media is paid for the number of slots or spaces utilised.

[11] *Direct versus indirect benefits*

Social advertising can be classified on the basis of the beneficiaries likely to gain from social advertising. Certain social advertisements bring benefit to the audience and in certain conditions it benefits some other party. The advertisements promoting regular check-ups for women above 40 years of age for cancer detection/prevention are likely to benefit the women themselves who take up tests regularly. Whereas a charitable institution working for aged people seeks donations from the citizen that will benefit the inmates of the institution and will not bring any direct benefit for the donors.

Thus, social advertising can be classified in multiple ways.

1.2.2.6 Challenges of Social Advertising

Today social advertising and commercial advertising suffer similar problems such as dull sensitivity, immunity to advertising messages, scarce attention and increasing clutter. One of the many challenges faced by social advertiser is difficulty in communicating about social causes to the masses. Absence of proper communication about social problems leads to ignorance and misunderstandings about the concept per se and aggravates the problem in question. Further, not all social campaigns are effective enough to achieve their objectives. There are many reasons why social campaigns fail in spite of the noble cause for which they are undertaken. Some of the factors responsible for this failure are:

- *Advertiser related factors*

There could be several advertiser related factors responsible for not getting the desired response. Any advertising campaign requires good research in order to have clear understanding of the target audience. Since social advertising aims at bringing about behavioural change it becomes even more empirical to understand the factors that motivate the target audience to bring about the desired action. Such a genuine research is mostly missing.

Secondly the advertisers who undertake social advertising, particularly the corporate sector often take it as an image enhancement exercise and lack deeper commitment to the underlying social causes. This is obvious from the meagre advertising budget sanctioned for the social issues in comparison to the advertising budget sanctioned for the commercial advertising. The lack of eye for detail and organisation of the social advertising in a comprehensive manner further illustrates their indifference towards the underlying social issues. For example many companies take up anti-smoking issues but fail to provide any concrete measures to deal with problems that smokers may experience physically and mentally when they actually quit smoking. It is also noticed the advertisers' link social cause with their regular brand advertising because it is a new or creative way to appeal to customers or it helps to break the clutter and some times enables the advertiser to score over the competitors but the genuine concern for the society is missing.

- *Audience related factors*

One of the greatest problems that social advertisers face is that of apathy and defensiveness from the target audience. Audiences may be indifferent because they fail to identify with the situation and its importance, further, they may have had no previous involvement with the concerned issue. Audiences may be defensive due to the costs and inconvenience involved in bringing about behavioural change. For example, buying and using helmets could be both costly and inconvenient for two-wheeler riders.

- *Message related factors*

Message factors relates to the content and conduct of presentation. The messages that do not convey real motivating benefits to target audience in an attention getting way are not effective. Advertisements fail because they often lack cause-appeal match and creativity. Advertising messages are also ineffective when they fail to provide any easy way to respond positively.

- *Credibility factors*

The credibility of the communicator determines the acceptance of any communication. When the credibility of the communicator is high it results in acceptance of the message leading to intended behavioural change. When issue-celebrity match is lacking in social advertising celebrity communicator's credibility is poor. Consequently the acceptance of the message is affected and there is no or limited behavioural change.

- *Media related factors*

The success of social campaign largely depends upon the media associated factors. Selection of media and media vehicles, media schedule that comprises of suitable timing, ample repetition and duration of the entire campaign, all play a decisive role in the fate of the advertising campaign. All these factors have to be carefully selected considering the target audience and concerned social issue. Social campaigns fail due to drawback in any of these factors.

- *Issue related factors*

Social issues differ in many respects. Some social advertisements call for behavioural changes, which bring about immediate benefits, while others benefit in the long run. Adoption of behavioural changes promoted through some social advertisements provide benefit at individual level while others provide benefits at social level, yet others provide both individual and social benefits. Some issues call for individual action and some for collective action, yet others call in for both. Issues, which provide long-term benefits only, benefits at predominantly social level or demand for collective action, pose a major advertising challenge.

1.3 Conclusion

The argument whether advertising is a mirror of society or whether a shaper of the society continues, but it cannot be denied advertising influences our society and affects us in multiple ways. The social advertising is a holistic side of advertising that has a role beyond the marketing environment. Social advertising promotes ideas to alter behaviour for the benefit of individuals, groups or society as a whole. However, social advertising is affected by multiple factors and to be effective it has to use elements of business marketing. And this poses a challenge of combining marketing and sociology to the social advertisers who have a daunting task of making effective social advertisements.

2
SOCIAL ADVERTISING IN INDIA

2.1 Introduction: Social Advertising in India

Compared to developed countries such as US and UK social advertising is of recent origin in India.[1] Around late 1960s, with increasing socio-economic problems and popularization of television, social advertising was given prominent role by government to address the issue of family planning. Since then they have become part and parcel of Indian advertising.

In recent years social advertising has been leading the advertising industry in terms of volumes in India.[2] Acccrding to the data released by Mumbai-based television measurement agency TAM Media Research Pvt. Ltd., commercials with social messages took up 2,800 hours of television broadcast time in the first six months of 2008, a rise of 18.5 per cent over the same period in 2007 indicating social advertising were on rise. The similar trend was observed in years 2006 and 2007 too. According to advertising inventory data for the year 2006 compiled by TAM

---

[1] Shipra Kundra, *Introduction to Advertising and Public Relations*, 1st edu., Anmol Publications, New Delhi, 2005, pp. 74-75.

[2] Priyanka Mehra, "Riding on Discounted Rates, Govt Ad Rules TV", *Hindustan Times*, Mint, 21, August 2008.

[3] Anusha Subramanian, "Changing Face of Social Advertising in India", *Business Today*, February 2007.

Adex, social advertising was the top advertising category of advertisements on television. Social advertisements saw a 90 per cent growth in volumes on television over January-November 2005 for the same period in 2006.[3] In 2007, social advertising topped the list at some 4,960 hours of airtime, compared with 3,965 hours that aired commercials by mobile phone services companies, followed by consumer goods, soft drinks and two-wheeler advertisements. In the year 2006, social messages were aired for 3,130 hours that grew by as much as 58 per cent in 2007.

2.2 Social Advertisers in India

In India host of social advertisers such as Government and its ministries, NGOs, corporate, media and advertising agencies regularly flaunt their social advertisements. Following is the brief summary of the nature of social advertising carried by different advertisers in India:

2.2.1 Government

Government and its various ministries lead the social advertising scene in India. Eight of the top ten advertisers in the social advertising category are done by government. In the year 2007, the government leads the social advertising chart, accounting for 83 per cent of the social advertisements aired on television while the non-government sector contributed mere 17 per cent. The government's share on social advertising was largely utilised for airing health awareness advertisements, which accounted for 50 per cent share of total airtime. The Health ministry had an annual budget of Rs 160 crore for the year 2007 for information, education and communication on social issues.[4]

However, the impressive volumes this category represents is not reflected in the value of the government advertisers pay for the

---

[4] Sharma Sanchita, "Big B is Social Ad Superstar," Hindustan Times, New Delhi, January 03, 2008.

airtime compared with what a company or industry segment has to pay as they are largely on the back of discounts and bonus airtime. Since government gets enormous discounts from networks, as most of the private channel owners have a special government rate card that is different from all other categories. Government is offered deals which are 20 to 40 per cent below the market rates depending upon the arrangement between government and the channel owner. The low advertising rate for social messages are agreed to by networks which use these advertisements to service their own corporate social responsibility initiatives. State-owned broadcaster Prasar Bharati, that manages close to 30 per cent of the government's advertising spends, offers 60 to 250 per cent of bonus airtime depending upon the volume of business. Considering the potentials of television medium, government is routing its social advertising towards television, from radio spots and print space which were its primary channels of advertising so far.

One prominent feature of government's social advertising is the use of celebrities for promoting the messages, who are lending their support for the social causes without any charge.[5] According to former Health Minister Anbumani Ramadoss celebrities are important for social messaging as they help establish brand connect. In the Indian context, many celebrities from diverse fields such as films, sports and creative arts have associated themselves with several social causes, government as well as nongovernmental, such as immunization, vegetarianism, literacy awareness and timely payment of income tax. Famous actress Shilpa Shetty, actors Vivek Oberoi and Boman Irani promote social issues such as quitting smoking, proper treatment of animals and conservation of petroleum resources. Popular cricketer and former

---

[5] Sanchita Sharma, *op. cit.*

[6] "Shah Rukh May Campaign Against Smoking — Health Ministry Keen to Rope in Bollywood Star", *Business Line*, *The Hindu*, 15, November 2005.

captain of the Indian cricket team Anil Kumble promoted vegetarianism for People for Ethical Treatment of Animals (PETA).

For the government programmes such as the National Rural Health Mission and Routine Immunisation, celebrities were used to garner initial attention and later unknown people were used to carry the health message across. The health ministry has been consistently using celebrities like Amitabh Bachchan for Pulse Polio and Rahul Dravid and Sachin Tendulkar's efforts to spread the message of HIV/AIDS among many others.[6] So far the ministry as well as the media planners have been satisfied with the feedback that they have been receiving for such celebrity endorsed social issues. The superstar Shahrukh Khan too, has appeared in National Rural Health Mission's programme urging India to participate in the immunization programme. Actor Vivek Oberoi also promotes 'DOTS' a treatment on tuberculosis through social advertising for the ministry. Following the health ministry, the tourism ministry too roped in a film celebrity for their Incredible India campaign.[7] The tourism ministry appointed Aamir Khan as a brand ambassador to sensitize people to preserve India's rich cultural heritage and to teach them to welcome foreign tourists.

A government in power, spending lavishly on advertising is a common practice in India. But the spending may not only target health issues. In an election year convincing the potential voters may just top the chart with all health and welfare issues taking the back seat.[8] In the year 2004 when National Democratic Alliance (NDA) government was in power it launched 'India Shining' campaign which was estimated to be about Rs.200 crore worth campaign. In spite of this extravagant advertising expenditure the

---

[7] "Aamir Khan to be Face of Incredible India", Times of India, 8, August 2008.
[8] Rajeev Banerjee and Delshad Irani , "Bharat Nirman vs. India Shinning", Brand Equity, *The Economic Times*, 4, February 2009.

NDA lost the elections. In 2009 too the Congress led United Progressive Alliance (UPA) government has a similar campaign running under the name 'Bharat Nirman'. Sources close to the campaign say that close to Rs. 200 crore has been spent on this campaign under various heads. More than million seconds of airtime and 8,00,000 column centimeters of print space have already made the government single largest consumer of air time and media space on major media. Both the campaigns were highly political in nature highlighting the government's achievement though the only difference being 'India Shining' was largely about urban India and 'Bharat Nirman' was about rural India. Though both the governments insisted that they were not political campaigns but merely public service ones, ultimately they were conducted out of taxpayer's funds that were being misused.

Table 2.1

Spending on 'Bharat Nirman' under different Ministries and Schemes (Period: Jan 2007 to Jan 2009)

Product	Rs. Crore
Bharat Nirman	14
Ministry of Consumer Affairs	35
Ministry of Health and Family Welfare	14
Ministry of Human Resource Development	0
Ministry of Labour Employment	1
National Rural Health Mission	52
Rashtriya Gramin Rojgar	5
Total (at market value)	**121**

Source: TAM data and channel ad rates.
Actual campaign spend likely to be Rs. 71 crore since DAVP gets 60% discount on Doordarshan.

- **Directorate of Audio Visual Publicity (DAVP)[9] – Government's agency**

Post Independence the foremost in Indian social advertising is the Directorate of AudioVisual Publicity (DAVP), a part of the

Ministry of Information and Broadcasting the sole mass communication agency of the Indian government.[10] The aim of the Ministry is to educate, inform and to some extent entertain the people. While doing this it also aims to create awareness about the country's development potentials and its problems to solicit the public's participation in the Government's programmes and policies to bring about social change and economic development. The DAVP is the nodal multi-media advertising agency of the central government of India. It caters to the communication needs of all Central ministries/departments and around 200 Public Sector undertakings and autonomous bodies and provides them a single window cost effective service. It informs and educates the people, both rural and urban, about the government's policies and programmes and motivates them to participate in development activities. As the only and biggest advertising agency in this field the Ministry of Information and Broadcasting has a comprehensive set-up of its mass media units with its regional and branch offices in different parts of the country. As the central agency of the government, the DAVP publicizes the policies, programmes and performances of various ministries departments and autonomous bodies through the widest range of communication media such as press advertising including printed material like folders, posters, brochures, etc., and outdoor publicity items like hoardings, transit advertising, etc. As a service agency, it endeavurs to communicate at grass roots level on behalf of various central government ministries. DAVP has been working as a catalyst of social change and economic growth over the years. It has been instrumental in creating awareness amongst masses on socio-economic themes, seeking their participation in developmental activities and for eradication of poverty and social evils.

---

[9] DAVP Annual Report 2006-2007.

[10] Meenakshi Chouhan, *The Social Ad Challenge*, Anmol Publications, New Delhi, 2002, pp. 111-123.

The origin of DAVP can be traced to the times of Second World War. Immediately after the outbreak of Second World War, the erstwhile government of India appointed a Chief Press Advisor. Besides other things, advertising was also the responsibility of the Chief Press Advisor. A post of Advertising Consultant was created in June 1941 under the Chief Press Advisor. This is where DAVP has its roots. On 1, March 1942, the Advertising Consultant Office became the Advertising Branch of the Department of Information & Broadcasting. Following the expansion in its scope, functions and activities, this Advertising unit was declared an Attached Office of the Ministry of Information & Broadcasting on 1, October 1955. The office also assumed the name of Directorate of Advertising and Visual Publicity. DAVP was further declared as Head of a Department on 4, April 1959. By virtue of this declaration, financial and administrative powers were delegated to DAVP. Following are the major objectives of DAVP:

- To perform the functions of a multi-media advertising agency for the central government.
- To act as service agency for central government ministries/ departments to meet their publicity needs including production of media inputs as well as dissemination of messages/information.
- To help central government departments in formulating communication strategies/media plans and help implement them at the grass-root level by providing multi-media support.

DAVP uses full spectrum of communication channels to reach out to the urban and rural masses. The channels of communication used are:

1. *Mailing of Publicity Material* - Mass Mailing Wing of DAVP primarily deals with dispatch of printed material to various crosssections of people in different parts of the country. The

Wing is one of the biggest set ups of its kind in the country and presently maintains an address bank of 16.50 lakh addresses spread over 564 categories.

2. *Outdoor Publicity* - Outdoor Publicity Wing uses the medium of hoardings, bus-panels, kiosks, wall paintings, banners, animation displays, decorative railings, cinema slides, metro display boards, metro train inside panels etc. to spread messages.
3. *Printed Publicity* – The printed publicity wing looks into the planning/production and supervision of print jobs, viz.,multi-colour posters, folders, brochures, calendars, diaries, booklets, stickers, wall-hangers, table calendars and other miscellaneous items of printed publicity. Besides Hindi and English, DAVP produces printed publicity material in Tamil, Telugu, Kannada, Malayalam, Marathi, Gujarati, Bengali, Assamese, Oriya, Punjabi, and Urdu.
4. *Audio and Visual (AV) Publicity* - The AV Cell of DAVP undertakes publicity campaigns through radio and video sponsored programmes, jingles and audio-video spots on AIR (All India Radio), Doordarshan, private satellite television, radio channels and Directorate of Field Publicity (DFP) units on various issues of social relevance and national importance. Various campaigns on the National Rural Health Mission for Ministry of Health and Family Welfare on various health related issue are being broadcast/telecast on AIR, Doordarshan and private television channels. A number of weekly sponsored radio programmes on various developmental issues are produced by DAVP and are broadcast from various AIR stations. These programmes are of 15-30 minutes duration and produced in Hindi and regional languages in interesting drama format. These are broadcast all over the country through Primary Channels and Commercial Broadcasting Service (CBS) stations of AIR. DAVP also uses the AV media to give publicity to variety of social issues.

5. *Exhibitions* - Distribution of publicity mate DAVP has a network of 35 Field Exhibition Units spread all over the country. The Field Exhibition Units of DAVP act as a vital communication link between the government and the people. The field functionaries hold exhibitions on social and developmental themes to far-flung areas of the country to disseminate information about the policies and programmes of the central government. Exhibition wing arranges exhibition on variety of issues. Apart from this DAVP Field Units organised exhibitions in famous melas and festivals like Trissur Pooram Festival in Kerala, Nauchandi Mela at Meerut, Puri Rath Yatra, Chandausi Mela, Sonepur Mela, Gaya Peterpakash Mela, Arogya Mela at India Trade Promotion Organisation (ITPO), Dussera Festival at Mysore and Perfect Health Mela at Sekh Sarai.
6. *Print Advertisements - Release of press advertisements*: As the central agency of the Government, the DAVP publicizes the policies, programmes and performances of various ministries departments and autonomous bodies through the widest range of communication media through press advertising. It uses nearly 3000 newspapers and periodicals for press advertising.

Thus DAVP has been enormously contributing to the general welfare through its number of channels. However, in the recent times DAVP is routing its social advertising towards television, from radio spots and print space which were its primary channels of advertising so far, possibly due to the potentials of television medium.

• Doordarshan – Governments' Platform for Social Advertising[11]

Doordarshan being the sole public service television broadcaster has been playing a leading role in the socio-economic development of the country since it's beginning in 1959.

At present when about 300 television channels are beaming programmes from within and outside the country, there is immense competition to Doordarshan for attracting more and more viewers by adopting all sorts of methods. As a result the responsibility of Doordarshan in providing healthy media support to socio-economic development of the country has gained even more significance.

Present terrestrial coverage of Doordarshan is 79.1 per cent area and 91.4 per cent population of the country. In the bouquet of Doordarshan DTH (Direct To home) service (DD Direct Plus) there are 36 television channels and 20 radio channels and it is a free to air service.

According to Indian Readership Survey TV Report 2006 (Round 2) there are 212.7 million television homes in the country. About 56 per cent television homes in the country have cable connections. The corresponding percentage in urban and rural areas is 70 and 42 respectively. Doordarshan is trying to reach those television homes having no cable and satellite connection, through its DTH service 'DD Direct Plus.'

From the very beginning Doordarshan has earmarked a sizeble chunk of its time for telecasting various socio-economic development activities of the country. Agriculture programme, programmes for rural development, women, children, family welfare, adult education, youth, civic sense and public awareness, science and technology, special programmes during natural calamities like flood, earth quake, epidemics,etc., are some of important programmes for socio-economic development of the country. Doordarshan News channel provides news and current affairs programmes on the development taking place in different parts of the country and in various fields.

Lok Seva Sanchar Parishad now a defunct organisation, was promoted by Doordarshan and the Ministry of Information and Broadcasting. This organisation was to act as a catalyst in

- - - - - - - - - - - - - - - - -

[11] "Doordarshan's Role in Socio-economic Development", Press Information Bureau, Ministry of Information and Broadcasting, Government of India, 14, August 2007.

developing social advertising which could be supported by both government and private organisations. Its first assignment, financed by the government to the tune of Rs 4 lakh was the film on national integration, *Torch of Freedom* created by Suresh Mullick, former Creative Head of O&M Advertising. The music was composed by Louis Banks, featuring cricketers like Gavaskar, Kapil Dev, Srikkanth, India's chess champion V. Anand, female athlete PT Usha, Badminton player Padukone, and many well known sports persons representing different parts of the country running with a blazing torch through the length and breadth of India. This video was first shown on Doordarshan in 1980s on the eve of the 40th anniversary of India's Independence. The film was highly appreciated and made every Indian feel proud of the country and of the young people who had brought such glory and respect to the country. This film was followed by another on the same theme of national integration. This film was called 'Ek Sur' and it had a national integration track which was sung by a galaxy of well-known musicians, singers and film personalities such as Bhimsen Joshi, Lata Mangeshkar and Sharmila Tagore. Unfortunately, this organisation which subsequently received funding from the Ford Foundation did little of note and the government wasted a wonderful opportunity of bringing together public and private funds with the best communication talent within the country to convey to the citizens of this country, areas of social importance.

In order to manage such development programmes more efficiently Doordarshan created two separate wings namely Development Communication Division (DCD), and Narrowcasting. Narrowcasting deals with agriculture and allied subjects whereas DCD was set up in 2001 particularly to discharge Doordarshan's social responsibility of highlighting development-oriented issues and to cater to the communication needs of government departments and public sector undertakings. The concept was born out of a need to generate revenue by securing funds from government partners including ministries, departments and public sector undertakings. The unique revenue generation scheme envisaged flow of earnings by selling airtime at competitive rates.

The DCD made a promising start with a bi-media, radio and television campaign for the Ministry of Rural Development (MoRD). The rural development campaign was on a large scale. It was conceptualized with the objective of optimum utilization of resources in Prasar Bharati (programme, engineering and research) while building on the strengths of the network in terms of reach and access to rural audiences. The Division took on this huge challenge to rediscover the role of the Public Service Broadcaster and tap creative in-house potential.

The prime objective of the rural development campaign was to create awareness among the target audience. It focused on creating awareness about various schemes of the ministry in areas as housing, roads, drinking water and sanitation. As many as 150 stations of AIR and 32 Kendras of Doordarshan were involved in producing and broadcasting content to create awareness about various schemes of the ministry that targeted 6,00,000 villages through programmes in 29 languages and dialects. The effort resulted in production of 1008 programmes. Doordarshan also experimented with the production of public service advertisements. Exchange of success stories across various linguistic regions and cultural zones contributed to the success of these campaigns. It encouraged viewers to follow practices for preserving natural resources. The Audience Research survey indicated awareness generation amount 69.4 per cent of the target audience on the rural development.

To tackle AIDS/HIV, one of the most dreaded epidemics of the recent times, DCD entered into partnership with the British Broadcasting Corporation World Service Trust (BBCCWST) and the National AIDS Control Organisation (NACO) in 2001. The collaboration aimed at promoting social development through the effective use of media. To begin with, a campaign on HIV/AIDS was launched in Delhi, Rajasthan and Uttar Pradesh. The campaign was first telecast in June 2002 and included public service advertisement (sports), production and telecast of a detective drama serial "Jasoos Vijay" and a youth television show "Haath Se Haath Mila". DCD took the initiative to bring 'Jasoos Vijay' to the national channel on prime time slot. This marked the commercial success of Jasoos Vijay. The division introduced regional language versions of Jasoos Vijay and dubbed it in seven languages to reach every nook and corner of the country. The DCD also enjoys the distinction of being a partner in the Global Media AIDS Initiative (GMAI) launched by the UN (United Nations) Secretary General Kofi Anan in January 2004. It was also actively involved in the National Summit on HIV/AIDS chaired by the prime minister of India. Internationally acclaimed cinestar Richard Gere attended the summit as a special invitee.

While collaborating with GMAI, the DCD also partnered with Heroes project a national HIV/AIDS initiative. DCD has been a partner with UNICEF (United Nations International Children's Fund), Kaiser Family Foundation, Asian Institute of Broadcast Development, Ford Foundation and European Union. DCD also collaborated with MTV, the music channel for World AIDS Day Summit. This was an exciting collaboration as it offered a meeting ground for two channels with diametrically opposite characteristic, one known for its sobriety and other for plain fun and entertainment. The collaboration also witnessed repackaging and adaptation of software and locations. These partnerships continue to focus on capacity building and exchange of best practices undertaken by organizations to fight against HIV/AIDS.

The DCD launched 'Kalyani' on behalf of the Ministry of Health and Family Welfare in May 2002. It was initially launched for one year as a weekly programme on the eve of World No Tobacco Day, in Assam, Bihar, Chhattisgarh, Jharkhand, Madhya Pradesh, Orissa, Rajasthan and Uttar Pradesh to create awareness on malaria, HIV/AIDS, cancer, tuberculosis, iodine deficiency, tobacco related and water borne diseases. In subsequent years, other issues such leprosy; blindness control and food safety were added. Highly interactive, innovative formats, unique presentation style, integrated approach and pioneering initiative of setting up Kalyani health clubs proved the efficacy of the campaign in no time. It paved the way for another weekly programme, Kalyani II on reproductive child health in October 2002. Kalyani II marked the addition of the hill State of Uttranchal to eight other Kalyani receiving states. Eventually Kalyani was telecast four times a week with two repeats from 21 stations of Doordarshan in three languages and six dialects. The response to Kalyani has been overwhelming since, as is evident from its impact on the target audience across nine most backward and densely populated States.

Another partnership thats worth a mention was in 2001 with the Department of Administrative Reforms and Public Grievances, Union Ministry of Personnel, Public Grievances and Pensions for the production and telecast of a series of documentaries on best practices in e-governance in India. It was titled 'Cascading quality governance'. The campaign was aired in 2003 and included 12 documentaries. These documentaries were telecast on DD National and in 12 States in an equal number of languages through Doordarshan Kendras. The Kendras that documented these documentaries were Bangalore, Guwahati, Mumbai, Kolkata, Bhubaneshwar, Sri Nagar, Thiruvannthapuram, Jallandhar, Ahmedabad, Chennai, and Hyderabad.

On behalf of Insurance Regulatory Development Authority of India (IRDA), DCD launched a campaign to create awareness among people about benefits of insurance. The campaign was telecast by 10 Kendras in 10 states in an equal number of languages and dialects.

The Department of Company Affairs, Ministry of Finance commissioned DCD for a campaign called "Paisa Hamara Faisla Hamara" on investor awareness and education. This was an interactive phone in programme with investors at one end and experts at the other, designed for addressing grievances of the investors. The programme focused on themes such as safe investments, companies where investments should be avoided, difficulties faced by the investors and agencies for redressing grievances and rights of investors. This was telecast across six Kendras in Ahmedabad, Chennai, Hyderabad, Kolkata, Lucknow and Mumbai.

DCD also initiated a multi-media campaign for the Department of Consumer Affairs to generate awareness on consumer rights. The campaign features the popular programme 'Jaago Grahak Jaago' which has done great public service. The programme has apprised consumers of the tricks used by mischievous persons, traders, businessmen and service providers to cheat them. The campaign also informs consumers about product safety, product defects, food adulteration, and environmental hazards. In addition, several public service advertisements on consumer rights are telecast from eight Kendras in eight states in an equal number of languages and dialects.

DCD has handled other meaningful campaigns for the Department of Birth and Death under the Ministry of Home Affairs. The campaign is aimed at generating awareness on the importance of Birth and Death registration. Under the campaign, a series of programmes were produced and telecast from four Kendras in four states. Twentyone Kendras were linked to provide inputs for yet another series of 'Jan Kerosene Yojana'. DCD has also campaigned on issues like women empowerment, trafficking, elementary and adult education, science and technology, rural development, environment and forest, productivity council and income tax. Some other initiatives introduced by DCD are 'Grameen Bharat' (on rural development), 'Bhoomi' (on environment), 'Janjatiya Darpan' (on tribal affairs), 'Khel Khel Mein Badalo Duniya (on petroleum conservation), 'Jaljivan' (on water conservation), 'Aatmaja' (on female infanticide), Aparjita' (girl child). Continuing its efforts to promote health literacy, the Division has been producing programmes for campaigns on Pulse Polio and Blood Donation.

From five partners and nine campaigns in the year 2001-02, DCD has come along way with 61 campaigns in the year 2005-06. This sevenfold increase in just five years is noteworthy. The government campaigns by the division during this period have contributed to 850 per cent growth in revenue. The campaigns by DCD have resulted in qualitative and quantitative improvement of in-house productions using Doordarshan's creative talent and infrastructure. Previously, ministries and departments depended on private producers for their production and Doordarshan only ran their own campaigns. But the Division succeeded in reviving in-house productions by tapping talent from the right quarters and with the right support from the Prasar Bharati management. In the process of strengthening in-house production capabilities, the division also assumed responsibilities for upgrading skills of creative teams and improving coordination among various wings as programming, engineering, administration and research at the headquarters and in the field. Fifty such training workshops have been designed and conducted by the division, some with BBC (British Broadcast Corporation) trainers, and at the Film and Television Institute of India, Pune.

The DCD works as a bridge between government ministries and departments on one hand and Doordarshan on the other. DCD focuses on the specific objective of fulfilling the communication needs of these client departments. DCD functions as a single window marketing division and a production house for government ministries and public sector undertakings. It offers turnkey solutions covering all aspects of media planning, software production, scheduling and impact evaluation. Within a short span of its inception, DCD has succeeded in revitalizing in-house production activities within Doordarshan.

"Kalyani I" and "Kalyani II, are the major campaigns being produced and telecast continuously since 2002 from 8 and 9 states respectively. This programme has made a significant impact on the target audience as is evident from the reported attitudinal change and social activism. Children, and women, who are among the members of "Doordarshan Kalyani Clubs", are taking the television messages further through inter-personal communication and social activism. Health Secretaries of the state governments, doctors and other health workers, NGOs, academicians, opinion makers and public at large have recognized the impact made by this campaign. 'Kalyani' and another initiative of DCD on HIV/AIDS awareness, detective series 'Jasoos Vijay'– were presented to UN's Secretary General at launch of Global Media AIDS Initiatives in January 2004 and to the prime minister of India at HIV/AIDS National Media Summit in January 2005. 'Kalyani' have brought Doordarshan national and international acclaim through GATES Malaria Partnership, Commonwealth Broadcasting Association (CBA) Awards, 2004, nomination for the prestigious ROSE D'Or Awards of Switzerland, 2005 (HIV/AIDS), 31st RAPA (Radio and Television Practitioner's and Advertiser Association Awards) in 2005, UNFPA (United Nations Fund for Population Activities) Laadli Media Awards for Western Region, 2006-07 and UNFPA Laadli Media Award Eastern Region, 2007. Other awards for the programmes of DCD include the Commonwealth Broadcasting Association Awards, 2003 (HIV/AIDS; Haath Se Haath Mila), Indian Telly Awards, 2004 (best public service spots, HIV/AIDS), Indian Telly Awards, 2003 for Best Thriller ('Jasoos Vijay'HIV/AIDS), Doordarshan Annual Awards for best spot of the year, 2002 (anti tobacco) and best serial of the year, 2002 (Rural Development).

In short, Doordarshan and particularly its DCD has proved to be a significant contributor in providing programmes that are need based, effective and useful for the audience and play an important role in the socio-economic development of the country. In this respect it certainly proves to be a channel with a social service vision, and this perhaps is the biggest difference between Doordarshan and other profit oriented private channels operating in the country.[12]

2.2.2 Contribution of Other Media in Social Advertising

Apart from the government private media too make their contributions towards social advertising. It is worth noticing that though the private media owners, in general are primarily profit driven, they too have shown commitment to social welfare in their own way. The Indian media has been contributing responsibly while addressing social issues. Media have articulated their own ways and means to exhibit social concern. Some media owners are providing free slots on radio stations or television channels while newspapers are providing free spaces for public service advertising. There are other media owners who have gone ahead and started their own initiatives to address the social problems. Media in some cases have also acquired the role of advertisers and launched their advertising campaigns, while some have contributed by recognizing and appreciating the role of those social advertisers who have actually done social good by awarding or rewarding their work.

One common way in which media makes its contributions is by providing free space or slots for running social advertisements.[13] Amongst those who have provided subsidized or free slots/space for social advertising are the television channels, ranging from the domestic ones like Zee, Sony, STAR to international ones like Discovery (a practice initiated by Doordarshan) and BBC.[14] The media have also contributed by way of launching social programmes and social advertising voluntarily on the issues which according to them need attention.

Zee Entertainment Enterprises was founded in October 1992, which is India's first and largest fully integrated media and entertainment company.[15] Recognizing its social responsibility, Zee Entertainment Enterprises launched 'Zee Touch India' initiative

- - - - - - - - - - - - - - - -

[12] Ibid.

which enables corporations to air social films on all channels owned by Zee TV, without paying for the airtime. This is mainly to do away with the financial constraints that corporations suffer while espousing social causes. The public service advertisements telecast to date on its various channels include campaigns for breast cancer, visually impaired, HIV/AIDS and Pulse Polio. Apart from airing campaigns for free Zee Touch has another initiative under the name 'Zee Jagran', a programme that showcases charitable endeavors taking place in the society. Any organisation that aims to make world a better place can partner with Zee and get recognition for itself and support for the work it is doing. Along with these efforts Zee TV with its numerous entertainment channels, reaching over 500 million viewers, had woven HIV/AIDS awareness messages into its top entertainment programmes and reality shows. Storylines of prime time shows highlighted concerns and issues related to the youth. In addition to this, the Network, through its regional channels, reached out to viewers in small towns and cities as well.

Indian government figures indicate that there are more than five million people living with AIDS/HIV in India. Two Indians become infected with HIV every minute and one in every six new HIV infections worldwide occurs in India. India is at a critical point in its epidemic, with AIDS/HIV poised to spread quickly. It is widely recognised that large-scale prevention interventions could help to avert a HIV epidemic in India. For many years India has been taking desperate steps to control AIDS / HIV, considering the way this deadly virus has taken its toll on Indian population. Many broadcasting and press media have been instrumental in bringing about AIDS awareness by partnering with NGOs. Star TV,[16] in

---

[13] S. Sharma and R. Singh, *Advertising Planning and Implementation*, Prentice Hall of India Private Ltd., New Delhi, India, 2006, p. 62.

[14] Alice Guram, "Social Ads from India Make It to London Festival", *Indian Express*, 15, November 1998.

[15] www.zeetelevision.com

India, has established a media partnership with the Heroes Project since 2004 to reduce HIV/AIDS stigma and raise awareness of its prevention through television and mobile phone media. Heroes Project is a national HIV/AIDS initiative, launched in July 2004 to work with media organisations and societal leaders in India. The project saw many television channels and publishing houses supporting the cause in their own way. STAR India's five-year airtime commitment is worth US$ 23.16 million, reaching an estimated 70 million viewers and garnering nearly 50 per cent of the media exposure on HIV/AIDS. It is the largest non-governmental public service campaign in India, which has engaged nearly one hundred film and sports celebrities including Amitabh Bachchan and Rahul Dravid and trained nearly 500 writers and producers in creating HIV/AIDS messaging. Their Public Service Advertisements (PSA) has been aired over 11,500 times across STAR India channels.

The Heroes project has many such partnerships with different media in India. The Heroes Project saw following major partnerships:

1. Sony TV embedded relevant HIV/AIDS messages into storylines of their most popular and youth-centric programmes, such as Indian Idol and detective thriller CID.
2. MTV India, Indian subsidiary of MTV networks Asia Pacific, a popular music channel among urban youth partnered with Heroes Project to incorporate HIV/AIDS messaging in their programmes as well as air Heroes public service advertisements. The project provided informational material and had special events to raise HIV/AIDS awareness amongst Indian youth. MTV as their own independent contribution even recognized the efforts of the team behind film 'Phir Milenge', Hindi cinema's first mainstream movie on the subject of HIV/AIDS by awarding them MTV Staying Alive Award, at MTV India's

---

[16] Heroes Project, Star Care, www.startv.com

biggest flagship award event MTV IMMIES (Indian Music Excellence Awards 2004).

3. The SUN Network, a leader in south Indian channels with 20 television channels had a sustained mass media campaign that played a critical role in influencing social attitudes and behavious towards HIV/AIDS in south India.
4. To equip its readers with accurate information on HIV/AIDS, *Dainik Jagran* one of the largest read daily in India, contributed in terms of periodic editorials and advertising space inventory of 4,000 sq. cm (valued at Rs. 9.3 million). Besides reaching out through its 25 editions in 8 Indian states, the group has designed on the ground events under its forum called 'Jagran Pahal'. Collaborating with Heroes Project, this forum features AIDS awareness camps, voluntary check ups, etc., at rural centers in regions where AIDS is on the rise. *Jagran* also deploys its popular website, jagran.com for AIDS awareness.
5. *The Hindustan Times* one of the wellknown newspaper, also disseminated in-depth information on HIV/AIDS through a sustained media campaign. Besides regular news reports the media campaign included an interactive weekly column. The group's popular website (HindustanTimes.com) featured a special micro-site on HIV/AIDS called 'Surviving AIDS'.
6. A pioneer in AIDS journalism, the Hindu group was engaged with filling gaps in reporting and analysing the problem of HIV/AIDS in India. They incorporated content on HIV/AIDS in their 'Newspaper in Education (NIE) programme' for schools. In addition, *The Hindu* has lent its AIDS journalism expertise for developing regional journalistic capability and in agenda building, by means of workshops and journalism school modules.
7. NDTV a popular news, business and entertainment channel has been quite prompt towards the social issues grappling India. NDTV's features and debate shows provided an ideal platform for open discussions on issues surrounding HIV/AIDS. As part

of its association with the Heroes Project NDTV ran HIV/ AIDS focused shows and screened short films based on AIDS.

Additionally in crunch situations media has contributed in all possible ways to provide aids and bring things to normalcy. In times of major accidents, earthquakes, war and floods various media groups have provided with help-lines and updated information, mobilized funds, food and clothes and delivered necessary assistance to the deserving victims.

In the wake of the terror attacks in Mumbai on 26th November 2008, one of the biggest attacks of the recent times, Indian news media have been very instrumental in becoming the change agents. Various initiatives have been launched to create awareness about terrorism and to find solutions to some of the key issues which could prevent India from facing a similar situation in future.[17]

Network18's English news channel CNN-IBN in association with Hindustan Times group launched their own agenda against terrorism called, 'Citizens against terror'. 'Aaj Tak' a News channel, too launched 'Declare War on Terror' to bring all Indians together to fight and counter terrorism in all forms. In response to the terror attacks a television channel under NDTV group, NDTV Profit launched a campaign to try and find answers to terror-based issues like security, intelligence, infrastructure, corporate activism and crisis management from the corporate world of India.

Newspaper daily Daily News & Analysis (DNA) launched its own initiative called 'Eyes & Ears People Protection Group' to encourage people to report anything suspicious in their surroundings to DNA. The India Today Group[18] launched an initiative 'Declare War on Terror' forum under the aegis of its non-profit foundation CARE TODAY. It started from five cities Mumbai, Delhi, Jaipur, Ahmedabad and Bangalore with people taking a pledge to defeat the terrorists and their motives. [19] The

---

[17] Puneet Bahri Bedi, "Attack Aftermath: Media Houses Initiate Fightback Against Terror," www.exchange4media.com, 4, December 2008.

forum intends to bring about change in policy and law. It aimed at studying and presenting detailed proposals for upgradation of anti-terror institutions. Moreover, it intends to serve as a watchdog body to demand efficiency, governance and alertness from civic administration. It aims at ensuring that the heroes in the war are honoured. It is determined, through debate and discussion, to try and build a national consensus on this issue. Above all, it will strive to ensure that the issue of terrorism does not fade away from the public domain and the national agenda. Mumbai-based daily tabloid *Mid-Day* launched a campaign 'Enough',

Radio stations too showed their concern and anguish over Indian government's apathy towards these attacks; Red FM launched its campaign 'Enough is enough', Mumbai station Big 92.7 FM of Anil Dhirubhai Ambani Group (ADAG) undertook a special drive 'Mumbai Halla Bol' to urge each and every Mumbai citizen to join them and speak up against terrorism. Additionally, ENIL's Radio Mirchi 98.3 FM initiated a 15day campaign 'Be alert but don't be prejudiced' appealing all to practice communal peace.

Apart from lending free air time and partnering with NGOs, media has also contributed by positioning as advertisers. Aaj Tak one of the leading Hindi news channels, pioneered the role of advertiser[20] by creating its own social advertising campaigns, where a protagonist addresses the various social evils like corruption, eve-teasing and smoking in public places. These advertisements were regularly aired on its channels. These social advertisements made by Code Red Films were honoured with the prestigious Radio and Television Advertising Practitioner's Award (RAPA) awards at the 29th All India RAPA Awards in the Public Service Advertising category.

Thus in the recent past, Indian media has been playing a pivotal

[18] "Over 94000 Join India Today Group's Movement Against Terror", *India Today*, 13, December 13, 2008.

[19] Ibid.

role in addressing social issues in crisis and otherwise. They have emerged as an effective change agent playing their part quite successfully.

2.2.3 Contribution of Corporate Towards Social Advertising

The Indian corporate have been actively involved on social front and social advertising in India is on the rise. The year 2008 should be considered one of the most phenomenal years considering India Inc's brand initiatives. Social awareness and proactive initiatives, driven by the corporate India, reached a new high for the mass awareness, assertion and action.[21] Times Group's Lead India/Teach India campaign and Bureau of Energy Efficiency's energy efficiency certification initiative signaled a beginning to this tone of 'awakening' early in the year. Followed by host of brands which have successfully woven their brand with a social idea—right from Tata Tea's electoral awareness campaign Jago Re!, Idea Cellular's 'What an Idea' campaign highlighting rural education and political accountability, Security and Exchange Board of India's investor awareness programme to SBI and ICICI Bank's consumer education series and ministry of consumer affairs''Jago Grahak Jago'. Though the year ended on a sad note due to the terror attacks on Mumbai, the financial capital of India, it spurred a series of social advertisements and campaigns demanding for accountability in loud voices against terror attacks.

For several years Indian private corporate have integrated philanthropy into their overall corporate goals. They usually allocate a percentage of their annual budgets to a variety of causes to which they contribute money, expertise or promotional know-how. Socially responsible activities enhance the image and stature of the company among its many publics and indirectly

---

[20] "Aaj Tak bags four RAPA awards", www.agencyfaqs.com,, 24, May 2004

[21] Bhanu Pande and Amit Sharma, "The Year of Mass Awareness, Assertion and Action", *The Economic Times*, 25, December 2008.

contribute to the company's commercial objectives, creating a win-win situation for the company and for society.

In recent times Indian firms are carrying social advertising as their basic responsibility, for example a manufacturer of alcohol like Seagram promoting social advertising for awareness about drunken driving or Reliance energy advertising on saving energy. Maruti Udyog has been promoting safe driving. Finland's telecom giant Nokia launched "why talk while driving?" commercial to educate Indians about mobile etiquette. United Breweries has been promoting sensible and socially responsible drinking.[22]

While some organisations take a cause marketing route some other companies adopt a social cause which is not connected to their brand in any way. Tata Tea, the market leader within the tea category, fulfilled its social responsibility to create awareness about the problems that India faces, and to initiate positive action to help society break free from apathy by tying up with Janagraha for the 'Jaago Re' campaign[23]. Founded in 2001, Janaagraha is a NGO working on social awakening, with citizens and their governments to impro e the quality of life in cities and towns, by addressing issues of urban governance[24]. The Jaago Re is a bid to awaken the entire country and to facilitate "One Billion Votes" campaign on-ground. The campaign was targeted at the youth, who would be urged to stand up against social apathy. With plans to create awareness in colleges and organisations in 35 cities across the nation, One Billion Votes will create a platform to help the people vote. The take away message of their on-ground and online campaign being, "If on Election day you're not voting then you're sleeping".

---

[22] Sujoy Bosu, "Social Ads: The Way to a Consumer's Heart", *Times of India*, 13, August 13, 2001.
[23] Saurabh Turakhia, "Tata Tea Brews Up Big Bang Social Advertising Campaign," Hindustan Times, 13, November 2007.
[24] www.jaagore.com

Profit oriented businesses adopt different measures to discharge their social responsibilities. Some companies use social advertising in order to generate goodwill by merging social idea with their product's sales appeals like Nirodh with family planning, Indian Drugs and Pharmaceuticals Limited's effect on health problem, McDowell with drunken driving.[25] Companies such as Seagram and Bacardi address issues like drunken driving.[26] Idea Cellular has been celebrating the power of ideas that can bring about social change through their commercials and according to them that reflects their brand ethos and allows them to differentiate from others. This social theme that they have adopted is rather in line with the general mood of the nation of social consciousness. In these cases the social cause is related to the product they promote.

Some companies set apart some budget for public service advertising (PSA) as a part of their corporate social responsibility.[27] While some other companies are adopting social advertising in a rapidly changing environment as a new and creative way for engaging stakeholders.[28] In such cases companies address the social issues by associating the sale of their product with a social edge, termed as 'Cause Marketing'. Such messages aren't just about corporate social responsibility but aimed to appeal to consumers. The companies promote their advertisements wherein there is a promise made to prospective buyers that in case they buy the brand then a pre-determined percentage of the profit will be utilised for some social welfare. Many wellknown companies like Britannia industries, ITC Ltd., Hindustan Unilever Ltd. have latched on to such strategies. Commercials for ITC's products such as Sunfeast biscuits speak

---

[25] Ibid.

[26] Shunu Sen, "In Society's Interest",*Business Line's Catalyst*, 31, August 2001.

[27] S. Y. Quraishi, "Cave of Flickering Shadows," *The Indian Express*, 07, Oct 2008.

[28] Priyanka Mehra, "Ads with Social Pitch Pay More", *Hindustan Times, Mint*, 4, June 2007.

of how the sale and purchase of these will help the company fund water-conservation efforts and Aashirvaad wheat flour will provide employment for people in rural areas.[29] Hindustan Unilever was an early adopter of this trend with its campaign, featuring activist film actors Shabana Azmi and Revathi, for Surf Excel Quick Wash detergent that tried to sell soap on the promise that it would require less water (by as much as two buckets). Since then, the company has sold detergent and soap on such promises as scholarships for poor children (Surf Excel, again), and personal and environmental hygiene (Lifebuoy).

The social welfare here becomes a peg and the consumers buy brand with a feeling that using the brand is a virtue and in this way they are discharging their social responsibility.[30] In this way company reaps dual benefits, at one end they are promoting themselves as a responsible corporate, concerned about society which helps them earn positive image whereas on the other hand commercial advertising with a social edge helps get positive evaluation for the brand and ultimately sell more units. A survey in Europe by market research firm Gfk NOP found that consumers were willing to pay a 5-10 per cent premium for products sold by 'ethical' companies. Another international survey, by public relations firm Weber Shandwick, found that social causes, especially ones that have to do with the environment, affect how consumers make decisions, including their "speed to action", or time between the message and the purchase.

Thus, social concern as an advertising strategy and creative execution is emerging as the latest trend among advertisers to sell their ware.[31] Several environmental factors could be attributed for this trend. In the first place public service undertakings were conceived with an inherent motive of public-good and there was no

---

[29] Ibid.

[30] "New face of Social Advertising", www.rediff.com, 29, November 2005.

[31] Ibid.

competition. But with more corporate jumping into the fray it became imperative for public service undertakings to communicate that they were socially responsible and social advertising became a form of corporate social responsibility. Several large institutions have used social advertising as a strategy to cut through competition during recession, or to project their image as that of a philanthropist.[32] Secondly social advertising gives a human face to the brand and protects it in the face of negative publicity and brands are awakening to this reality. The trend of social advertising is increasing across brands and categories because it is seen as an effective way to break clutter. This is however only possible if the company and social cause fit with each other.[33]

India Inc. had been showing keen interest in welfare of the society yet their commitment is still not instrumental in bringing about the required change in the society. Considering the volume of social issues requiring serious attention, it is felt that companies are not advertising enough.They are more keen on gauging the marketability of social issues rather than finding solutions to long-standing problems and its ironic that the budget for social advertisements is culled from what the consumer pays.[34]

2.2.4 NGOs and Non Profit Organisations

There are non-profit organizations in India that undertake social advertising with specific objectives in their stated mission. A cancer society like CPAA promotes healthy social practices and informs and educates the public through social messages. These are social causes that fulfil the prime objectives of such a non-profit organisation that sponsors them and marketing these causes is their major reason for being. Many organisations involved in social welfare such as houses for destitute, handicaps and aged

[32] Sujoy Bosu, *op. cit.*

[33] "New Face of Social Advertising," *op. cit.*

[34] Sujoy Bosu, *op. cit*

and hospitals are involved in social advertising. Organisations like NACO relies heavily on social advertising to disseminate information on various issues related to AIDS/HIV like promoting healthy sex practices through use of condoms, to fight with social stigma associated with AIDS /HIV patients, to prevent mother-to-child transmission and so on.

2.2.5 Contribution of Advertising Agencies Towards Social Advertising

Advertising agencies in India also contribute towards social advertising.[35] Since there are no set parameters for charity, every advertising agency has its own ways and means of contributions. Agencies usually contribute towards social advertising through subsidized fees for creative work or for no fee at all. Some agencies have a special department working for social advertising. Lintas, a reputed advertising agency, when under Alyque Padamsee, who is currently chairman of London Institute of Personality Development, used to keep 1 per cent of their profits to make public service advertisements. They had special units with the mandate to create social communication messages which can be sponsored by interested parties. In Lintas no charges were made for the creative work done, which was the contribution of the agency to society. The advertising agencies through social advertising get an opportunity to discharge their social responsibility. In case of Ogilvy & Mather (O&M) India who has done its share of social welfare, with campaigns for the CPAA, the Jaipur Foot Association, Indian Association for Promotion of Adoption and Child Welfare, among others the practice is little different. When it comes to charging the client for social advertising considers the clients and if the NGO in question does not have a budget the agency does not charge for the creatives though they usually ask for reimbursements of actual expenses incurred.

[35] "Moves that tweak attitudes", *Financial Express*, 30 September 2007

In their personal capacity too, many of the creative people are involved in social welfare. As one grateful mother of a special abilities child reveals Prasoon Joshi, executive chairman and regional creative director, South and South-East Asia, McCann, Prahlad Kakkar, advertising filmmaker, Piyush Pande, among others, took time out to do half-day sessions on filmmaking with a group of special abilities children, free of cost.

Following are some of the contributions made by the advertising agencies:

- The advertisement shown on several television channels made by Piyush Pande of O&M Advertising, focusing on the fact that smokers don't have much time to live is effective since it targets the younger generation who are still making the decision whether to smoke or not. O&M has been regularly associated with making social advertisements for different advertisers. O&M had made a very impressive social advertising for National Literacy Mission to encourage adult education.[36]

- The advertisement created by Contract Advertising with the message "Every cigarette pack comes with an expiry date. . . . . Smoking kills" put up on hoardings effectively drives home the point that smoking decreases the life expectancy. Contract Advertising also made series of advertisements, which appeared in newspapers like *Indian Express* and *Loksatta* (a Marathi Daily) regarding passive smoking. The advertisements depicted how often smokers endanger the lives of non-smokers by smoking in their presence.

- Varsha Chawda of SOMAC, the Social Marketing & Communication wing of Lowe, created outdoor ad showing the word "BREASTS" in mirror image. The message "Check in the mirror at least once a month" emphasised the importance of Breast Self Examination in diagnosis of breast cancer at the earliest possible stage when it is curable.

- Trikaya Grey devised an advertisement showing a tongue protruding out of a mouth. The copy, extending over the tongue says "Cut here". A coupon was provided for mailing to CPAA for information on cancer. This advertisement, which appeared in *Loksatta* a Marathi daily, was highly effective since a number of enquiries were received in response to this advertisement.

- Mudra started its 'Child domestic work-awareness' media campaign through billboards, after conducting intensive research involving 2,000 children engaged in domestic work. The communication attempts to heighten the fact that child domestic workers most often do the kind of work that adults ought to do. The campaign idea, 'domestic work isn't child's play', is dramatized by replacing the home setting where they do their chores, with toy houses – complete with a kitchen set, bathroom set, bedroom set, etc., that typically children play with. The agency has used bus shelters, bus panels and hoardings at prominent places, followed by a print campaign in select magazines.
- The social division of a well known advertising agency Leo Burnett, Leo Hope, works with an NGO, Prerana. They have made use of mass media such as television and press advertising for addressing the issue of child trafficking. The communication works on the insight that the girl child from a village is often lured with false promises to big cities, where she becomes a victim of child crimes.
- Rediffusion-DY&R Brand Communications made a campaign on child prostitution issued in public interest.

---

[36] Shunu Sen, *op. cit.*

Made by the trio, Adrian Mendonza, Parag Tembulkar and Mangesh Rane, this film was a sensitive portrayal of a real-life story picked up from police files. This film was made in-house by Rediffusion to fulfil their social responsibility without charging any money. Fortunately Mumbai daily Afternoon Courier & Dispatcher sponsored the campaign and showed their commitment to the social cause. Rediffusion India had assisted Mumbai Police and Punjab Police with their advertising dealing on issues such as traffic signals safe driving, road signs, safety at home, neighbourhood watch schemes and highway safety.[37]

The advertisements made by various advertising agencies for CPAA were made with no fees at all or they claimed only reimbursements for expenses incurred.[38]

Though advertising agencies have shown their support to such endeavours yet the objective is not always social. Firstly advertising agencies consider this as a platform to showcase their creativity.[39] Social advertising also gives the creative heads from agencies a free hand as the work is mainly pro bono.[40] The best advertising talent is taking up the challenge to make advertising with social messages that are targeted at creating awareness about AIDS, family planning, child abuse, drug abuse, adult literacy and environmental conservation. Many of these have been admired for their aesthetic excellence. The volume of such films has also increased as more companies support causes or initiatives to enhance their people-friendly image or corporate social responsibility. In these types of advertisements, the subject matter itself has an inherent dramatic quality. In the hands of a talented creative person, this drama can be amplified to stunning effect.[41] Besides the social service organizations involved are not so preoccupied with things like 'brand architecture','advertising proposition' and 'discriminator', the creative person is free to give

[37] Alice Guram, *op. cit.*

full rein to his or her creativity. (Contrast this with what happens in a typical commercial brand advertising scenario: Where the real challenge is not in creating great advertisements, but in getting them past the client). As a result agencies find it easy to work with NGOs compared to mainline clients since they are often less rigid and more amenable to good creative ideas, which allows for better advertising. And this, in turn, has an effect on mainline clients, as they look at the agency's good work and notice the ideas in mainline advertising too.[42]

Some agencies have a different point of view while working on social ideas merged with commercial product / services.[43] Advertising agencies and advertisers adopt socially centric theme with its emphasis on powerful human values due to the rising paranoia about the state of the advertising industry. Advertising has always been on the verge of being marginalized and keeps losing out to branded entertainment like public relation and other events. And advertising campaigns that deal with social agendas is the best way to become significant and save the business by integrating it into the social fabric and into society's value system.

Thus, advertising agencies have been instrumental in the field of social advertising and have been making social advertisements out of their sense of moral responsibility.

2.2.6 International Aid for Social Issues and Social Advertising

At international level too India receives assistance from international agencies for various social causes. The International

---

[38] Cancer Patients Aid Association, Monthly report, December 2000.

[39] Pervin Malhotra, *op. cit.*

[40] *Ibid.*

[41] Sumanto Chattopadhyay, "Some of the Most Outstanding Cannes Winners Were in the Social Categories Cannes Special!", www.afaqs.com, June 23, 2003.

[42] N. Shatrujeet, "Cannes 2003: Implications for India - Part II", www.agencyfaqs.com, 01, July 2003.

and United Nations agencies that provide significant technical and material assistance to India include the following:[44]

- *The United Nations*

The United Nations has been providing India funds for various social causes. India receives assistance for national level family welfare scheme under UNFPA and other issues such as literacy, girl child and drug addiction.

- *United Nations International Children's Fund*

The UNICEF assistance to India has been in the Maternity and Child Health programmes and Expanded programmes on Immunization . The assistance has been in the form of supplies and equipments for medical aids like syringes and vaccines for pediatric units of districts and sub-districts hospitals, publicity materials, and in the form of in-service training and health education.

- *World Bank*

India has been receiving World Bank assistance in the area projects that were aimed at improving health and family welfare, reducing fertility and reducing maternal and child mortality and morbidity.

- *World Health Organisation (WHO)*

The WHO is the main UN agency collaborating with India for promotion and development of various fields of health. India is the founder member of the WHO. WHO provides assistance to its member states on a biennium basis.

- *Norwegian Agency for International Development (NORAD)*

---

43 Paul Josy, "Socially Active Advertising Idea on a High", *The Economic Times*, 1, Jan 2008.

44 Chauhan, Meenakshi, *op. cit.*

India has been receiving partial financial support from the Royal Government of Norway for implementing postpartum programme in Urban and Semi Urban areas of the country.

- *Danish International Development Agency (DANIDA)*

India receives assistance from DANIDA for expansion and improvement of rural services delivery infrastructure.

- *United States Agency for International Development (USAID)*

Under the agreements signed from time to time with the USAID, the government has been receiving assistance for undertaking demographic analysis and development studies. The assistance is also utilised for activities such as expansion and improvement of basic health, efforts for special preventive health, family planning, providing nutrition services and other relevant social causes in rural and urban areas. The voluntary organisations also receive financial assistance for their objectives.

Thus, many international agencies have been liberally providing monetary as well as non-monetary assistance to India in order to address the social issues.

2.3 Assessing the Social Advertising in India

Social advertising in India is changing drastically almost without exception.[45] In the recent years it is slickly produced and expensively mounted. Social advertising in India is witnessing massive increase in the levels of professionalism. One reason for this could be the fact that the work is mostly pro bono and creative people get a free hand while working with this genre of advertisements. The change could also be because organizations are willing to pay for social campaigns and the planning, execution and evaluation of social campaigns are accorded the same importance as regular commercial ones in some cases. John Hopkins Centre of Communication's AIDS Campaign 'Jawan Hoon Nadaan Nahi' created by FCB ULka was Rs. 10 crore campaign. The absolute sums of money being spent on social advertising have increased substantially and the budgets in case estimated could run into several hundred crore, especially if one monetises the media exposure. The reason for this treatment for social advertising could be further attributed to the way social causes are defining corporate vision and brand stances and hence, they are seen as part of total branding exercises.

Though social advertising is getting highly professional, it suffers from its own version of haves and have nots[46]. It is generally observed voluntary organisations interested in working for the society pick up issues such as AIDS and HIV positives where funds are liberally sanctioned. Whereas issues devoid of funds like illiteracy among children or care of thalassaemic patients rarely get any attention. This secondary treatment is observed from media too, that shies away from non-glamorous social issues. AIDS is a huge celebrity enterprise and organisations try to portray celebrities as caring individuals who need to be taken seriously. But celebrities use such campaigns as vehicles to improve their own public image with little conviction about what they are saying to the camera. The welfare sector in India is beginning to assume the complications and the intrigue of the corporate world since the advertisers too are seen using the welfare messages to camouflage their commercial motives.

It is also observed, barring few instances most of the social advertisements appear to be unimpressive in nature in India. The fate of various good cause social advertising aimed at educating or admonishing the masses is lost because they have not been introduced in the manner to make an impact[47]. And one of the simple way of achieving this is by using the services of popular personalities. The UK government had run some successful campaigns to spread messages on social awareness among the

- - - - - - - - - - - - - - - - - - -

[45] Anusha Subramanian, *op. cit.*

[46] Jaisinghani Bella, "The Hysteria of Activism", *Times of India*, 3, December 2006.

South Asian communities by using Indian film-stars and television stars. Dr Vilas Deshpande, deputy director, state health information, education and communication, feels government advertises the social issues with limited budgets and as a result the impact of social advertising is also limited. Several social advertising lack emotions and are not made in a way that would generate interest. There is a dire need to localise advertising and make it as per the audience's strata and cultural constraints. If social advertising is spruced as brand advertising is and if it is made in a subtle fashion it will bring about the necessary change in the society.

The irony of the social scene in India is tnat the social advertising is criticised for its quality and impact yet it impresses international juries and industry experts, especially in the past few years. Some of these advertising are so ingenious and creative that they corner a fair share of awards on the global stage. Indian social advertising has been internationally applauded quite regularly in recent times. Rediffusion-DY&R Brand Communications had secured nine finalist entries at the London International Awards. Of these nine, four campaigns were nominated in the social campaign category. While two films made for Maruti Udyog Ltd. urged viewers to obey traffic rules, the film made for a Mumbai-based non-governmental organisation focused on the gruesome aspects of child prostitution. Another film, Flower Child, was from the Novartis campaign. The campaign on child prostitution initiated by Rediffusion was sponsored by Mumbai daily Afternoon Courier & Dispatcher.

BBDO's campaign 'Open your mind' for Essar won India's first International Pencil Award at the One Show Awards in New York.[48] The agency has to its credit many popular advertising campaigns like 'Jaago' campaign for Tata Tea and a social

---

[47] Devayani Shahane, "Social Advertising: Don't Condone It, CONDOM It", *Times of India*, September 6, 2001.

campaign for Idea Cellular.

Mudra Delhi won a Silver at the AME Awards (Advertising and Marketing Effectiveness) of the New York Festivals 2005 for its 'Save Water' campaign, RMG David's 'Nest' campaign for WWF won a couple of awards at the ABBYs, One Show Pencil, Young Guns, and London International, where locally produced public service campaigns had charmed the local/international jury.[49]

A media relations campaign aimed at promoting the consistent use of condoms as part of safe sex practices and family planning in India was chosen for the 2007 United Nations Grand Award for outstanding achievement in public relations. The Grand Award was established in 1990 to recognise excellence in campaigns that address UN priority issues. The campaign, 'Condom Bindaas Bol', was designed to address a decline in condom use and sales across eight northern Indian states — Bihar, Chhattisgarh, Delhi, Jharkhand, Madhya Pradesh, Rajasthan, Uttaranchal and Uttar Pradesh that account for 45 per cent of the condom market in India and make up 40 per cent of India's population. The award was presented as part of the 2007 IPRA Golden World Awards at a ceremony in London. The social campaign, created by Delhi based Weber Shandwick, is a joint effort of PSP-One, a United States Agency for International Development (USAID) project, ICICI Bank, and the Indian Health and Family Welfare Ministry.[50]

It is to be further noted that pubic service advertising has been dominating as far as the India's supremacy is concerned in the global advertising scenario. More than a third of the 29 nominations in Print and Outdoor at the Cannes International Advertising Festival 2003[51] were public service/social awareness

---

[48] Josy Paul ,*op. cit.*

[49] Devina Joshi, "What Drives Public Service Campaigns – Conscience, Money or Awards?," www.agencyfaqs.com, 25, July 2005.

[50] "United Nations Public Information Department, Global Public Relations Association to Honour Publicity Campaign on Condom Use for Safe Sex, Family Planning," Press Release, Note No. 6096, www.un.org, 20, August 2007.

advertisements. Of the four Lions in Print and Outdoor, three were for public service advertisements (for CPAA), while only one (Coke) was for a mainstream advertiser. India's Film shortlist too had a clear public service tilt. In the year 2004 too, of the seven Indian entries that had been nominated in Press, four carried public service/social awareness messages for NGO clients. In the Outdoor category, of the 17 short-listed entries from India, while four were directly for NGOs, six were for mainstream clients and brands - with themes centnred at social awareness and safety. And two of the four Lions that India won in the same year were for social awareness advertisements. Thus Indian advertising depends heavily on public service category when it comes to sending entries to the most prestigious Cannes International Advertising Festival.[52]

While award-winning entries deserve to be congratulated, there are quite a few industry insiders who feel that some of these advertisements are produced with the objective of grabbing awards, and have little to do with the effectiveness of the commercial. The criticism is not actually about public service advertising. It is about the fact that these advertisements were hardly seen by anybody Many senior people from the field acknowledge the existence of 'awards obsession' in the industry and in fact in some cases public service advertisements are made first and then they look out for a sponsor. There is no unanimous opinion about whether public service is charitable or commercial; some experts believe it to be charitable because there is no money in it on the other hand some believe it to be as professional as any commercial advertising.[53]

2.4 Conclusion

In a nutshell social advertising in India is characterised by contributions from all participants, headed by government followed by corporate, media, advertising agency and celebrities as well.

- - - - - - - - - - - - - - - - -

[51] N. Shatrujeet, *op. cit.*

[52] N. Shatrujeet, "Cannes 2004: India's Showing Draws Mixed Response," www.agencyfaqs.com, 28, June 2004.

The social advertising in India is on rise and is gaining recognition for its creativity at international level. Whether social advertising is done for self-aggrandisement or for the greater good but as long as the public is benefiting from them it should be encouraged.

[53] Devina Joshi, *op. cit.*

3

Studying the Influence of Social Advertising with Reference to Youth

3.1 Introduction - To the Study

Any advertising to accomplish its objectives involves correct understanding and treatment of many factors like content and tone of advertising message, selection of media and media vehicle, timing and repetition of the advertisements. Failure from any of these would ultimately mean the failure of the entire advertising exercise. In social advertising these factors acquire even more importance than commercial advertising. In commercial advertisements the functional goal often could be restricted to creating awareness or to increase sales without necessarily altering the consumer's predispositions and attitudes. Whereas social advertising by and large aims at bringing about more permanent attitudinal or behavioural change among its audience and therefore its goal are even more difficult to accomplish. Before carrying social advertising several factors need to be analysed in-depth so that they can be effectively used to bring about the desired change. The book is an attempt to present how the various factors affecting the effectiveness of social advertising were evaluated. Various variables are evaluated in this book like celebrities, appeals, repetition, clutter and the media used for social advertising. According to authors these variables contribute in a major way to the success or failure of social advertising. The present research work tries to investigate the role of these variables individually in social advertising and how they affect the recall of social advertising. The authors have attempted to investigate the causative factors that influence the response of youth towards social advertising.

While observing the social advertising scene in India and in particular in Mumbai it was noticed that different advertisers like International bodies, government and their ministries, private companies, non-governmental organizations conduct advertising on various social issues. Each of these organisations has its own set of media which includes a varying mix of television, radio, newspaper, magazines, banners and hoardings. The impact of such social advertisements on the opinion and attitudes of youth was to be studied. The authors employed a controlled laboratory technique to yield meaningful outcome. Since in the controlled laboratory test like in the present case the authors had control on what was being shown and also on how many times it was shown. The authors could maintain uniform degree of exposure to the social advertisements in the subjects. This was achieved by presenting absolutely new or unseen advertisements in the presentation so that all the subjects were at the same level of awareness or rather unawareness.

Secondly there are various factors that need to be considered while creating and presenting social advertising. After careful observation of content and conduct of social advertising in India and Mumbai, and considering the limitations of time and practicality the authors ascertained five areas of study. Thus the present endeavor tries to seek answers for the following questions:

- Does social advertising with celebrity as a source result in better recall compared to social advertising without celebrity?
- Does social advertising with fear as an appeal result in better recall compared to social advertising without fear appeal?
- Do exclusively shown social advertisements result in better

recall compared to social advertisements shown amidst clutter of general advertising?

Does social advertisements presented on audio-video medium like television result in better recall compared to social advertisements presented on non-audiovideo medium like posters?

Does social advertising shown repeatedly result in better recall compared to social advertising not repeated at all?

3.1.1 Variables under Study

A Variable is an empirical property that takes two or more values. As Nachmias and Nachmias put it, if a property can change in value or kind, it can be regarded as a variable.[1] In most of the cases the research is focused on cause-effect relationships that start with an effect and then the causes for it are searched. The variable which represents the cause is termed as independent variable. The variable that is the effect or is the result or outcome of another variable is the dependent variable. Thus the variable expected to explain change in the dependent variable is referred to as the independent variable. The independent variable is also known as explanatory variable. Independent variable is considered as the presumed cause of changes in the values of dependent variable. Processwise, the dependent variable is the expected outcome of the independent variable. Independent variable and dependent variable are also termed as predictor and criterion variables respectively.[2]

In the present research the following independent variables and dependent variables were measured:

a) Independent variables

The study measured five independent variables namely:

- - - - - - - - - - - - - - - - -

[1] D.Nachmias and C. Nachmias, *Research Methods in the Social Sciences*, New York, St. Martins Press, 1981, p. 1.

- Celebrity as a source in advertising
- Fear appeals in advertising
- Clutter as a barrier to communication
- Effectiveness of audio-video medium such as television for social advertising
- Repetition as an aid to memory

In order to measure these five variables individually, following five studies were designed:

Table 3.1
Details of Studies

Sr. No.	Factors under study
Study One	Impact of celebrity as a source in social advertising
Study Two	Impact of fear appeals in social advertising
Study Three	Impact of noise/clutter on recall of social advertising
Study Four	Effectiveness of television in social advertising
Study Five	Impact of repetition on recall of social advertising

Study One: Impact of celebrity as a source in social advertising

Study One was designed to evaluate the impact of celebrity in social advertising. In order to achieve this, four social advertisements with celebrities were pitched against a set of four social advertisements without celebrities through audio-video presentation. A study specific questionnaire based on the advertisements presented was used to study the responses for further analysis and comparison.

Study Two: Impact of fear appeals in social advertising:

Study Two was an attempt to analyse the impact of fear appeals in social advertising. To evaluate whether social

---

[2] D. K. Lal Das, *Designs of Social Research, Rawat Publications*, Jaipur, 2005, p. 30.

advertisements with fear appeals make more impact, social advertisements that had fear or disturbing appeals were shown along with social advertisements that appeals other than fear like humour or information. Four advertisements on each, fear based and non-fear based appeals were shown in the audio-video presentation. A study specific questionnaire based on the presentation was used to seek the responses.

Study Three: Impact of noise/clutter on recall of social advertisements

Study Three aimed at evaluating the negative impact of noise or clutter on social advertising. The audio-video presentation was made comprising four social advertisements that were shown amidst clutter of commercial advertisements and there were another set of four social advertisements that were shown exclusively without any clutter. A study specific questionnaire was used to seek the responses and determine the impact.

Study Four: Effectiveness of television in social advertising

The objective of Study Four was to evaluate the effectiveness of audiovideo medium like television compared to non-audio-video medium like posters for social advertising. For achieving this objective the audio-video presentation included four social advertisements and their responses were compared with the response of the four social advertisements that were shown through posters. The responses were obtained using study specific questionnaire.

Study Five: Impact of repetition on recall of social advertisements

Study Five was conducted to study whether repetition has an impact on the audience. To investigate this four social advertisements were repeatedly presented and four social advertisements were presented just once in the audio-video presentation. The responses to repeated and non-repeated social advertising were acquired using study specific questionnaire.

b) Dependent variables

The study measured two dependent variables namely:

- Recall of social advertising.
- The attitude towards social advertising.
- Recall of social advertising : The organisation that initiates the message must develop some method for determining whether its mass communications are, in fact, received by the intended audience, understood in the intended way and successful in achieving the intended objectives.[3] Post-tests are used to evaluate the effectiveness of an advertisement that has already run and to see which elements, if any, should be changed to improve the impact of future advertisements. Recall is a type of post-test that is conducted to determine whether consumers remember seeing a commercial, whether they can recall its content and to assess the commercial's influence on consumers' attitudes toward the product and their buying intentions. *Recall* refers to measures of the proportion of a sample audience that can recall an advertisement.[4] This approach involves asking an individual to recall what advertisements he or she viewed in a given setting or time period. Then, in progressive steps, the subject is asked to identify information about the advertisement. Some of the parts of an advertisement that can be tested for recall are product name or brand, firm name, tagline, product attributes and so on.[5]

The audience can be tested using an approach called unaided recall. In unaided recall, only the product or service name may be given and the subjects are asked to name or recall, the

---

[3] Leon Schiffman and Kanuk Leslie Lazar Kanuk, *Consumer Behaviour*, Prentice-Hall India, New Delhi, 2000, pp. 288-89.

[4] Rajeev Batra, John G. Myers and David A. Aaker, *Advertising Management*, 5th ed., Prentice Hall India, New Delhi, 2004, pp. 466-468.

[5] Kenneth E Clow. and Donald Baack, *Integrated Advertising, Promotion and Marketing Communications*, Pearson Education Inc., 2002, pp. 487-88.

advertisements they saw or heard the previous evening, without being given any other prompts or memory jogs. The second type of recall test is the aided recall method. In aided recall, the respondent is prompted by showing a picture of the advertisement with the sponsor or brand name blanked out.[6] Aided recall means that consumers are prompted by being told the product category and, if necessary names of specific brands in that category. The respondent does not know which brand or advertisement is being tested. When the consumer states that he or she does recall seeing a specific brand being advertised, then he/she is asked to provide as many details as possible about the advertisement. At that point, no further clues are given regarding the advertisement content.

Most researchers believe the unaided recall approach is superior to other evaluative tests because it identifies the times that an advertisement has become lodged in the person's memory.[7] Unaided recall is also better than aided recall because some people may respond to a prompt by saying they do indeed remember an advertisement, even when they are uncertain. Recall scores are almost always higher when the aided recall method is used. Some advertisement agencies use both methods. First, they use unaided recall to gather basic information. Then the researcher follows up with prompts to delve deeper into the memories that are present, even if it takes a little help to dig them out.

Thus recall tests are valuable instruments used in recall testing to gauge whether advertisement has the potential to move into a person's long-term memory and affect future purchase decisions. On the plus side, it is considered that recall tests can assess the advertisement's impact on memory.[8] In present research both aided

- - - - - - - - - - - - - - - -

[6] Rajeev Batra, John G. Myers and David A. Aaker, *op. cit.*, pp. 466-68.

[7] E. Clow Kenneth and Donald Baack, *op. cit.*, p. 487.

[8] G.Belch and M. Belch, *op. cit.*, p. 642.

recall and unaided recall were measured in each of the five studies conducted.

- The attitude towards social advertising.

The topic of attitudes has been one of the most important subjects of study in the field of consumer behaviour.[9] Attitude is a central concept in the entire field of social psychology and theories and methods associated with its explanation and measurement have largely evolved from the work of social psychologists and psychometricians. Allport Gordon W., for example has stated that "Attitude is probably the most distinctive and indispensable concept in American social psychology. No other term appears more frequently in experimental and theoretical literature."[10]

Though social psychologists do not agree on any precise definition of an attitude, one of the common definitions generally accepted is given by Allport:

Attitude is a learned disposition to respond to an object or class of objects in a consistently favorable or unfavorable way.

The most widely held view of the structure of an attitude is that it is made of three closely interrelated components: cognitive (awareness, comprehension, knowledge), affective (evaluation, liking, preference) and conative (action tendencies such as intentions, trial or purchase). Attention is usually focused on the middle (affective) component, assessing the degree of positive or negative feelings towards an object. The underlying assumption is that this overall liking component is based on the cognitive component (beliefs and knowledge about the brand) and then leads to the intention to try (or lack of it).[11] From the advertisers point of view it is important to know how overall attitude is measured and to understand the basis on which it is formed, in order to develop an

---

[9] David L. Loudon and Albert J. Della Bitta , *Consumer Behaviour*, 4th edu., Tata McGraw Hill, New Delhi, India, 2002, p 422.

[10] Gordon W. Allport, "Attitudes", in C. A. Murchison (ed.), *A Handbook of Social Psychology*, Clark University Press, Worcester, MA, 1935, pp. 798-844.

[11] David L. Loudon and Albert J. Della Bitta, *.op. cit.*, pp. 422-25.

advertising campaign that strives to increase the favourability of attitudes towards brands.

In the present research the attitude towards social advertising is measured directly by asking the sample to indicate, whether he or she liked or disliked the advertisements. The authors have measured cognitive component by assessing the awareness of the sample about social advertising carried on in India and affective components, by assessing whether the sample has liked the social advertisements shown in the presentation or not. The conative component of the attitude that deals with any behavioural change in the sample due to these social advertisements is however excluded from the present research.

3.1.2 Tools for Data Collection

For all the five studies mentioned above two tools were used, questionnaire and audio-video presentation. Accordingly five sets of questionnaires and five audiovideo presentations were prepared as per the need of the study. A plethora of social issues confront modern urban youth. Also social issues differ in their relevance for youth as well as their extent of publicity they receive in the media. The authors have made an attempt to cover issues, which differ in relevance as well as publicity in the audio-video presentation. Hence the presentation includes issues like anti-smoking, AIDS/HIV awareness and use of condoms which are directly concerned with youth and are highly publicized. However several other youth related social issues like anorexia, eve-teasing, drunken driving, use of mobile phones while driving, second hand smoke, which are acute, but rarely publicized are also a part of the presentation. Some of the issues like female feticide, domestic violence, population, polio, which may not have direct relevance to youth are also used in order to gain an insight into their attitude towards such social issues. Some neglected social issues like loneliness among elderly in Mumbai and maintenance of cleanliness in city, were included with an effort to create awareness among youth.

Table 3.2
The Social Issues Addressed in Audio-Video Presentation

1 Road accidents	Don't drink and drive
	Avoid using mobile phone while driving
2 Tobacco	Second hand smoke kills
	Anti smoking
3 AIDS/HIV	Importance of sex education
	Use of condoms
	Abstinence and promotion of responsible behaviour
4 Women related issues	Anorexia
	Eve-teasing
	Female feticide
	Domestic violence
5 Cleanliness	Keep Mumbai clean
6 Threat to elderly in city	Spend time with elderly
7 Polio eradication	Pulse polio awareness
8 Rising population	Population control

The rationale behind considering and including these issues in the presentation is based upon the severity of the issues. The social issues are explained with a brief background

1. Road Accidents

Road traffic crashes are a routine occurrence on roads throughout the world. Road traffic crashes kill 1.2 million people each year and injure millions more, particularly in low-income and middle-income countries. Many millions more are left with disabilities or emotional scars that they will carry for the rest of their lives. Children and young adults are among the most vulnerable. A combination of physical and developmental immaturity among children, and inexperience and youth-related lifestyles further increase the risk of young road users – particularly males – to road traffic collisions. Every hour of every day, forty youngsters die as a result of road traffic crashes. Every day just over 1000 young people under the age of 25 years are killed in road traffic crashes around the world. Road traffic injuries are the leading cause of death globally among 15–19-year-olds, while for those in the 10–14-years and 20–24-years age brackets they are the second leading cause of death. The emotional and practical impact on the victim's families and caregivers is considerable. In India there is a road accident every 100 seconds. One person dies on the road every seven minutes. Over 1000 people are injured every 24 hours! No wonder then that India accounts for the second largest number of road accidents in the world.

Road traffic injuries are a public health epidemic that costs countries millions of dollars / rupees. However, there is evidence of what can be done effectively to cut the volume of deaths and injuries linked to road traffic crashes. Bringing about a reduction in the road traffic toll among youth requires both political will and financial investments in prevention efforts targeting young people. Investments in various Public awareness campaigns can reduce the likelihood of an injury or fatality occurring due to drunken-driving. By presenting drunken–driving as socially unacceptable and by stimulating social pressure against the practice the publicity campaigns can bring about a widespread change in attitudes and behaviour. With a view to address these rising levels of road safety violations and to convert these concerns into positive behavioral changes, the advertisement on road safety message revolving round the use of seat belts and avoiding use of mobile phones while driving was included. The advertisement focused on the casual habit of many car users to attend their mobile phone while driving and the divided attention ultimately exposing them and pedestrians on the road at risk. In order to inculcate social responsibility awareness of disadvantages of alcohol and encouraging them to be accountable for their own actions, the advertisement on not driving when they were drunk was included in the presentation. The advertisement tries to remind consumers that their irresponsible behaviour is not only inviting risk for their own life but also for the others who depend on them.

2. Women Related Issues

Following women related issues were addressed in the audio-video presentation since everyday, women are subjected to violence in many forms. If unchecked, worldwide, an estimated one in five women will be a victim of rape or attempted rape in her lifetime. About 1 in 4 women will be abused during pregnancy, which puts both mother and child at risk. One in three will have been beaten, coerced into sex or otherwise abused, usually by a family member or an acquaintance. So several aspects related to women such as violence against women, female feticide, anorexia and eve-teasing were addressed through social advertisements.

Violence kills and disables as many women between the ages of 15 and 44 as cancer. And its toll on women's health surpasses that of traffic accidents and malaria combined. Gender-based violence is perhaps the most widespread and socially tolerated of human rights violations. Gender-based violence is preponderantly inflicted by men on women and girls which is a major human rights and public health concerns. It encompasses, a wide range of abuses, from physical, sexual and psychological violence occurring in the family and in the general community, including battering, sexual abuse of children, dowry-related violence, rape, female genital mutilation and other traditional practices harmful to women. The consequences of gender-based violence are devastating. Survivors often experience life-long emotional distress, mental health problems and poor reproductive health. Abused women are also at higher risk of acquiring HIV. Women who have been physically or sexually assaulted tend to be intensive long-term users of health services. The impact of violence may also extend to future generations: Children who have witnessed abuse, or were victims themselves, often suffer lasting psychological damage. So an advertisement focused on the issue of domestic violence is included in the Presentation.

In a country like India where many go hungry, Anorexia is unknown to most. But psychiatrists in urban areas are reporting cases of 'Anorexia Nervosa,' the so-called slimming disease that can cause sufferers to starve themselves to death. Anorexia is a dreaded illness where a person deliberately eats a bare minimum to keep one's body weight at painfully thin levels. This craze of young girls striving for the perfect figure was essentially a Western concept but has now transcended to most cultures. The concern is that this disorder is now on the rise in India, with not only young girls, but urban women and men and young boys too in its foray. To create awareness regarding this, the issue of anorexia was included.

Of all the gruesome crimes that take place against women, the molestation of women in public places is perhaps one of the most serious unnoticed crimes in urban India. Molestation is criminalized not just because it bodily violates the integrity of a woman, but also it is an affront to her dignity. Sexual violence apart from being a dehumanizing act is also an intrusion of the right to privacy and sanctity of a female. It is a serious offence to the women's honur and self-esteem. This advertisement is based on the general role people should adopt while in public. It stresses the need on how people should not be apathetic to the social evils happening around them and behave in a socially responsible manner to fight issues such as eve-teasing.

One form of violence against women is discrimination of women on the basis of gender to such an extent that a female baby is abandoned immediately after her birth or worse still she is killed in the womb before she sees the light of the day. There have been growing instances of female feticide in India and the blame is on misconceptions and superstitions attached with the male-child and also the technology, which is-being misused to detect the sex of babies in the womb.

One concern associated with female feticide crippling the country is abandoning of female infants immediately after they are born. The increasing practice of pre-natal selection as well as disowning baby girls indicates that male preference is predominant among all communities and all socio-economic sections of the society. Even the major metropolitan cities, which have higher incomes, higher female literacy rates and more women participating in the work force along with more liberal social values, are no different from others when it comes to this trend. Delhi, the political capital and Mumbai the commercial capital of the country have sex ratios of merely 865 and 898 females respectively per 1000 males in 0 to 6 years age group. These ratios are much below the already low national ratio of 927 females to 1000 males. To highlight the discriminative treatment a female fetus or child gets in India these issues were included in the presentation.

3. AIDS Awareness

Considering that globally young people constitute a third of all new HIV infections and 33 per cent of infections in India are in the 15-29 age group, it is important to reach young people with prevention messages before they become sexually active. With this objective following social advertisements addressing several aspects of AIDS were included in the audio-video presentation.

Young People are the key determinants of the future course of the HIV epidemic. The behaviours they adopt now and those that they maintain throughout their lives will determine the direction of the AIDS/HIV epidemic for decades to come. The advertisement targeted at urban youths in the age group of 15-19 year old, repositions perceived "old fashioned value" such as delaying sexual initiation, as a new and acceptable norm. The advertisement grounds in the realities of youth, recognises the challenges that young people face especially women, with peer pressure and the difficulty of refusing a sexual advance.

In order to raise AIDS/HIV awareness, promote safer sex, and enable youth to choose safer lifestyle options popular comedians were used in the ads. The information attempts to disseminate the information in a humorous manner. The advertisements dispels four common AIDS/HIV related myths which include "HIV/AIDS spreads by sharing food", "HIV/AIDS spreads by touching," "HIV/AIDS spreads via swimming pool" and "HIV/AIDS spreads through mosquito bites". The advertisements were supposed to easily connect with the youth because of its humour, non-preachy and yet educative approach.

In India, awareness about condoms is high but their us age is very low. The advertisement attempts to popularise condoms by emphasising that only caring men use condom. The campaign does not advertise any specific brand of condoms but promotes the entire category.

There is a dire need to equip the young people with prevention, education and life skills for promoting healthy and safe behavior and practices among them. This advertisement has several young people discussing about the need of correct and timely information on sex and sexual health as a protection against AIDS. The advertisement skilfully uses youth to voice the different aspects of AIDS and sex related concerns understanding the role of peers in influencing the behaviour of youth.

4. Cleanliness

Mumbai is the financial and commercial capital of India and its functioning and development is critical to India's development since it generates a large share of national tax revenues. However its economy and quality of living has stagnated rather worsened and the decline is quite steep. Slums have proliferated and congestion, pollution and water problems have skyrocketed. Municipal Corporation of Greater Mumbai (MCGM), the primary agency responsible for urban governance in Greater Mumbai with its limited resources is unable to provide a safe and hygienic environment to the ever-increasing population, exposing the Mumbai's residents to huge health risk.

The advertisement based on the disastrous consequences of 26 July 2005. This was the day when the entire city of Mumbai was lashed with heavy rainfalls for two consecutive days. The effects were disastrous and led to the loss of thousands of lives and homes. The advertisement tries to awaken the citizens to their responsibility of maintaining the city. The Mumbai citizens by curbing their habit of throwing plastic bags, paper and other litter on the streets that clog the drains, will not only keep their streets clean but also avoid a 26th July situation.

One more advertisement was included to support the cause of cleanliness. The advertisement included famous and responsible citizens of Mumbai appealing for co-operation of the Mumbai residents in keeping the city clean. The public-service communiqué urges people to understand the civic problems and teaches them the merits of keeping their homes and the city clean.

5. Anti Smoking

Tobacco use is a serious public health challenge in several regions of the world. It has assumed the dimension of an epidemic resulting in enormous disability, disease and death. In addition to damage to personal health, tobacco use results in severe societal costs like reduced productivity, health care burden, environmental damage and poverty of the families. Tobacco is one of the biggest killers in the world; tobacco kills one person every six seconds. Tobacco kills a third to half of all people who use it, on average 15 years prematurely. Today, tobacco use causes 1 in 10 deaths among adults worldwide. Second-hand smoke also has serious and often fatal health consequences. Children exposed to second hand smoke are at an increased risk of asthma development and aggravation, impaired lung function, ear and respiratory infections, more coughs and colds and developing lymphoma.

With a billion population, consisting of 230 million youth and with about 250 million tobacco users consisting of 194 million men and 45 million women and many more potential smokers India poses itself as a prime target for the tobacco giants from industrialised countries. In India, tobacco consumption is responsible for half of all the cancers in men and a quarter of all cancers in women, in addition to being a risk factor for cardiovascular diseases and chronic obstructive pulmonary diseases. India also has one of the highest rates of oral cancer in the world, partly attributed to high prevalence of tobacco chewing. Advertisements based on ill effects of smoking on one's own health and that of family members through passive smoking were included in the presentation.

6 Issue of Elderly

A substantive percentage, 77 million of India falls in the category of aged population, i.e. above 60 years and within the next 25 years, India's grey population will ratchet up to 177 million. Considering the current condition in which the elderly live or are rather made to live, with insecurity, injustice and abuse, it is a clear indication that ageing has become a major social challenge. Various NGOs, and autonomous organisations, including police are rendering valuable services to protect the vulnerable elderly. In Mumbai city, orgainsations like Dignity Foundation, HelpAge India and Mumbai Police offer helplines exclusively for the senior citizens, The helpline of Mumbai Police 1090, a 24 hours service, has 393 doctors, 152 hospitals and 1,419 volunteers registered with it. But in spite of these efforts spate of murders of senior citizen have been on rise, in most of the cases robbery being the prime motive. Isolation and frail health exposes them to assaults and other such criminal acts. The senior citizens plight is a social concern and it can be tackled if society extends support. The issue of safety and loneliness can be best resolved by increasing awareness. Public awareness can make the senior citizens aware of their own rights. In order to sensitize the youth with the concerns of the aged and promote better understanding of ageing issues this advertisement was included.

7. Polio Eradication

The world is about to turn the page on poliomyelitis, a viral disease that cripples young children since the dawn of civilization. The disease has vanished in most corners of the globe at the turn of the 21st century. As many as 209 countries, territories and areas have succeeded in cutting down wild poliovirus cases to nil by 2003. Among them, 134 have been certified polio-free after maintaining zero case performance for three consecutive years. Yet polio continues to menace the health and lives of children in seven countries: Afghanistan, Egypt, India, Nigeria, Niger, Pakistan and Somalia, the last frontiers of humankind's battle against the virus.

At the same time, the areas of transmission are more concentrated than ever - 98 per cent of all global cases are found in India, Nigeria and Pakistan. Mass immunization campaigns are conducted regularly to combat the largest polio epidemic in recent history. The publicity through mass media using popular personalities helps give momentum to the issue.

8. Population Control

The problem of one billion and ever-growing Indian population struggles to make a living. There are struggles in their daily chores and ironically they revolve round issues such as a bucket of water, treatment at government hospital, employment. Population and related health issues have to be addressed within the framework of women's rights and social development. There is dire need of communication and advocacy initiative for a balanced, planned and stable population. Reducing gender imbalances in population, investing for the current and future population and reaching the goal of a family size of two per couple are the key communication objectives in order to tackle the issue of population. In order to draw the attention of the youth to such a long standing yet critical issue the advertisement on population control was included in the presentation.

3.1.3 Data collection and analysis Data has been collected from both sources primary and secondary. The secondary data was collected from marketing and advertising books and research journals available in various libraries. Thorough literature review on the subject allowed the authors to examine the existing research work in this area and varied methodologies through which past research had been conducted. Articles appearing from time to time in newspapers and magazines allowed the authors to be abreast with the happenings in the field of advertising and social advertising in particular. The various official sites of Indian and foreign private, government and non-governmental organisations were a great aid in providing vital information, social and general advertisements that were eventually used in the audio-video presentations.

The focus of the primary data was youth. Youth has been particularly selected for several reasons. Firstly, the sheer proportion of this segment in the population calls in for attention. Size-wise youth dominates the Indian population; of the one billion population of India in the year 2000 half comprised of youth of less than 25 years.[4]

Secondly youth is one of the most fascinating and complex stages of life at both personal and social level. Mental and physical well-being and development during these formative years can be directly attributed to immediate environment where in parents, teachers and peers play a pivotal role. However with changes in lifestyle and growing impact of Westernization the parent's and teacher's influence is replaced with overpowering media. Television, radio and Internet are the new sources of education and information. Similarly research is full of instances of positive and negative influence of advertising on the youth. So when media and advertising used together in the form of social advertising they are likely to entertain and educate simultaneously.

Further youth of any country represents its dreams and aspirations; it's a promise for better tomorrow. The development of youth into mentally and physically healthy individuals by providing them conducive environment is a basic responsibility of any country. In the era of globalization youth faces innumerable challenges on local and global fronts. More so in a developing country like India, wherein multitudinous problems are resolved and fabricated everyday, youth is besieged by plethora of issues. Majority of the youth issues are directly and obviously related to the changing society around them. This not only connotes the problems created by the youth but also the problems faced by them. And as such for any country it becomes utmost necessary that these issues are resolved by proper understanding.

The primary data is collected from youth in Mumbai. In all 700 youths studying in various degree colleges of Mumbai were

[12] www.yuva.nic.in

selected for the survey and audio-video presentations. After the data collection, when the questionnaires were scrutinized, there were 37 forms that were incomplete in some respect and had to be discarded. So the total sample finally consisted of 663 subjects. The minimum target for each study was 100 youths. For each of the five studies mentioned above a unique set of youths was utilised. The data collected was thoroughly researched for extracting significant findings and for determining appropriate interpretations and conclusions.

Following is the step-by-step manner in which the recall of the social advertisements shown in the presentation was analysed for each study individually:

[1] Number of social advertisements per study, correctly recalled from each set in aided and unaided category was calculated.

[2] Means were calculated for number of social advertisements from each set, per study, correctly recalled in aided and unaided category.

[3] Paired samples T-test were conducted for comparing the recall of social advertisements between the sets under both aided and unaided conditions, per study.

[4] Percentages of social advertisements under each set, under each study, recalled in aided and unaided conditions were calculated.

[5] z-tests were performed to measure the significance of the difference between percentages of social advertisements in each set of each study, under aided and unaided conditions.

3.2 Understanding the Youth

For the five studies conducted five distinct set of sample were used and following is the brief description of the sample presented studywise:

3.2.1 Size of the Sample

The size of the sample used for each of the study conducted is as follows:

Table 3.3
Studywise composition of the sample

Study No.	Details of the study	No. of subjects	%
Study One	Impact of celebrity as a source in social advertising	141	21.27
Study Two	Impact of fear appeals in social advertising	124	18.70
Study Three	Impact of noise/clutter on recall of social advertising	118	17.80
Study Four	Effectiveness of television in social advertising	136	20.51
Study Five	Impact of repetition on recall of social advertising	144	21.72
	Total	663	100.00

Source: Compiled from primary data.

Graph 3.1
Studywise composition of the sample

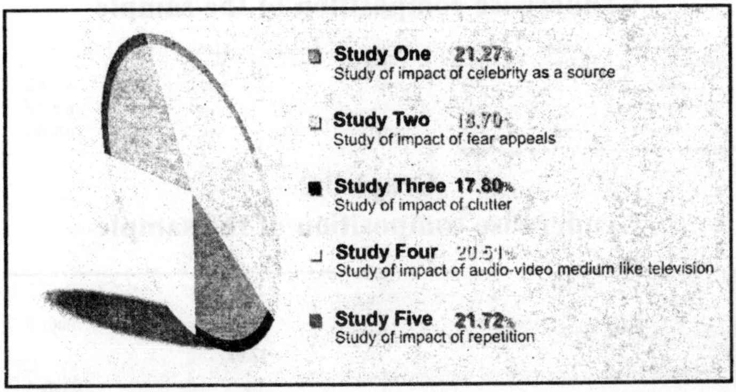

As indicated in Table 3.3 and Graph 3.1, Study Five had the maximum number of subjects of 144, which contributed 21.72 percent to the total sample size. Study Three had minimum number of subjects of 118 that made a contribution of 17.80 percent to the total sample size. Study One had the sample size of 141 subjects (21.27 per cent), Study Two had the sample size of 124 subjects (18.70 per cent) and Study Four had the sample size of 136 subjects (20.51 per cent).

3.2.2 Personal Profile

A very basic but useful a priori demographic segmenting variable is age. Consumers of different ages process information differently and they have special needs as far as the way in which the information is communicated. Research suggests that men and women process information from advertisements differently and therefore gender becomes an important demographic variable. The sample's personal profile was thus assessed on factors such as gender and age.

a) Gender wise profile of the sample

The gender wise composition of the sample for the studies was as follows:

Table 3.4

Genderwise composition of the sample

Sr. No.	Gender	Study One	Study Two	Study Three	Study Four	Study Five	Total	%
1	Male	31	61	69	59	60	**280**	**42.23**
2	Female	110	63	49	77	84	**383**	**57.77**
	Total	141	124	118	136	144	**663**	**100.00**

Source: Compiled from primary data.

Graph 3.2

Genderwise composition of the sample

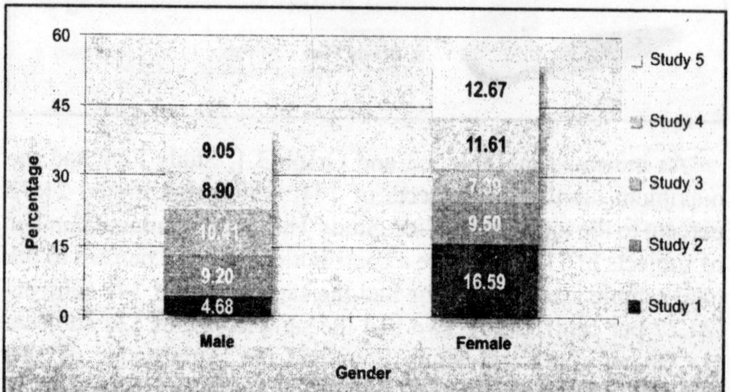

As seen in Table 3.4 and Graph 3.2, the total sample of 663 subjects consisted of 280 males (42.23 per cent) and 383 females (57.77 per cent). The gender wise composition indicated that either of the gender did not excessively dominate the sample. Study One was the only study that was dominated by females over males, whereas all other studies had almost fair share of males and females.

b) Agewise composition of the sample

The sample was made up of degree college students and their age ranged between 17 to 21 years. Table 3.5 gives age-wise composition of the sample.

Table 3.5
Agewise composition of the sample

Sr. No.	Age	Study One	Study Two	Study Three	Study Four	Study Five	Total	%
1	17 years	24	5	7	14	17	**67**	**10.11**
2	18 years	57	41	61	42	55	**256**	**38.61**
3	19 years	31	46	39	50	56	**222**	**33.48**
4	20 years	16	25	10	29	15	**95**	**14.33**
5	21 years	13	7	1	1	1	**23**	**3.47**
	Total	**141**	**124**	**118**	**136**	**144**	**663**	**100.00**

Source: Compiled from primary data.

Graph 3.3
Agewise composition of the sample

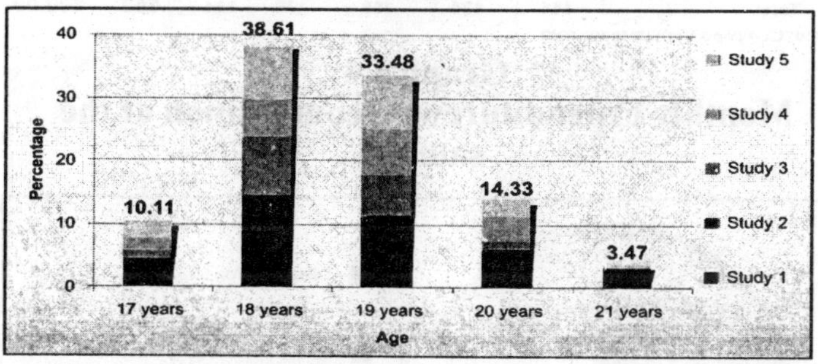

The age wise composition of the sample as indicated in Table 3.5 and Graph 3.3 was made up of 67 subjects (10.11 per cent) of 17 years, 256 subjects (38.61 per cent) of 18 years, 222 subjects (33.48 per cent) of 19 years, 95 subjects (14.33 per cent) of 20

years and 23 subjects (3.47 per cent) of 21 years. Thus considering the age, sample consisted of youth ranging between 17 to 21 years of age which was marginally dominated by 18 year old subjects.

3.2.3 Income-expenditure profile

The income-expenditure profile was analysed on the basis of the sample's monthly expenditure, the items on which money was spent and the source from where the money was generated to take care of these items.

a) Monthly expenditure pattern

The question on monthly expenditure was included to get an idea about youth'spending habit. This question tried to assess the general economic background of the subjects.

Table 3.6
Monthly expenditurewise composition of the sample

Sr. No.	Monthly expenditure pattern (in Rupees)	Study One	Study Two	Study Three	Study Four	Study Five	Total	%
1	Less than 500	58	51	18	83	75	**285**	**42.99**
2	Between 500 – 1500	63	50	46	29	40	**228**	**34.39**
3	Between 1500 – 3000	15	15	31	12	20	**93**	**14.02**
4	More than 3000	5	8	23	12	9	**57**	**8.60**
	Total	**141**	**124**	**118**	**136**	**144**	**663**	**100.00**

Source: Compiled from primary data.

Graph 3.4
Monthly expenditurewise composition of the sample

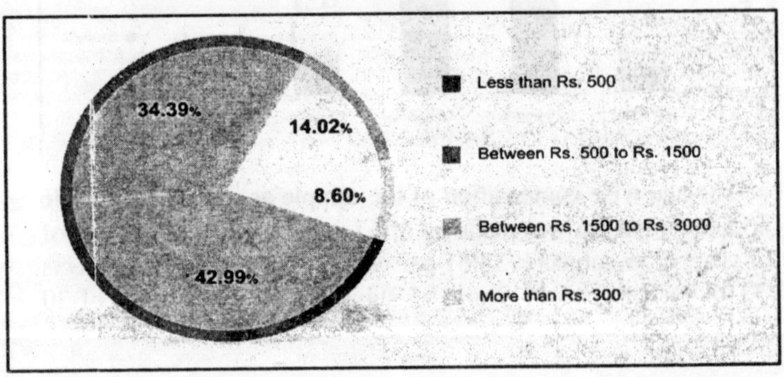

Monthly expenditure wise distribution of sample as revealed in Table 3.6 and Graph 3.4 indicated that 285 subjects (42.99 per cent) spent below Rs. 500, 228 subjects (34.39 per cent) spent between Rs. 500 and Rs. 1500, 93 subjects (14.02 per cent) spent between Rs.1500 and Rs. 3000 and 57 subjects (8.60 per cent) spent more than Rs. 3000 per month. If the monthly expenditure is considered as an indicator of the subject's economic background then the overall background of the subjects seemed to be low where almost 43 per cent of the subject spent less than Rs. 500 a month.

b) Source of income

There is a growing trend of students taking up employment when still studying. Particularly in Mumbai many employment avenues have opened up due to growth of outsourcing and retail sector. To gauge the subject's sources of income different options were provided in the questionnaire.

Table 3.7

Source of incomewise composition of the sample

Sr. No.	Source of Income	Study One	Study Two	Study Three	Study Four	Study Five	Total	%
1	Allowance from parents/pocket money	118	87	109	109	118	**541**	**81.60**
2	Employment	8	19	4	14	11	**56**	**8.45**
3	Pocket money and employed	7	6	2	4	5	**24**	**3.62**
4	Other sources: Tuitions / shares	8	12	3	9	10	**42**	**6.33**
	Total	**141**	**124**	**118**	**136**	**144**	**663**	**100.00**

Source: Compiled from primary data.

Graph 3.5

Source of incomewise composition of the sample

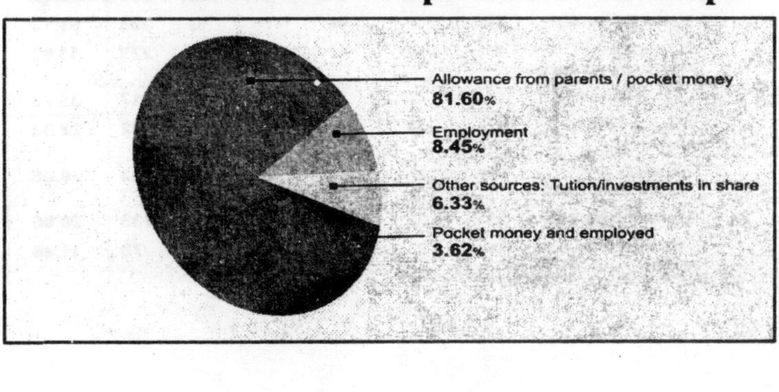

The study of sample's sources of income as shown in Table 3.7 and Graph 3.5 indicated that 541 subjects (81.60 per cent) were not employed and received monthly allowance from their parents for regular expenditures commonly termed as pocket money. There were 56 subjects (8.45 per cent) who were formally employed and 24 other subjects (3.62 per cent) got monthly allowance in spite of being employed. There were 42 subjects (6.33 per cent) who took tuitions or invested in shares to generate income. Thus the majority of the sample was not employed and was entirely dependent on their parents for their monetary requirements.

c) Spending pattern

In order to understand youth better it was important to understand their needs and what they are spending on. To facilitate this a list of items on which youth could possibly spend their money on a regular basis was provided and the subjects were supposed to tick across the appropriate options. The subjects were also required to write down those items / activities on which they regularly spent in case those items were not mentioned in the list. Following is the analysis of the items / activities on which the subjects were found to be spending on regular basis:

Table 3.8
Monthly spending pattern of the sample

Sr. No.	Items / Activities	Study One	Study Two	Study Three	Study Four	Study Five	Total	%
1	Food, refreshment etc.	129	108	112	119	134	**602**	**90.80**
2	Traveling	121	96	96	90	106	**509**	**76.77**
3	Mobile phone bills	79	67	68	56	69	**339**	**51.13**
4	Movies / audio / video compact discs	45	42	62	38	36	**223**	**33.63**
5	Clothes and shoes	54	47	48	36	32	**217**	**32.73**
6	Partying / outings / socializing	31	28	46	21	26	**152**	**22.93**
7	Cosmetics and fashion accessories	30	27	20	20	36	**133**	**20.06**
8	Internet / cyber café	29	22	35	25	22	**133**	**20.06**
9	Contribution towards house	18	25	2	14	17	**76**	**11.46**

10	Petrol/diesel, vehicle maintenance	6	11	–	2	11	30	4.52
11	Books	3	–	16	3	3	25	3.77
12	Fees	2	2	–	–	–	4	0.60
13	Hostel rent	–	–	4	–	–	4	0.60
14	Medicine	–	–	–	–	2	2	0.30
15	Newspaper	–	–	–	–	1	1	0.15
16	Sports	–	–	–	–	1	1	0.15

Source: Compiled from primary data.

Graph 3.6
Monthly spending pattern of the sample

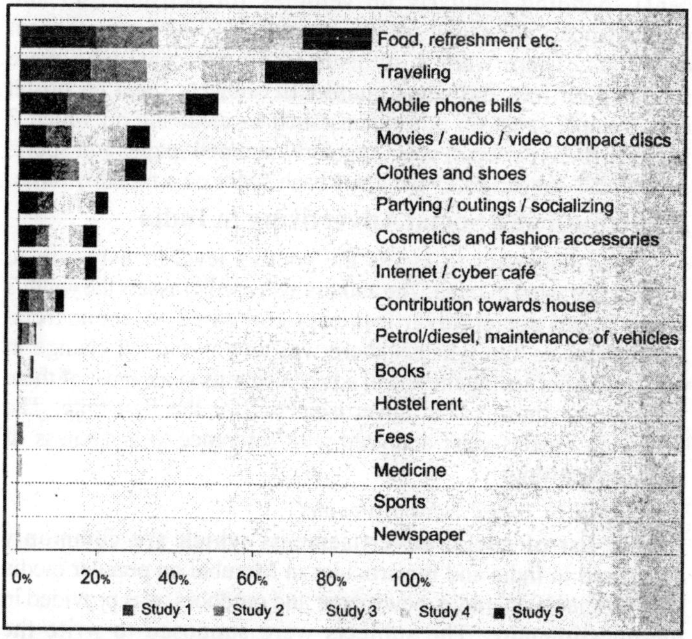

As indicated in Table 3.8 and Graph 3.6 the subjects spent their monthly allowance / pocket money on the following items / activities. There were 602 subjects (90.80 per cent) and 509 (76.77 per cent) spending on food / refreshments and traveling respectively. Mobile phone was another common item on which 339 subjects (51.13 per cent) spent regularly. There were 223 subjects (33.63 per cent) spending on movies / audio and video compact discs. There were 217 subjects (32.73 per cent) spending regularly on clothes and shoes. It was found that 152 subjects (22.93 per cent) indulged in partying and socialising on a regular basis. There were 133 subjects (20.06 per cent) spending on fashion accessories and equal number of subjects was found to be spending on accessing Internet. Of the total subjects, 76 subjects (11.46 per cent) who were employed shared their income towards their household responsibilities. There were 30 subjects (4.52 per cent) spending regularly on vehicles for petrol/diesel and maintenance. Of the total sample 25 subjects (3.77 per cent) spent on books. There were 4 subjects (0.60 per cent) who were spending on fees and equal number of subjects spent on hostel rent. Sample spent on other items such as medicine on which 2 subjects (0.30 per cent) spent regularly and newspaper and sports on which 1 subject (0.15 per cent) each spent on a monthly basis.

3.3 Youth and Social Advertising in India

It was important to assess the youth's level of exposure to social advertising in India. The authors also tried to assess the youth's views about social advertisements compared to commercial advertisements and whether there was any attitudinal change in the youth after seeing the social advertisements since most of them were seeing those social advertisements for the first time. The following aspects were analyzed with reference to awareness of social advertising:

Recall of social advertisements

The list of social advertisements which are commonly advertised in India and in particular in Mumbai on popular media such as television, radio, newspaper and outdoors, was provided in the questionnaire. The subjects were supposed to write the corresponding details that they could recall in terms of media on which the advertisement had appeared, the message or slogan used and the celebrity if at all involved. The sample's response is as follows:

Table 3.9
Sample's exposure to social advertising in India

Sr. No.	Social Issues	TV	Radio	Print	Outdoor	Celebrity	Message	Total
1	Polio eradication	472	119	71	97	236	110	**1105**
2	AIDS	426	140	139	155	83	26	**969**
3	Family planning / population control	295	84	78	102	24	86	**669**
4	Girl child literacy	251	66	64	151	16	65	**613**
5	Cleanliness	216	51	65	162	55	28	**577**
6	Vaccination	276	70	51	77	52	13	**539**
7	Timely payment of Service / Income tax	333	55	82	45	5	15	**535**
8	Anti-tobacco	211	68	75	130	17	20	**521**
9	Getting girls married after the age of 18	269	76	81	32	21	6	**485**
10	Women empowerment	165	37	61	149	7	37	**456**
11	Respecting national anthem	182	58	41	165	9	–	**455**
12	Banning plastic bags	173	73	113	82	6	6	**453**
13	Saving monuments / national property	271	41	37	41	7	16	**413**
14	Consumer awareness	229	73	55	19	11	11	**398**
15	Eradicating child labour	211	49	80	39	9	–	**388**
16	Expectant mother care	184	62	51	22	24	3	**346**
17	Not misleading foreign tourist	197	27	30	23	2	33	**312**
18	Fund raising / donations	129	46	64	45	13	8	**305**
19	National integration	131	39	54	46	6	6	**282**
20	Supporting social cause by purchasing Brand	143	38	43	21	7	16	**268**
21	Care during diarrhea	83	14	31	21	2	2	**153**

Source: Compiled from primary data.

The responses in Table 3.9 clearly indicated that the subjects mostly remembered social issues that enjoyed overall high media publicity in India like Pulse polio, AIDS awareness and family planning campaigns.

Exposure to social advertising

The level of exposure of the sample was assessed by providing the subjects with options to choose from. The options ranged between seen most of the social advertisements frequently to never seen any of them. The responses to this question were as follows:

Table 3.10
Exposure to social advertisements shown in the audio-video presentation

Sr. No.	Exposure to social advertisements	Study One	Study Two	Study Three	Study Four	Study Five	Total	%
1	Seen most of them frequently	12	6	4	22	12	56	**8.45**
2	Seen some of them very often	20	29	22	39	10	120	**18.10**
3	Seen some of them sometimes	49	57	34	57	52	249	**37.55**
4	Rarely seen any of them	46	22	46	20	43	177	**26.70**
5	Never seen any of them	14	10	12	6	19	61	**9.20**
	Total	**141**	**124**	**118**	**144**	**136**	**663**	**100.00**

Source: Compiled from primary data.

Graph 3.7
Exposure to social advertisements presented in the audio-video presentation

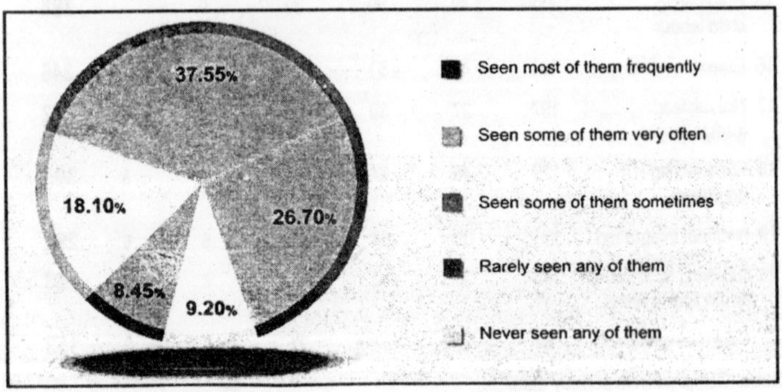

As revealed in Table 3.10 and Graph 3.7 the subject's exposure to the social advertisements shown in the presentation was limited. There were 61 subjects (9.20 per cent) who reported they had never seen any of these advertisements at all, whereas 177 subjects (26.70 per cent) reported they had rarely seen the social advertisements shown in the presentation, 249 subjects (37.55 per cent) had seen some of these advertisements sometimes and 120 subjects (18.10 per cent) had seen some of these advertisements often. There were only 56 subjects (8.45 per cent) who reported having seen these advertisements quite often. Thus the exposure of the social advertisements among the sample was limited.

- *Social advertisements in comparison to commercial advertisements in the audio - video presentation*

It was important to assess the subjects' views on how they perceive social advertisements especially in comparison to commercial advertisements that they had seen in the presentation. The subject's opinion on social advertisements in comparison to commercial advertisements was as follows:

Table 3.11
Social advertisements in comparison to commercial advertisements

Sr. No.	Opinion on social advertisements	Study One	Study Two	Study Three	Study Four	Study Five	Total	%
1	Better than commercial advertisements	83	89	48	88	80	388	**58.52**
2	On par with commercial advertisements	48	25	52	47	46	218	**32.88**
3	Not as effective as commercial advertisements	10	10	18	9	10	57	**8.60**
	Total	**141**	**124**	**118**	**144**	**136**	**663**	**100.00**

Source: Compiled from primary data.

Graph 3.8
Social advertisements in comparison to commercial advertisements

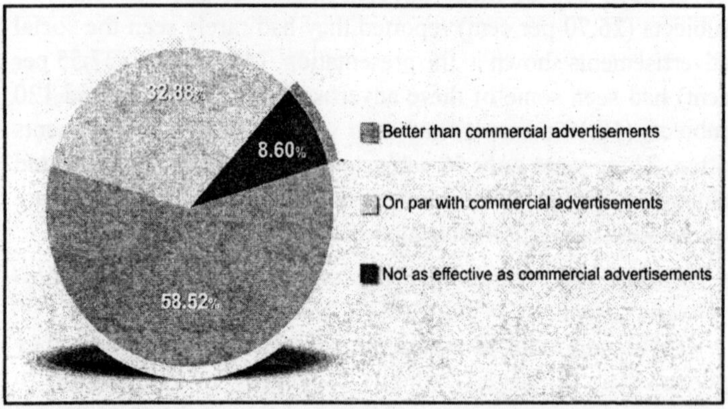

As seen in Table 3.11 and Graph 3.8, when the subjects were asked to compare the social advertisements with commercial advertisements that they had seen in the presentation, 388 subjects (58.52 per cent) felt that the social advertisements were better than the commercial advertisements while 218 subjects (32.88 per cent) felt they were on par with commercial advertisements. A comparatively small number of 57 subjects (8.60 per cent) felt that the commercial advertisements were better than social advertisements. Thus the subjects did not find these social advertisements lacking on any grounds when compared to commercial advertisements. In fact most of them found social advertisements to be better than the commercial advertisements shown in the audio-video presentation.

- ### Impact of social advertising

The impact of social advertisements from the presentation on the subjects was studied. This was very important to assess whether social advertisements are influential. It was equally important to get an understanding of the degree of this impact. To enable this, the subjects were provided with several options that ranged from no effect at all to willingness to fight for these issues. The response of the sample with this respect was as follows:

Table 3.12
Impact of social advertising on the sample

Sr. No.	Impact	Study One	Study Two	Study Three	Study Four	Study Five	Total	%
1	Interested in knowing more	43	30	25	30	36	164	**24.74**
2	Increased awareness	16	14	15	16	13	74	**11.16**
3	Gained knowledge	45	55	41	60	51	252	**38.01**
4	Willingness to fight for issues	33	23	29	38	35	158	**23.83**
5	No effect at all	4	2	8	0	1	15	**2.26**
	Total	**141**	**124**	**118**	**144**	**136**	**663**	**100.00**

Source: Compiled from primary data.

Graph 3.9
Impact of social advertising on the sample

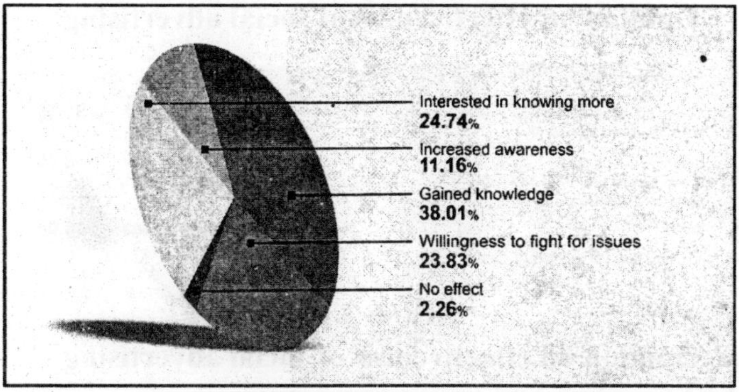

Table 3.12 and Graph 3.9 indicate the degree of impact social advertisements from the presentation had on the sample. A considerable number of 164 subjects (24.74 per cent) felt they were interested in knowing more about the social issues. There were 74 subjects (11.16 per cent) who felt that the social advertisements increased their awareness. Whereas 252 subjects (38.01 per cent) felt that they have gained knowledge and given a chance a 158 subjects (23.83 per cent) were even willing to fight for the social cause. A small number of 15 subjects (2.26 per cent) did not

seem to gain anything from the presentation in comparison to 648 subjects (97.74 percent) on whom there was some positive impact of the social advertisements. The subjects indicated varying degree of attitudinal change in response to the exposure of social advertisements. A substantial number of them gained knowledge and some of them had shown their willingness to fight for the issues given an opportunity. This stands as a testimony to the strong influence of social advertising.

- *Effectiveness of conducting social advertising in India*

The subject's views on social advertising promoted in India in terms of whether it makes an impact or it is ignored, were analyzed.

Table 3.13
Opinion on effectiveness of social advertising

Sr. No.	Effectiveness of social advertisements	Study One	Study Two	Study Three	Study Four	Study Five	Total	%
1	Social advertising must be done frequently	130	106	103	140	128	607	91.55
2	Social advertising is a waste and are generally ignored	11	18	15	4	8	56	8.45
	Total	141	124	118	144	136	663	100.00

Source: Compiled from primary data.

Graph 3.10
Opinion on effectiveness of social advertising

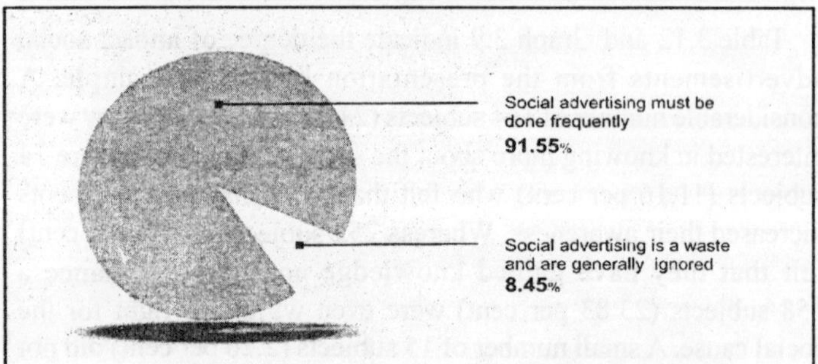

As indicated in Table 3.13 and Graph 3.10, 607 subjects (91.55 per cent) felt that social advertising is effective and must be done more frequently in India. Advertisements are generally neglected by the audience and therefore 56 subjects (8.45 per cent) felt that social advertising was a waste and ineffective. This is an indication that the sample was dissatisfied on the way social advertising is promoted in India and they were in favour of more frequent social advertising.

- *Adequacy of issues covered through social advertising in India*

A more direct question was asked to assess the adequacy of issues covered though social advertising in India. The subjects' views were assessed by providing them two statements based on social advertising in India of which they were to select the appropriate one.

Table 3.14
Opinion on adequacy of social advertising in India

Sr. No.	Social advertising in India	Study One	Study Two	Study Three	Study Four	Study Five	Total	%
1	Social advertising is adequately done in India	50	28	30	38	34	180	**27.15**
2	Social advertising is limited and must cover more issues	91	96	88	106	102	483	**72.85**
	Total	**141**	**124**	**118**	**144**	**136**	**663**	**100.00**

Source: Compiled from primary data.

Graph 3.11
Opinion on adequacy of social advertising in India

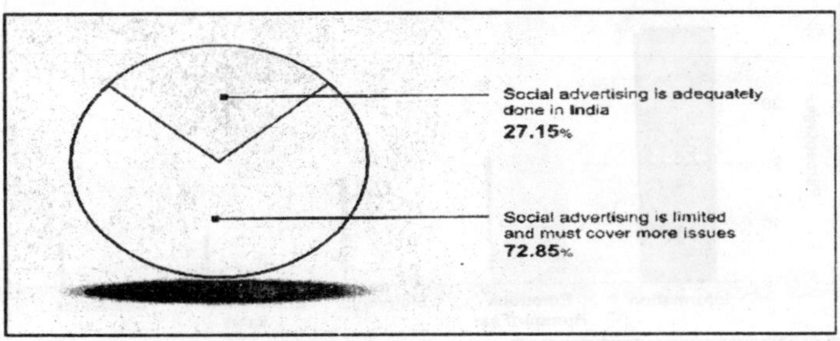

From Table 3.14 and Graph 3.11 it is obvious that a considerable number of 483 subjects (72.85 per cent) felt that social advertising in India is not enough and it must cover more issues, there were 180 subjects (27.15 per cent) who felt that in India social advertising is satisfactorily conducted. This is an indication that social advertising has to be done more frequently.

- *Essential elements of social advertising*

The subjects were required to write the element which they felt contributes the most to the effectiveness of social advertisements. The subjects were provided with several options to choose from.

Table 3.15
Essential elements of social advertising

Sr. No.	Most essential element in social advertising	Study One	Study Two	Study Three	Study Four	Study Five	Total	%
1	Information	45	55	35	76	73	284	**42.84**
2	Emotions – humour / fear	47	25	35	24	21	152	**22.93**
3	Simplicity	24	16	25	30	18	113	**17.04**
4	Entertainment value	16	8	13	10	16	63	**9.50**
5	Celebrities	9	20	10	4	8	51	**7.69**
	Total	**141**	**124**	**118**	**144**	**136**	**663**	**100.00**

Source: Compiled from primary data.

Graph 3.12
Essential elements of social advertising

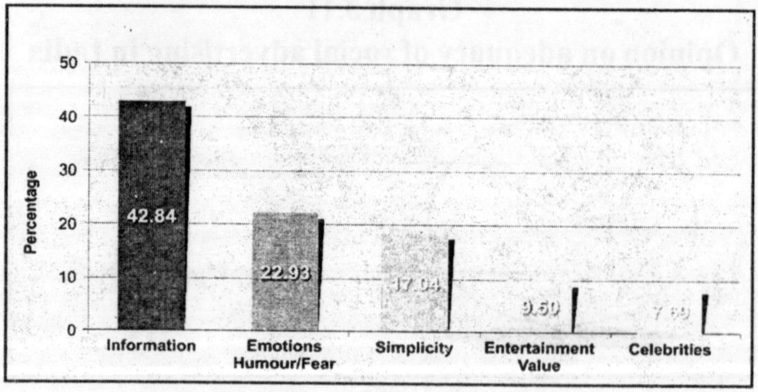

Table 3.15 and Graph 3.12 indicate that of the five different options provided, 284 subjects (42.84 per cent) felt that the most important feature of social advertisement is its informative content. There were 152 subjects (22.93 per cent) who felt emotions in social advertising makes advertising interesting. Simplicity and straightforwardness was rated important by 113 subjects (17.04 per cent) whereas 63 subjects (9.50 per cent) felt entertaining value of social advertising is more important. A comparatively small number of 51 subjects (7.69 per cent) felt celebrities make social advertising more appealing. This is an indication that subjects look up to social advertising as a source of information and therefore according to them information is the most essential element of social advertising.

- *Responsibility of conducting social advertising in India*

In India social advertising is sponsored and promoted by different entities like government, private companies, non-governmental organisations and media. The subjects were asked to select which entity is primarily responsible for conducting social advertising in India.

Table 3.16
Responsibility of conducting social advertising

Sr. No.	Entity/Agency	Study One	Study Two	Study Three	Study Four	Study Five	Total	%
1	Government / Ministry	62	77	70	80	82	371	**55.96**
2	Media	44	23	21	25	32	145	**21.87**
3	NGO	32	24	22	36	19	133	**20.06**
4	Private companies	0	0	5	3	2	10	**1.51**
5	Other - Citizen	3	0	0	0	1	4	**0.60**
	Total	**141**	**124**	**118**	**144**	**136**	**663**	**100.00**

Source: Compiled from primary data.

Graph 3.13
Responsibility of conducting social advertising

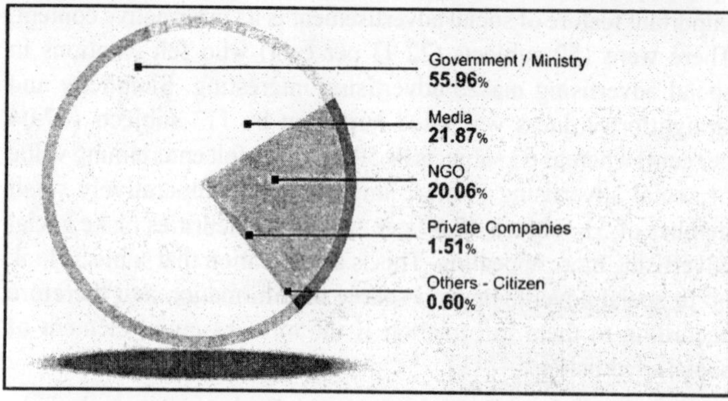

Table 3.16 and Graph 3.13 indicate that there were 371 subjects (55.96 per cent) who felt that government and its various ministries are responsible for promoting social advertising. There were 145 subjects (21.87 per cent) who felt media was responsible, whereas 133 subjects (20.06 per cent) felt non-governmental organisations were responsible for sponsoring social advertising. A small number of 10 subjects (1.51 per cent) felt corporate sector was liable for conducting social advertising and 4 subjects (0.60 per cent) suggested even citizens are responsible in some way for conduct of social advertising. Thus according to the sample, social advertising in India is the prime responsibility of the government and its various ministries, followed by media and various NGOs.

- *Issues that need to be addressed through social advertising in India*

When asked about the issues advertised in India, the subjects felt social advertising is not adequately done in India. The subjects showed their concern for many social issues which need to be focused through social advertisements. The subjects mentioned following social issues on which either there was no advertising or inadequate advertising in India:

Table 3.17
Suggested issues for social advertising

Issue	Suggestions
Health related issues	► Awareness against drinking / drugs / smoking ► Polio eradication ► TB / Jaundice / Cancer awareness ► Promoting hygienic food ► AIDS awareness
Issues related to women	► Ensuring women's safety in India ► Awareness against female feticide / discrimination suffered by girl child ► Promoting literacy particularly girl child literacy ► Abandoning inhumane practices of child marriage / Sati / Dowry ► Women empowerment ► Care of expectant mother ► Creating awareness against prostitution / rape
Awareness about safe driving practices	► Avoiding use of mobile phone while driving ► Avoiding drunken and rash driving ► Following traffic rules ► Use of helmets / seat belts for two/four wheelers
Awareness regarding environmental issues	► Awareness to minimize pollution and promote tree plantation ► Ban on plastic bags ► Promoting eco friendly products ► Conserving water
Awareness about various issues affecting quality of life in general	► Eradicating child labour ► Providing assistance to old people ► Poverty eradication ► Population control / family planning ► Providing sexual information to youth ► Awareness against censor ► Cleanliness awareness ► Providing employment opportunities ► Promotion of blood / eye donation ► Encouraging sports ► Preventing suicides ► Promoting social rights of people ► Resolving the menace of stray dogs ► Respecting elders ► Effective parenting ► Consumer awareness ► Ban on ragging ► Eradicating racism
Awareness about issues related to India	► Promoting national integration ► Awareness against corrupt politicians ► Awareness against corruption ► Promotion of Indian culture ► Awareness against terrorism / bomb blast ► Promoting tourism in India ► Awareness against cyber crime ► Timely payment of taxes

Source: Compiled from primary data.

As seen in Table 3.17 subjects mentioned host of issues which they feel must be addressed through social advertising. Many of the issues mentioned here are not at all advertised in India and several of the issues are derived from recent events taking place in India which need immediate attention such as molestation at public places, ragging and so on. This is an indication that subjects have given a sincere thought while mentioning these issues and are well aware of the state of affairs around them.

3.2 Conclusion

The present chapter was an attempt to understand the sample's views, which comprised of unemployed youth between the age group of 18 to 21 years of age, belonging to middle and lower strata of the society on different aspects of social advertising on various criterions. From the responses of the sample it was obvious that they had an overall positive attitude towards social advertising since the social advertising done in India is noticed and recalled. However, the sample seemed to be dissatisfied with the way in which social advertising is carried in India and expressed the need for increased frequency. The subjects suggested host of issues from diverse fields such as politics, health, sexual discrimination, safety measures and so on to be covered under social advertising in India. This study gave a valuable insight about the youth's attitudes towards social advertising.

4
Influence of Social Advertising with Celebrities on Youth

4.1 Introduction – Celebrities in Advertising

Source in advertising refers to the ones who actually present the advertising messages.[1] They are responsible for encoding the message in such a way that its meaning is interpreted by the target audience in precisely the intended way. The source of the communication has an enormous influence on how the advertising message is accepted by the target audience. When the source is well respected and highly thought of by the audience the message is much more likely to be believed and vice versa. Advertisers have variety of options to choose from while encoding their advertising messages, such as using words, pictures, spokespersons and special channels. The spokespersons refer to use of celebrities, experts or Chief Executive Officer (CEO) of the firms in advertisements. Consideration of an appropriate source for advertising is one of the important decision making area for the advertisers.Celebrity is one of the most commonly used advertising sources.

4.2 Assessing Literature on Celebrity Endorsements

A celebrity is any person who enjoys public recognition such as film stars, television personalities, popular entertainers and sports

[1] Clow Kenneth E. and Baack Donald, *op. cit.*, pp. 233-238.

[2] Friedman H. H. and Friedman L., "Endorser Effectiveness by Product Type," Journal of Advertising Research, 19(5), 1979, pp. 63-71.

persons. According to Friedman and Friedman[2] a celebrity endorser is an individual who is known to the public (actor, sports figure, entertainer) for his or her achievements in areas other than that of the product class endorsed. According to McCracken celebrity endorsement refers to any person who is publicly known and who appears in an advertisement with a product with the purpose of promoting the product.[3] An endorsement or testimonial is any advertising message that consumers believe reflects the opinions, beliefs or experiences of an individual, group or institution. The basic requirement of celebrity endorsers being that they must be qualified by experience or training to make judgments and they must actually use the product.[4]

Using well-known and admired people to promote products is a widespread phenomenon with a long marketing history. Celebrity endorsements began way back in the 19th century with UK's Queen Victoria endorsing Cadbury's Cocoa, which soon became a global practice for promotion in marketing communications strategy.[5] Even former U.S. President Ronald Reagan was a celebrity endorser, pitching several different products including cigarettes, during his acting days.[6]

Celebrities play the role of a source in the advertisements. From advertising point of view the source has an impact on how well it is received by the audience. The first attempt to synthesise the work on source and apply it to advertising and other marketing

---

[3] McCracken Grant, "Who Is the Celebrity Endorser? Cultural Foundations of the Endorsement Process," Journal of Consumer Research, 16 (3), 1989, pp. 310-321.

[4] Wells William, Moriarty Sandra and Burnett John, Advertising, Principles and Practice, 7th ed., Pearson Education Inc., 2006, pp. 341-342.

[5] Mukund A., Celebrity Endorsement, Trends and Cases, The ICFAI University Press, Hyderabad, pp. 158-160.

[6] Keller Kevin L., Strategic Brand Management, 2nd ed., Pearson Education Inc., 2007, p. 403.

[7] Percy Larry, Rossiter John R. and Elliott Richard, Strategic Advertising Management, 2001, pp. 151-163.

communication was the VisCAP model of source effectiveness introduced by Percy and Rossiter[7] in 1980. VisCAP is an acronym for four important characteristics of the source viz.: Visibility – how recognisable the person is from public exposure, Credibility - knowledge of the source, Objectivity - trustworthiness in communication, Attractiveness - likeability of the source, Power – sources' ability to instill compliance on the part of the target audience. Celebrity scores high on all these attributes and therefore becomes an important contender for the source.

Some researchers have recognised that audience's judgements about source mainly concern cognitive and affective dimension as depicted in Chart 4.1.[8] The cognitive dimension includes judgements about the power, prestige (from past achievements, reputation, wealth, political power or visibility) and competence (expertise) of the source. The affective dimension includes judgements about trustworthiness, attractiveness and dynamism.

Chart 4.1
Dimensions of Source Credibility

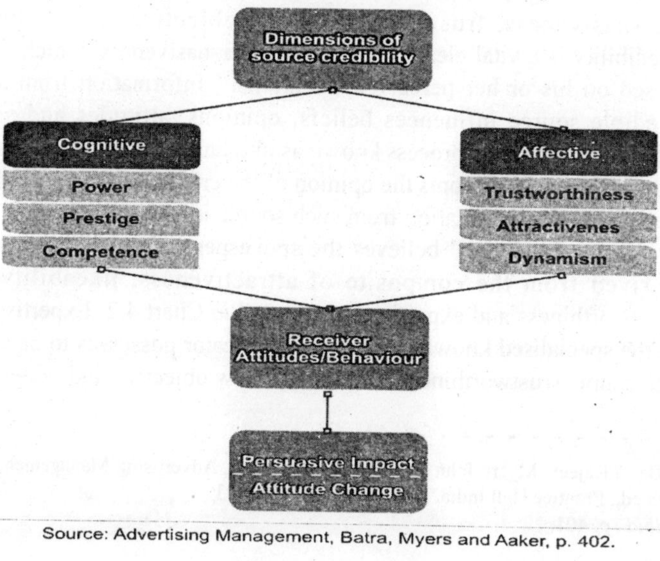

Source: Advertising Management, Batra, Myers and Aaker, p. 402.

There are two ways of thinking about an endorser's characteristics.[9] The traditional way is to think of an endorser as a source of the information in the advertisement, contributing to the acceptability of the content of the message because of the source's credibility or attractiveness. The second way is to think of the endorser as possessing some symbolic properties, which are transferred from the endorser to the endorsed brand through advertising and then from the brand to the consumer.

By celebrity credibility Ohanian[10] means the audience's perception of both the celebrity's expertise (how much the celebrity knows about the product area) and trustworthiness (how honest the celebrity is about what he or she says about the product). One of the most reliable effects found in communications research is that expert and/or trustworthy sources are more persuasive than sources that are less expert or trustworthy.[11] From the advertiser's point of view, the Source Credibility Model suggests that pursuing a celebrity endorsement strategy enables them to project a credible image in terms of expertise, persuasiveness, trustworthiness and objectiveness.[12] The credibility is a vital element in message persuasiveness, which is based on his or her perceived intentions.[13] Information from a credible source influences beliefs, opinions, attitudes and/or behaviour through a process known as internalisation. This occurs when the receiver adopts the opinion of the credible source out of belief that the information from such source is accurate.

However, Keller[14] believes the spokesperson's credibility is derived from the composite of attractiveness, likeability, trustworthiness and expertise as indicated in Chart 4.2. Expertise is the specialised knowledge the communicator possesses to back the claim. Trustworthiness is related to how objective and honest

---

[8] Batra Rajeev, Myers John G. and Aaker David A., Advertising Management, 5th ed., Prentice Hall India, New Delhi, 2004, p. 403.

[9] *Ibid.*, p. 401.

the source is perceived to be. Likeability describes the source's attractiveness. Qualities like candor, humor and naturalness make a source more likeable.

Chart 4.2
Composition of Source Credibility

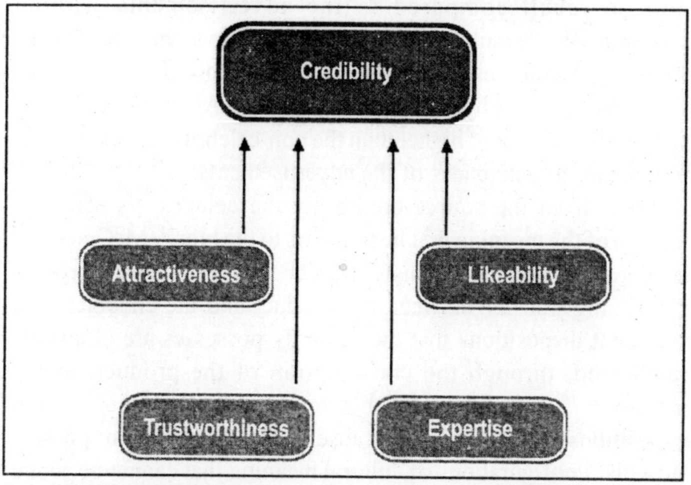

Source: Integrated Advertising, Promotion and Marketing Communications, Clow and Baack, p. 236.

Of all the benefits that a celebrity might contribute to a firm's advertising program such as fame, talent, credibility or charisma,

---

[10] Ohanion Roobina, "The Impact of Celebrity Spokespersons Perceived Image on Consumers' Intention to Purchase," Journal of Advertising Research, 31 (1), February-March 1991, pp. 46-54.

[11] McGuire William J., "The Nature of Attitudes and Attitude Change," in Handbook of Social Psychology, 2nd ed., G. Lindzey and E. Aronson (eds.), Addison-Wesley, Cambridge, 1969.

[12] Till Brian D. and Shimp Terence A., "Endorsers in Advertising: The Case of Negative Celebrity Information," Journal of Advertising Research, 27(1), Spring 1998, pp. 67-82.

[13] Schiffman Leon G. and Kanuk Leslie Lazar, *op. cit.*, pp. 331-332.

[14] Keller Kevin L., *op. cit.*, pp. 404.

celebrity credibility with the consumer audience is the most important,[15] as credibility affects a receiver's acceptance of the spokesperson and messages. A credible source is believable.[16] As per the study conducted by G. Muruganantham and Dr. S. Kaliyamoorthy,[17] celebrity endorsed television advertisements were high on recall compared to the advertisements without celebrities. While ranking the expected qualities in the celebrity, the credibility factor was ranked the highest, followed by likeability, recognition and physical attractiveness. Also the celebrity advertisements scored higher than the non-celebrity advertisements in terms of attractiveness of the advertisements.

Apart from the source credibility the celebrity is effective because of the meaning that he transfers to the brand. McCracken[18] developed 'A Meaning Transfer Model' that describes the process of meaning transfer between the product and the endorser. The congruent dispositions that the celebrity possesses are ultimately transferred, through the consumption of the product, to the consumer.[19] According to this model brands benefit from associations with endorsers because endorsers acquire or possess particular configurations of cultural meaning that cannot be found elsewhere and the cultural meaning that "resides" within the celebrity endorser, is passed on to the product or service being endorsed. It is widely assumed that celebrity endorsers bring the benefit of their symbolic images (i.e. their personal "meaning") to the products and services to which they lend their name and person.[20]

According to Erdogan, Baker and Tagg,[21] apart from the Source Credibility Model where the effectiveness of the message depends on the perceived expertise and trustworthiness of an endorser and

---

[15] Schiffman Leon G. and Kanuk Leslie Lazar, op. cit., pp. 331-332.

[16] Batra Rajeev, Myers John G. and Aaker David A., *op. cit.*, p. 403.

[17] Muruganantham G. and Dr. Kaliyamoorthy S., Indian Journal of Marketing, December 2006, pp. 20-24.

the Meaning Transfer Model popularised by McCracken, there is the Match-Up Hypothesis and the Source Attractiveness Model (McGuire) which contribute to the rationale of using celebrities for endorsements.

The Match-up Hypothesis states that the physical attractiveness of a celebrity endorser will enhance evaluations of the products characteristics only if the characteristics of the product match up with the image conveyed by the celebrity.

As per the Source Attractiveness Model the effectiveness of a message depends on the attractiveness of the source. The attractiveness encompasses similarity, familiarity and likeability of an endorser. The similarity is the resemblance between the source and the receiver, while familiarity is defined as knowledge of the source through previous exposure and likeability as affection for the source as a result of physical appearance or behaviour.[22] Source attractiveness leads to persuasion through a process of identification, whereby the receiver is motivated to seek some type of relationship with the source and thus adopts similar benefits, attitudes, preferences or behaviour.[23]

However it is essential that an appropriate fit between the celebrity and the product's target audience be considered. An associative link occurs when there is a fit between the product and the celebrity and the consumer will associate the celebrity with the product being endorsed and vice versa.[24] According to Kotler and Keller[25] celebrity associations can catapult even the most unlikely product to stardom, provided along with high appropriateness to the

---

[18] McCracken Grant, *op. cit.*

[19] Byrne A, Whitehead M. and Breen S., "The Naked Truth of Celebrity Endorsement," British Food Journal, 105 (4/5), 2003, pp. 288-296.

[20] Schiffman Leon G. and Kanuk Leslie Lazar, *op. cit.*, pp. 331-332.

[21] Erdogan B. Z., Baker M. J. and Tagg S., "Selecting Celebrity Endorsers: The Practitioner's Perspective," Journal of Advertising Research, 41, May-June 2001, pp. 39-48.

product the celebrity has high recognition and high positive affect. The most important attribute of the spokes person is his credibility.

According to Silvera and Austad,[26] an explanation for the success of celebrity-endorsed advertisements could be ascribed to consumers' faith in the celebrity's genuineness. The consumers believe that celebrities endorse products as a result of their true emotions towards the product and not because of the remuneration they receive. A famous person shapes the perceptions of the brand by virtue of the inferences that consumers make based on the knowledge they have about the famous person.[27] Celebrities represent an idealisation of life that their loyal followers or most of the general people imagine that they would love to live.[28] The celebrities add a touch of glamour to the brand either due to their dramatic roles or athletic accomplishments.

Research suggests three types of benefits of celebrity endorsement.[29] First endorsers enhance advertising readership (or viewership or listenership) scores.[30] Second endorsers can induce positive attitude change towards a company and its products in general, more credible the source, the more persuasive that source is likely to be.[31] Third, the personality characteristics of the endorser can get associated with the brands' imagery.

The research also points to an interesting connection between celebrity endorsement and youth. The correlation could be attributed to the celebrity's mystique or the aspirational values that

---

[22] Ibid.

[23] Belch G. and Belch M., *op. cit.*, p. 172.

[24] Till B. D., "Using Celebrity Endorsers Effectively: Lessons from Associative Learning." Journal of Product and Brand Management, 7(5), 1998, pp. 400-409.

[25] Kotler Philip and Keller Kevin Lane, Marketing Management, 12th ed., Pearson Education, Inc., Delhi 2006, p. 506.

[26] Silvera D. H. and Austad B., "Factors Predicting the Effectiveness of Celebrity Endorsement Advertisements," European Journal of Marketing, 38(11/12), 2004, pp. 1509-1526.

[27] Keller Kevin L., *op. cit.*, p. 403.

[28] Schiffman Leon G. and Kanuk Leslie Lazar. *op. cit.*, p. 331.

celebrities lend to the brand. Celebrities help create emotional bonds with the product and it is also observed this bond transfer is more profound for younger consumers as older consumers are not as likely to be influenced by celebrity endorsements.[32] One study conducted in Great Britain[33] indicated that celebrities held a greater appeal for the 15 to 24-year-old age bracket, 62 per cent of that group stated that a famous person in an advertisement would get their attention, though overall 55 percent of the consumers reported that a famous face was not enough to hold their attention. Another study found that college-age students were more likely to have a positive attitude towards a product endorsed by a celebrity than were older consumers.[34]

Research comparing the impact of advertisements with and without celebrity endorsers found that those featuring celebrities were rated more positively.[35] This was especially true among teenagers, who are more likely to project the celebrity's credibility to the advertising message and the endorsed product.

Review of literature on celebrity associations clearly concur that celebrities lend emotional or psychological benefits. These benefits are like essential pre-condition to the more obvious commercial objectives that marketers are expecting from such associations. Celebrity endorsers are more effective than non-celebrity endorsers in generating actual sales and for positively influencing the consumption of the products they are associated with.[36]

---

[29] Batra Rajeev, Myers John G. and Aaker David A., *op. cit.*, p. 405.

[30] Rudolph H., Attention and Interest Factors in Advertising, Printer's Ink, New York, 1947.

[31] Fireworker R. B. and Friedman H. H., "The Effects of Endorsements on Product Evaluation," Decision Sciences, 8, 1977, pp. 576-583.

[32] Clow Kenneth E. and Baack Donald, *op. cit.*, p. 233.

[33] Murphy Claire, "Stars Brought Down to Earth in Television Ads Research," Marketing, January, 1998, p. 1.

[34] Atkin Charles and Block Martin, "Effectiveness of Celebrity Endorsers," Journal of Advertising Research 23, February-March, 1983, pp. 57-61.

[35] *Ibid.*

Involvement of celebrity for endorsements does not mean they are a panacea for all marketing or advertising issues and they too bring along with them host of problems of their own. Several studies have shown instances where a high credibility source has been more of a liability than being an asset. Celebrity campaigns can sometimes be an expensive flop just as can happen with movies.[37]

It's true that a right source delivering a message helps facilitate brand awareness, but with celebrities as sources, there is always a risk of their fluctuating popularity negatively affecting the brand. Owing to unavailability of dates, sometimes long-term contracts are signed, but the celebrity's life might be over soon causing a mismatch between the celebrity's life cycle and that of the brand. Another issue with celebrities is lack of professionalism and being overly opportunist or insincere, like a celebrity might hold out for a larger fee at contract renewal time or simply withdraw.[38]

The credibility of a commercial source is problematic and usually is based on a composite evaluation of its reputation, expertise and knowledge.[39] If some event happens that affects the reputation of the celebrity, the negative publicity could backfire on the associated brand as well. A celebrity's behaviour may pose a risk to a company.[40] The celebrities might lose popularity or even worse, get caught in a scandal or embarrassing situation.[41] The trouble-either in their careers or in their personal lives can cause immense damage to the brand diminishing its market value.[42]

One of the major issues with celebrity endorsement from the marketers' point of view is that of vampiring, the celebrity being bigger than the brand.[43] With celebrities there is a risk of celebrity

---

[36] Mukund A., *op. cit.*

[37] Kotler Philip and Keller Kevin Lane, *op. cit.*, pp. 506-507.

[38] Joshi Sangita, "Face Value," The Hindu, April 24, 2003.

[39] Schiffman Leon G. and Kanuk Leslie Lazar, *op. cit.*

[40] Till Brian D. and Shimp Terence A., *op. cit.*

overpowering the brand.[44] Celebrities may distract attention from the brand in advertisement such that audience notice or remember the stars but have trouble remembering the advertised brand.[45] Multiple endorsements is the other problem associated with most-sought-after celebrities. Since there is a limitation to the number of celebrities who can resonate with consumers, popular celebrities are seen endorsing multiple brands in several categories. The over-exposure of celebrities leads to a fair degree of confusion and little room for credibility.[46] When a celebrity endorses a variety of products, his or her perceived credibility is reduced because of the apparent economic motivation underlying the celebrity's efforts.[47] The overuse of celebrity for endorsing multiple products can result into a possible devaluing of the celebrity amongst audience lacking any specific product meaning.[48]

Another peril associated with celebrity endorsement is that of celebrity clutter. Celebrities are used because they have stopping power that is they draw attention to advertising messages in a cluttered media environment.[49] In the fairly non-descript advertisements' clutter, celebrities give the brand differentiation and add recall to the advertisements in which they feature. However with surfeit of celebrities endorsing almost all conceivable product

---

[41] Kotler Philip and Keller Kevin Lane, *op. cit.*, pp. 506-507.

[42] McCracken Grant, *op. cit.*

[43] Shankar Smita, "Celebrity Endorsements: Is It the Only Survival Recipe for Marketers?," Indian Journal of Marketing, October 2006, pp. 3-5.

[44] Vyas Shuchi, "Chief Endorsement Officer," Brand Equity, The Economic Times, February 21, 2007.

[45] Keller Kevin L., *op. cit.*, p. 407.

[46] Shankar Smita, *op. cit.*

[47] Tripp C., Jensen T. D. and Carlson L., "The Effects of Multiple Product Endorsements by Celebrities on Consumers' Attitudes and Intentions," Journal of Consumer Research 20, March 1994, pp. 535-47.

[48] Keller Kevin L., *op. cit.*, pp. 404-405.

[49] Belch G. and Belch M., *op. cit.*, p. 173.

categories relevant or otherwise and worst the same celebrities endorsing multiple brands lead to celebrity clutter. All brands follow the same path of celebrity usage resulting in the death of differentiation and a poor recall of the brand and category.

To sum up, using celebrities in advertising is a creative strategy to break through clutter but several aspects need a careful consideration before selecting the celebrity. First is to consider the celebrity's popularity, physical attractiveness and expertise in the concerned field. Second it is important to consider celebrity with the image that matches with the image of the product or service being endorsed. Third and most importantly the celebrity's trustworthiness and conduct in personal life, since for audience celebrity's credibility is of utmost importance.

4.3 Study One: Influence of Celebrity in Social Advertising

From marketing and advertising perspective celebrities contribute in variety of ways. Celebrities association had been successful in garnering positive reactions from the audience. Considering the significant role that celebrities play in commercial communication, they are also commonly used in social advertising. There are host of celebrities in India and abroad lending their support for variety of social causes such as AIDS, Polio eradication, literacy awareness and so on. The present study was conducted on a similar premise, to analyse whether celebrities have an impact on youth and whether they make any positive contribution towards the recall of social advertising.

The objective of Study One was to evaluate the impact of celebrity in social advertising. In this study, eight social advertisements, four with celebrities and four without celebrities were presented to the subjects in order to evaluate the impact of celebrity in social advertising. The Table 4.1 gives details of the social advertisements used for this study:

Table 4.1
Social advertisements presented in Study One

Sr. no.	Social advertisements	
[1]	**With celebrity**	**Celebrity involved**
1	AIDS awareness	Ehsaan Qureshi – comedian – television
2	Cleanliness awareness	Ajay Devgan - film star
3	Polio eradication	Shahrukh Khan – film star
4	Promotion of condoms	Rohit and Manasi Roy – television actor couple
[2]	**Without celebrity**	
1	Anti-tobacco	
2	Awareness about not using mobile phone while driving	
3	Female feticide	
4	Spend time with elderly	

Source: Compiled from primary data.

The responses to the questions based on the impact of celebrity in the aided and unaided categories were carefully analysed in the following step-by-step manner:

[1] Number of social advertisements with celebrity and social advertisements without celebrity correctly recalled in aided and unaided category were calculated.

[2] Means were calculated for number of social advertisements with celebrity and social advertisements without celebrity correctly recalled in aided and unaided category.

[3] Paired samples T-test were conducted to compare recall of social advertisements with celebrities and social advertisements without celebrities under both aided and unaided conditions.

[4] Percentages of social advertisements recalled with celebrities and without celebrities under aided and unaided conditions were calculated.

[5] z-tests were performed to measure the significance of the difference between percentages of social advertisements recalled under aided and unaided conditions with celebrity and without celebrity.

The study specific questionnaire was one of the tools used for data collection. In this the subjects were required to recall the social advertisements that they had seen in the presentation in two categories, social advertisements with celebrities and social advertisements without celebrities. These two categories were further investigated under two conditions, viz. unaided and aided. Further the subject's overall opinion about use of celebrities and their contribution if any in social advertising was analysed.

4.3.1 Recall of Social Advertisements in Unaided Category

In the unaided category the subjects were supposed to recall and write the social advertisements that they had seen in the audio-video presentation. There was no clue or hint provided and they had to recall social advertisements on the basis of the issues addressed and the celebrities involved.

[1] *Recall of celebrity based social advertisements in unaided category*

The four social advertisements with celebrities consisted of two advertisements with film stars and two advertisements with television actors. Shahrukh Khan and Ajay Devgan were celebrities from films and Rohit and Manasi – actor couple and Ehsaan Qureshi a comedian, belonged to television. The recall of the social advertisements with celebrities was as follows:

Table 4.2

Recall of celebrity social advertisements in unaided category

Sr. No.	Social advertisements with celebrities	Recall	% recall
1	**Shahrukh Khan** – Eradicating Polio	122	**86.52**
2	**Ajay Devgan** – Cleanliness awareness	119	**84.40**
3	**Ehsaan Qureshi** – Aids awareness	56	**39.72**
4	**Rohit–Manasi Roy** – Use of condoms	49	**34.75**

Source: Compiled from primary data.

Graph 4.1
Recall of celebrity social advertisements in unaided category

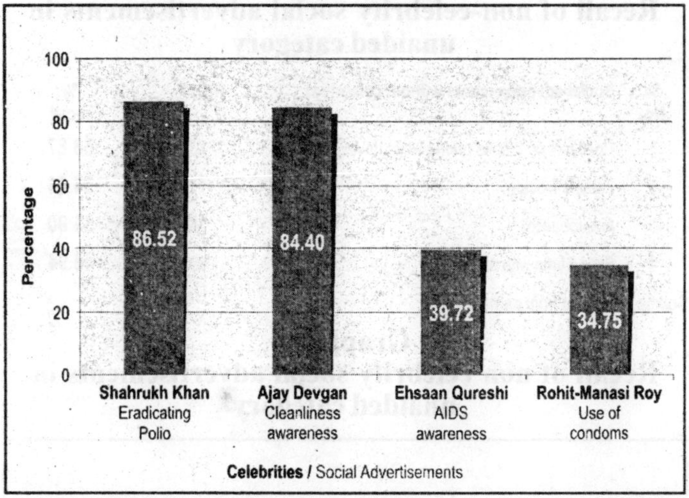

Table 4.2 and Graph 4.1 give the details of the recall of celebrity based social advertisements in unaided category. As per the responses, advertisements with popular film stars like Shahrukh Khan and Ajay Devgan had a significantly high recall of 122 subjects (86.52 per cent) and 119 subjects (84.40 per cent) respectively. The recall of these advertisements was high across both the categories with or without celebrities, indicating a high attention seeking ability of the celebrities. The advertisements with television actors Ehsaan Qureshi and Rohit and Manasi Roy were low in recall with 56 subjects (39.72 per cent) and 49 subjects (34.75 per cent) respectively.

[2] *Recall of non-celebrity social advertisements in unaided category*

There were four advertisements within the non-celebrity social advertisements category. The recall of these social advertisements was as follows:

Table 4.3
Recall of non-celebrity social advertisements in unaided category

Sr. No.	Social advertisements without celebrities	Recall	% recall
1	Don't talk on mobile phone while driving	83	**58.87**
2	Female feticide	77	**54.61**
3	Anti-tobacco	76	**53.90**
4	Spend time with elderly	69	**48.94**

Source: Compiled from primary data.

Graph 4.2
Recall of non celebrity social advertisements in unaided category

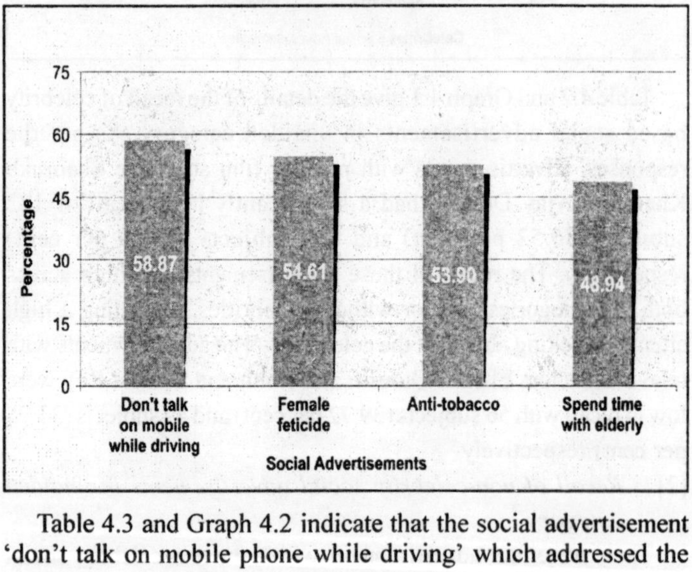

Table 4.3 and Graph 4.2 indicate that the social advertisement 'don't talk on mobile phone while driving' which addressed the

issue of increasing accidents due to talking on mobile phone while driving had the highest recall in this category with 83 subjects (58.87 per cent). The rest three social advertisements on female feticide, anti-tobacco and awareness about spending time with elderly were recalled by 77 subjects (54.61 per cent), 76 subjects (53.90 per cent) and 69 subjects (48.94 per cent) respectively.

[3] *Comparison between recall of celebrity and non-celebrity social advertisements in unaided category*

The comparison of recall of social advertisements with celebrities and social advertisements without celebrities yielded the following results:

Table 4.4
Recall of celebrity and non-celebrity social advertisements in unaided category

Sr. No.	Social advertisements in unaided category	Total recall	% recall
1	Celebrity social advertisements	346	61.35
2	Non-celebrity social advertisements	305	54.08

Source: Compiled from primary data.

Graph 4.3
Percentage recall of celebrity and non-celebrity social advertisements in unaided category

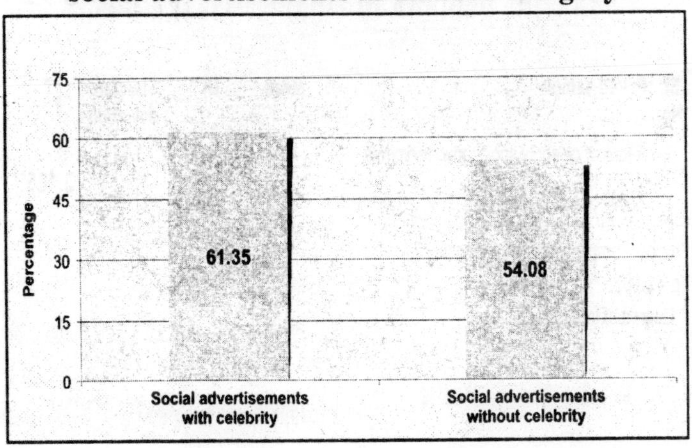

As · Table 4.4 and Graph 4.3, when the recall of celebrity social a. vertisements was compared with recall of non-celebrity social advertisements in the unaided category it was found that the overall recall of advertisements with celebrities was higher (61.35 per cent) than that for the advertisements without celebrities (54.08 per cent). The z-test revealed a significant difference ($z=2.47$), $p < 0.02$. Thus the social advertisements with celebrities had a higher impact on the recall of advertisements compared to that of social advertisements without celebrities in the unaided category. Also it was observed that the impact of celebrities from films had greater influence among the celebrity based advertisements compared to television based celebrities.

[4] *Paired sample T-test of recall in unaided category*

The paired sample T-test comparing mean recall of social advertisements with celebrities and social advertisements without celebrities in unaided category was as follows:

Table 4.5
Paired sample T-test of recall in unaided category

Sr. No.	Paired sample	Mean	Df**	Standard deviation	T
1	Recall of celebrity social advertisements	4.91	140	1.521	**3.105***
2	Recall of non-celebrity social advertisements	4.33	140	2.009	

Source: Compiled from primary data.

* $p < 0.002$.

** Degree of freedom.

Graph 4.4
Mean scores of recall of celebrity and non-celebrity social advertisements in unaided category

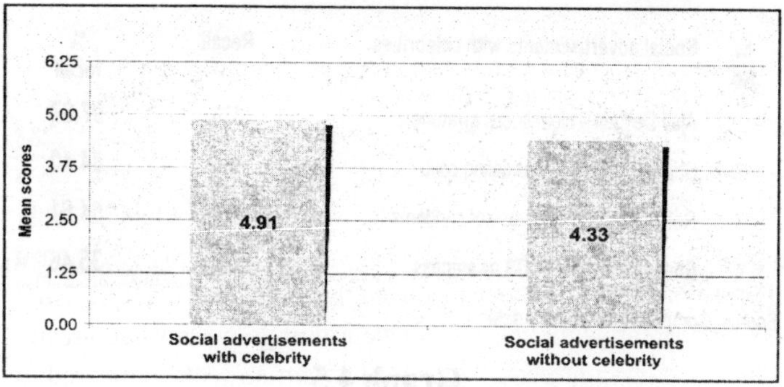

The paired sample T-test comparing mean recall of social advertisements with celebrities and without celebrities in unaided category as indicated in Table 4.5 and Graph 4.4 showed a significant difference, ($t = 3.105$) at a probability < 0.002. The mean recall of the social advertisements with celebrity ($m = 4.91$) was higher than the mean recall of social advertisements without celebrity ($m = 4.33$) in the unaided category.

4.3.2 Recall of social advertisements in aided category

In the aided category the subjects were supposed to recall the social advertisements with the help of some clues provided in the questionnaire for easy recall.

[1] Recall of celebrity social advertisements in aided category

The recall of the social advertisements in aided recall category when certain clues were provided to the subjects, in terms of name of the celebrity or the social issues that were advertised, was as follows:

Table 4.6
Recall of celebrity social advertisements in aided category

Sr. No.	Social advertisements with celebrities	Recall	% recall
1	Ajay Devgan – cleanliness awareness	138	97.87
2	Shahrukh Khan – eradicating polio	119	84.40
3	Rohit – Manasi Roy – use of condoms	77	54.61
4	Ehsaan Qureshi – AIDS awareness	50	35.46

Source: Compiled from primary data.

Graph 4.5
Recall of celebrity social advertisements in aided category

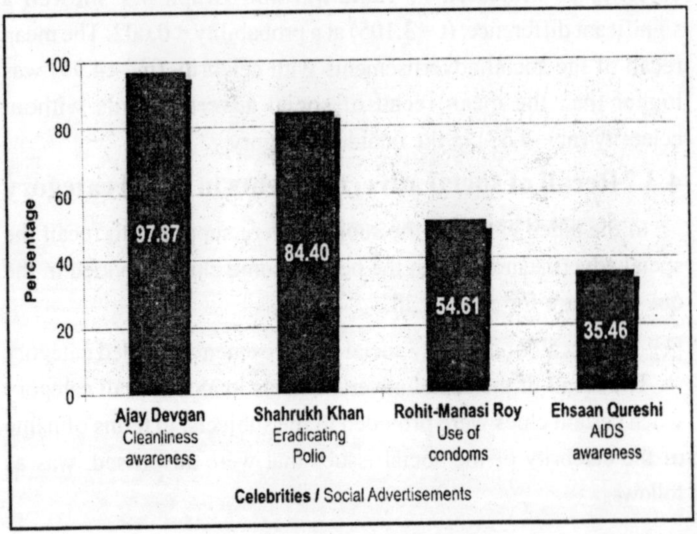

Table 4.6 and Graph 4.5 indicate that within the celebrity based social advertisements in the aided category, the advertisements with film stars had a higher recall just as in the case of unaided category. Ajay Devgan's cleanliness awareness advertisement had a recall from 138 subjects (97.87 per cent) and Shahrukh Khan's polio eradicating advertisement had a recall from 119 subjects (84.40 per cent). In comparison to social advertisements with celebrities from films, social advertisements with celebrities from television had a lower recall. Rohit-Manasi Roy's advertisement on promotion of condoms had a recall from 77 subjects (54.61 per cent) and Ehsaan Qureshi's AIDS awareness advertisement garnered a recall from 50 subjects (35.46 per cent).

[2] Recall of non-celebrity social advertisements in aided category

In the non-celebrity social advertisements aided category, clues based on the advertiser or the central issue / theme of the social advertisement was provided for easy recall.

Table 4.7
Recall of non-celebrity social advertisements in aided category

Sr. No.	Social advertisements without celebrities	Recall	% recall
1	Don't talk on mobile phone while driving	137	**97.16**
2	Spend time with elderly	127	**90.07**
3	Anti-tobacco	82	**58.16**
4	Female feticide	76	**53.90**

Source: Compiled from primary data.

Graph 4.6
Recall of non-celebrity social advertisements in aided category

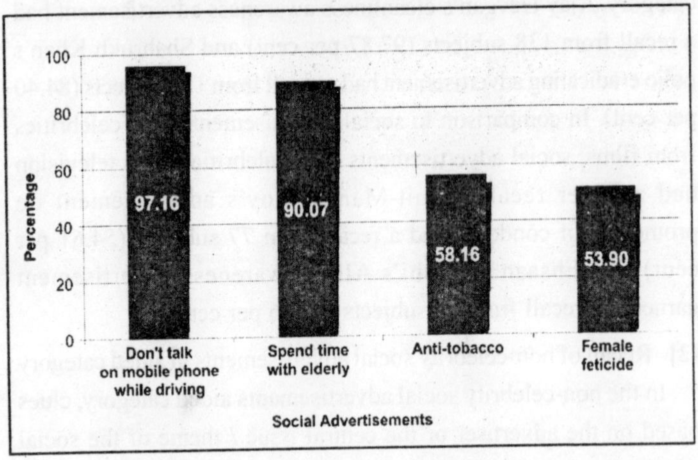

Amongst the non-celebrity social advertisements in the aided category, as indicated in Table 4.7 and Graph 4.6, two issues in particular, 'don't talk on mobile phone while driving' and 'spend time with elderly' were highly recalled by 137 subjects (97.16 per cent)and 127 subjects (90.07 per cent) respectively. Advertisements on tobacco awareness and female feticide had comparatively low recall from 82 subjects (58.16 per cent) and 76 subjects (53.90 per cent) respectively.

[3] Comparison between recall of celebrity and non-celebrity social advertisements in aided category

The comparison of recall of social advertisements with celebrities and social advertisements without celebrities in the aided category yielded the following results:

Table 4.8
Recall of celebrity and non-celebrity social advertisements in aided category

Sr. No.	Social advertisements in the aided category	Total recall	% recall
1	Celebrity social advertisements	384	**68.09**
2	Non-celebrity social advertisements	422	**74.82**

Source: Compiled from primary data.

Graph 4.7
Percentage recall of celebrity and non-celebrity social advertisements in aided category

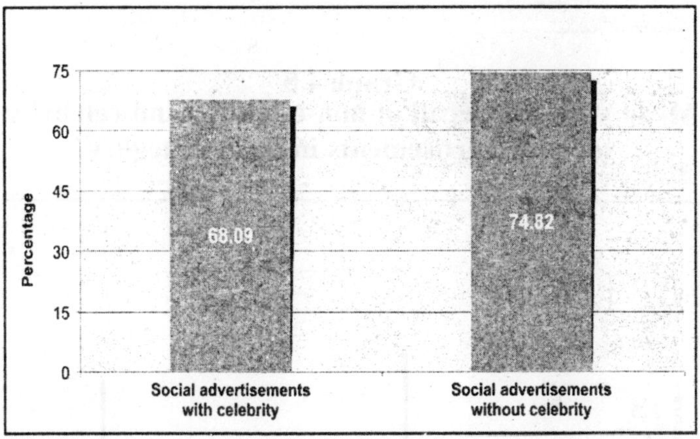

As indicated in Table 4.8 and Graph 4.7, when the recall of celebrity social advertisements was compared with the recall of non-celebrity social advertisements in the aided category, it was found that the overall recall of the celebrity social advertisements was lower (68.09 per cent) than the social advertisements without celebrities (74.82 per cent). The z-test revealed a significant difference ($z=2.51$), $p < 0.02$.

[4] Paired sample T-Test of recall in aided category

The paired sample T-test comparing mean recall of social advertisements with celebrities and social advertisements without celebrities in aided category was as follows:

Table 4.9
Paired sample T-test of recall in aided category

Sr. No.	Paired sample	Mean	Df**	Standard deviation	T
1	Recall of non-celebrity social advertisements	2.99	140	0.975	3.136*
2	Recall of celebrity social advertisements	2.72	140	0.949	

Source: Compiled from primary data.

* p < 0.002.

** Degree of freedom.

Graph 4.8
Mean scores of recall of non-celebrity and celebrity social advertisements in aided category

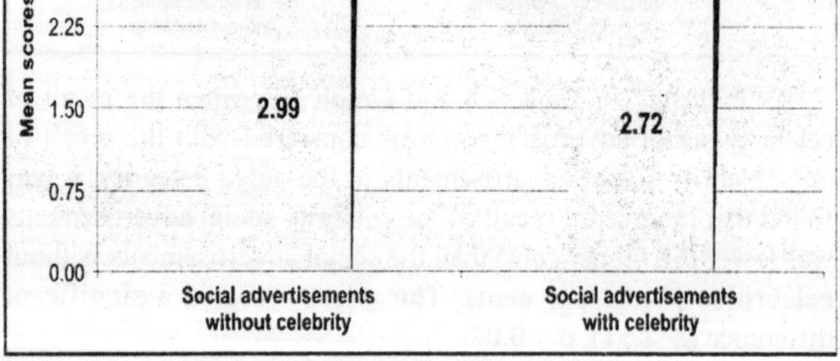

The paired sample T-test comparing mean recall of social advertisements with celebrities and without celebrities in aided category as indicated in Table 4.9 and Graph 4.8, showed a significant difference, (t = 3.136) at a probability < 0.002. The mean recall of the social advertisements without celebrities (m = 2.99) was higher than the mean recall of social advertisements with celebrities (m = 2.72).

4.3.3 Impact of celebrities

Apart from the recall of social advertisements with and without celebrities in the aided and unaided category the overall effectiveness of celebrities was also judged. The subjects were asked to recall celebrities featuring in Indian social advertisements. The subjects had to write their views on whether these celebrities were effective and capable of motivating the audience.

[1] Recall of celebrities

The subjects were asked to recall the celebrities that they have seen supporting social causes. This was asked in the general questionnaire before the subjects were shown the audio-video presentation. The subjects recalled 31 celebrities that were supporting different social causes in India. The recall for each of the celebrity was totaled and the following celebrities emerged at the top five position:

Table 4.10
Recall of celebrities from social advertisements

Sr. No.	Top five celebrities recalled	Field
1	**Amitabh Bachchan**	Film
2	**Shahrukh Khan**	Film
3	**Vivek Oberoi**	Film
4	**Baa** (Character from popular television serial)	Television
5	**Sachin Tendulkar**	Sports

Source: Compiled from primary data.

As seen in Table 4.10 the subjects recalled celebrities belonging to various fields such as films, television serials, sports and music. Amitabh Bachchan and Shahrukh Khan the popular film stars were significantly high on recall compared to other film stars, television actors and sports personalities who generally support the social causes. Here too, like in the unaided and aided category the recall of celebrities from films surpassed the recall of celebrities from other fields such as television or sports.

[2] Attitude towards celebrities in social advertising

It was important to assess the general attitude of subjects towards celebrities in social advertising. The subjects were therefore asked to give their opinion on celebrity's contribution towards social causes through social advertising. The probable reasons why celebrities are an integral part of social advertising were provided and the subjects had to choose amongst them the most appropriate option. In case the subjects felt any other reason was relevant they had an option to write so. Overall 87 subjects (61.70 per cent) indicated a strong preference towards use of celebrities in social advertising. The reasons why the subjects believed celebrities were effective are as follows:

Table 4.11

Celebrity's effectiveness in social advertising

Sr. No.	Reason why celebrities are effective in social advertising	Subjects	%
1	Celebrities provide required publicity	50	57.47
2	Celebrities have ability to mobilize public support	32	36.78
3	Celebrities have charismatic personality	5	5.75
4	Celebrities are trustworthy	–	–

Source: Compiled from primary data.

Graph 4.9
Celebrity's effectiveness in social advertising

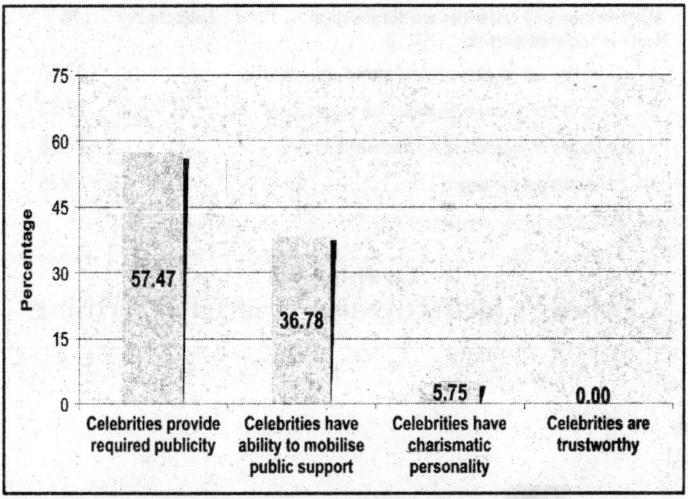

As revealed in Table 4.11 and Graph 4.9, of the total sample 50 subjects (57.47 per cent) felt that celebrities help in creating awareness about the cause and 32 subjects (36.78 per cent) felt celebrities are responsible for even getting the actual support of the general people for the social causes. None of the subjects felt that celebrities are trustworthy; while only 5 subjects (5.75 per cent) felt celebrities are effective because of their persona.

Celebrities are not effective in social advertising according to 54 subjects (38.30 per cent). Here too the subjects were provided with options to choose from, as to why they felt the celebrities were ineffective in social advertising. Incase subjects had any other reason why celebrities were ineffective in social advertising apart from the options provided they could write so. Following are the responses of subjects when compiled together:

Table 4.12
Celebrity's ineffectiveness in social advertising

Sr. No.	Reason why celebrities are not effective in social advertising	Subjects	%
1	Celebrities are not genuinely concerned about society	18	**33.33**
2	Celebrity's popularity overshadow the social causes	16	**29.63**
3	Celebrity's involvement is at superficial level only	15	**27.78**
4	Celebrities are not experts	5	**9.26**

Source: Compiled from primary data.

Graph 4.10
Celebrity's ineffectiveness in social advertising

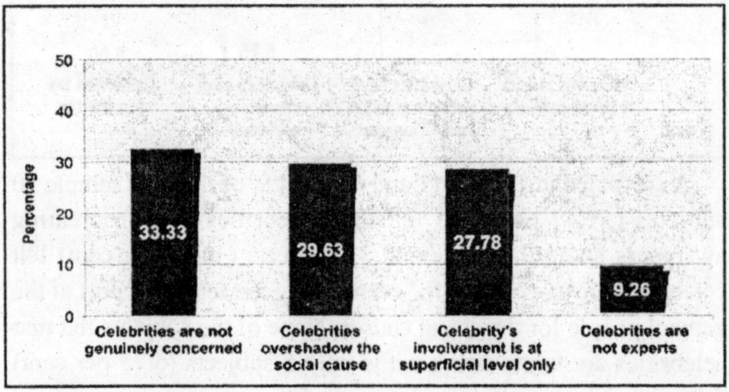

Table 4.12 and Graph 4.10 indicated that out of the total sample, 18 subjects (33.33 per cent) felt that celebrities support the social causes not of genuine concern but purely for monetary reasons whereas 16 subjects (29.63 per cent) felt that the celebrity's persona overshadow the real cause. There were 15 subjects (27.78 per cent) who felt that celebrities are involved only at superficial level and their concern does not go beyond acting in social advertisements. Celebrities are not considered experts in the field of social causes by 5 subjects (9.26 per cent) and therefore they are ineffective.

[3] Role of celebrity in motivating the target audience in social advertising

The views of subjects on whether celebrities contribute towards motivating the target audience were assessed through a dichotomous question on whether they agree or disagree to the statement. The response was as follows:

Table 4.13
Role of celebrities in motivating the target audience

Sr. No.	Celebrity's influence in motivating target audience	Subjects	%
1	Agree	119	84.40
2	Disagree	22	15.60

Source: Compiled from primary data.

Graph 4.11
Role of celebrities in motivating the target audience

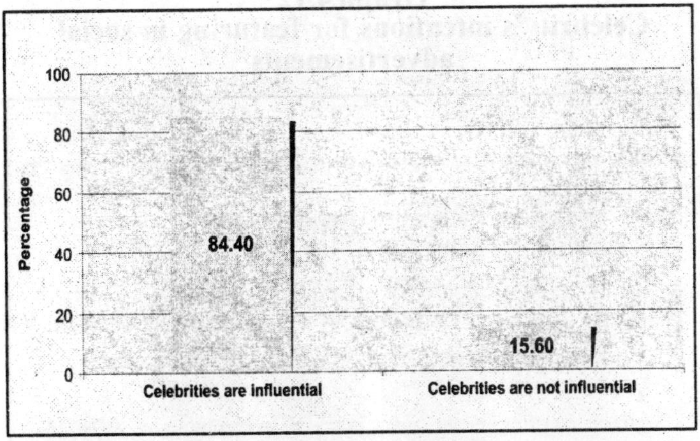

The response as seen in Table 4.13 and Graph 4.11 showed that 119 subjects (84.40 per cent) agreed that celebrities have an influence on the target audience and only 22 subjects (15.60 per cent) disagreed. From the responses it was obvious that majority of

the subjects felt that celebrities contribute positively towards motivating the target audience.

[4] Intentions of celebrities for featuring in social advertisements

The possible intentions why celebrities regularly feature in social advertising were provided to the sample. The subjects had to choose the most suitable reason or write the one he/she felt appropriate.

Table 4.14
Celebrity's intentions for featuring in social advertisements

Sr. No.	Reason why celebrities appear in social advertising	Subjects	%
1	For money	37	**26.24**
2	For creating an overall good impression	36	**25.53**
3	Personal reasons – like release of films	35	**24.82**
4	Out of genuine concern for society/issue.	27	**19.15**
5	Unsure	6	**4.26**

Source: Compiled from primary data.

Graph 4.12
Celebrity's intentions for featuring in social advertisements

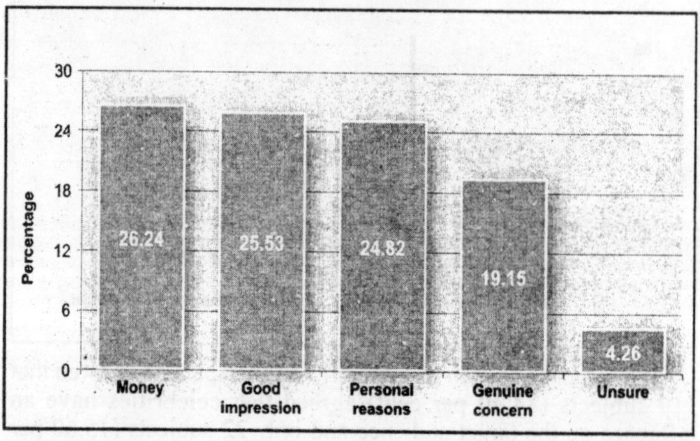

As seen in the Table 4.14 and Graph 4.12 the responses of the subjects were quite diverse. Of the total sample 37 subjects (26.24 per cent) felt that the celebrities are being paid for their services. There were 36 subjects (25.53 per cent) who felt that celebrities support social causes to maintain a good public image and 35 subjects (24.82 per cent) felt that there are personal reasons like garnering publicity for their upcoming movie or for combating negative publicity, for which celebrities want to be in a public eye. There were 27 subjects (19.15 per cent) who felt that the celebrities deliver social messages out of genuine concern for the society. A confused lot of 6 subjects (4.26 per cent) could not figure out as to why celebrities support social causes.

[5] Nature of social advertisements

The nature of social advertisements was assessed on four distinct criteria viz. genuineness, informative value, entertainment value and interest generated. The subjects had to write the most suitable option against each of the advertisements. The study of these elements gave an idea of how youth generally perceive social advertisements with celebrities and without celebrities.

Table 4.15
Nature-wise analysis of social advertisements with celebrities

Sr. No.	Social advertisements with celebrities	Genuine	Informative	Entertaining	Boring
1	**Shahrukh Khan** - eradicating polio	38	80	6	17
2	**Rohit – Manasi Roy** - use of condoms	39	75	7	20
3	**Ajay Devgan** - cleanliness awareness	48	77	12	4
4	**Ehsaan Qureshi** - AIDS awareness	21	51	67	2

Source: Compiled from primary data.

Graph 4.13
Nature-wise analysis of social advertisements with celebrities

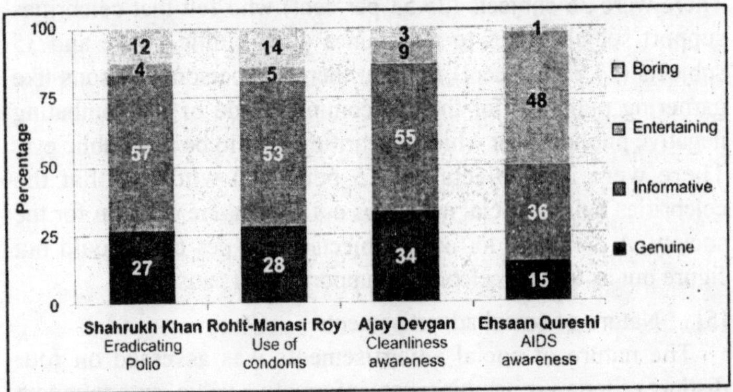

Social advertisements with celebrities registered a mixed response as seen in Table 4.15 and Graph 4.13. The social advertisements' informative quotient dominated the other elements. Celebrity involvement perhaps made the social advertisements appear more realistic since 'genuine' was the most selected element after information. Except the humorous advertisement by comedian Ehsaan Qureshi other advertisements were generally not rated as entertaining. The boring element was selected by very few subjects. One thing particularly noticed in these celebrity based social advertisements was that they were rated everything else but not boring which was perhaps the contribution of the celebrities.

Table 4.16
Nature-wise analysis of social advertisements without celebrities

Sr. No.	Social advertisements	Genuine	Informative	Entertaining	Boring
1	Spend time with elderly	44		33	9
2	Female feticide	59		6	2
3	Don't talk on mobile phone while driving	39		17	6
4	Anti-tobacco	47		18	8

Source: Compiled from primary data.

Graph 4.14
Nature-wise analysis of social advertisements without celebrities

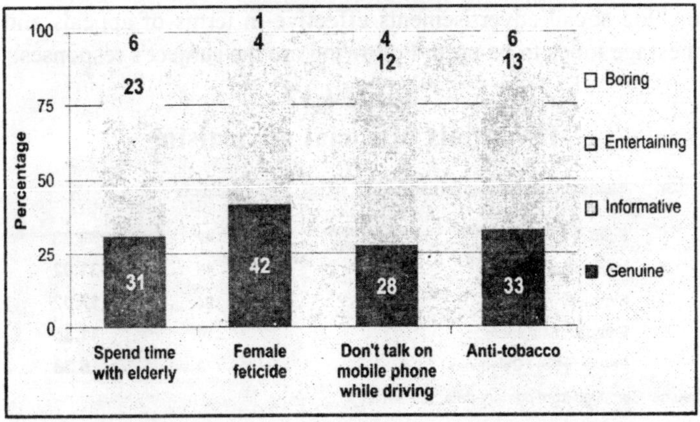

The analysis of social advertisements without celebrities as shown in Table 4.16 and Graph 4.14 indicated that these advertisements were also highly rated in terms of 'informative' and 'genuine' element. However when the responses were compared with the responses of the social advertisements with celebrities it was found that social advertisements with celebrities were rated higher in terms of 'entertaining' element which was missing in social advertisements without celebrities. Here too very few subjects felt that the social advertisements were boring. This is an indication that social advertisements overall garner a positive response perhaps because they are considered genuine.

[6] *Essentials of social advertising*

The questionnaire included questions on the subject's views on the manner in which social advertising must be conducted. The subjects had to choose from the given options to determine the most important element and effective manner of social advertising.

A. Important element in social advertising

In order to analyse the important element that makes social advertisements effective, subjects were provided with various options to choose from. Study of such elements can be helpful in making social advertisements effective in terms of appeals and message tones to be used. Following are the subject's responses:

Table 4.17
Essentials of social advertising

Sr. No.	Elements of social advertisements	Subjects	%
1	Emotions	47	**33.33**
2	Informative value	45	**31.92**
3	Simplicity	24	**17.02**
4	Entertainment value	16	**11.35**
5	Personalities / Celebrities	9	**6.38**

Source: Compiled from primary data.

Graph 4.15
Essentials of social advertising

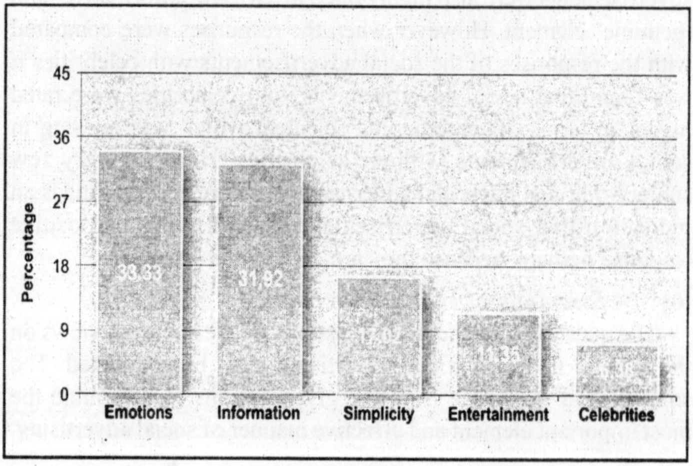

When asked about the most important element in the social advertisements the subject's responses were highly diverse as revealed in Table 4.17 and Graph 4.15. Emotional appeal was considered important element by 47 subjects (33.33 per cent). Whereas 45 subjects (31.92 per cent) felt the information quotient in social advertising was most important. Elements like simplicity and entertainment value were considered as significant by 24 subjects (17.02 per cent) and 16 subjects (11.35 per cent) respectively. Surprisingly the celebrities were considered important only by 9 subjects (6.38 per cent).

B. Nature of social advertising

The similar question was solicited in different manner and following were the responses:

Table 4.18
Effective form of social advertising

Sr. No.	Type of advertisements	Subjects	%
1	Celebrity advertisements	19	**13.48**
2	Informative advertisements	101	**71.63**
3	Humorous advertisements	21	**14.89**

Source: Compiled from primary data.

Graph 4.16
Effective form of social advertising

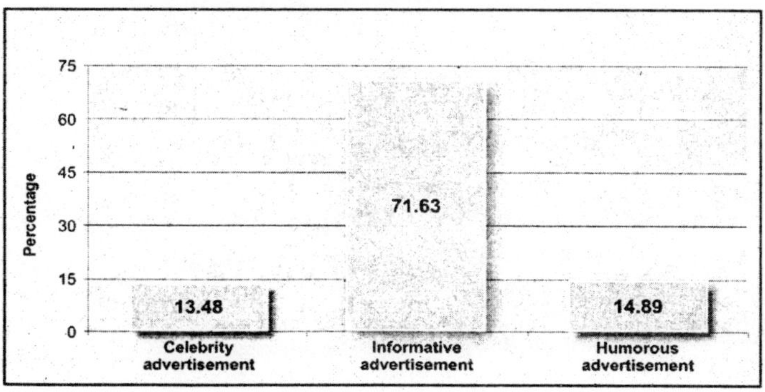

The same question about celebrity effectiveness when asked differently, the subject's response was still the same as seen in Table 4.18 and Graph 4.16. Of the total sample as many as 101 subjects (71.63 per cent) felt that they expect information from social advertising, 21 subjects (14.89 per cent) felt humour in advertising was important. There were 19 subjects (13.48 per cent) who felt use of celebrity was more vital for promoting social causes.

4.4 Conclusion

In this research study, the impact of celebrity was studied by comparing celebrity social advertisements with social advertisements without celebrity. The subjects as high as 62 per cent felt that celebrities in social advertising made an impact while rest of them felt otherwise. The subjects also felt that social advertising with celebrities contribute in motivating the target audience. As far as the recall of social advertising was concerned the celebrities definitely made a positive contribution. The impact of the celebrities was evident from the higher recall of social advertising with celebrities compared to social advertising without celebrities in the unaided category.

5

Influence of Fear Appeals in Social Advertising on Youth

5.1 Introduction to Appeals in Advertising

While developing the advertising campaign one of the most critical aspect of decision-making involves deciding the advertising appeal to be used in the advertisement. The advertising appeal refers to the approach used to attract the attention of consumers and influence their feelings towards the product advertised. Advertising appeals are used to communicate and influence the behaviour of the consumers.

The selection and application of appeals varies on the basis of the clients' preferences, objective of the advertising campaign, the nature of the product and the target audience to be reached. Advertising appeals are often classified as rational appeals, emotional appeals and moral appeals. Rational appeals are designed with the intent of appealing to the rational and logical aspect of the consumers' decision-making process. Then there is use of emotional appeals that attempts to stimulate consumer's feelings with the intent of evoking some desired emotional response. Moral appeals are the ones which attempt to draw attention to what is right and what is wrong.

Emotional appeals are related to the consumer's psychological or social needs that come into play while they make their purchase decisions. Many a times these emotional motives can be more important than attributes, functions and features of the product. Unlike rational appeals, emotional appeals are not preceded by careful analysis of the brand's functional or practical utility. Emotional appeals are designed to stir up some negative or positive emotions. The aroused emotions are those mental agitations or excited states of feelings which are suppose to motivate product interest and prompt the audience to behave in the desired manner.

The emotional appeals are further classified into positive emotional appeals and negative emotional appeals. The positive emotional appeals are the appeals based on feelings such as love, affection, joy and pride which users can feel / enjoy after buying or using the product. Negative emotional appeals are based on feelings such as shame, guilt, fear, rejection and embarrassment that motivate the audience to do things that they should do or stop doing things that they shouldn't be doing.

5.2 Assessing Literature on Fear Appeals in Advertising

Advertising is all about persuading and changing the attitude and behaviour of the target audience towards a predetermined goal. Since individuals are emotional beings many a times their purchase decisions in marketing are guided by emotions rather than pure functional benefits offered by different products and services. To seek benefit of this aspect of consumer behaviour many advertisers are seen using emotions to promote brands and influence the customer's psyche. Some studies also show that emotional advertising is better remembered compared to non-emotional advertising.[1]

Many feelings or needs can serve as the basis for advertising appeals designed to influence consumers on an emotional level. Positive emotions such as humor, love, joy and pride used in advertising can have favourable effect on people and put them in a positive frame of mind. While negative emotions such as fear, guilt and shame used in advertising can direct people to stay away from undesirable consequences.

Fear is an emotional response to a threat that expresses or at least implies, some sort of danger. Advertising sometimes use fear appeals to evoke this emotional, response and arouse individuals to take steps to remove the threat.[2] Some, like the anti-drug advertisements stress physical danger that can occur if behaviours are not altered. Others like those for deodorant, mouth-wash or dandruff shampoos threaten disapproval or social rejection.

In literature, fear appeal is described as "a persuasive communication attempting to arouse fear in order to promote precautionary motivation and self-protection action [e.g. stop smoking]. Fear arousal is an unpleasant emotional state triggered by the perception of threatening stimuli."[3] It is believed that the state of fear involves a physiological arousal that results in more cognitive, affective and behavioural attention directed to the threat; leading the individual to respond by trying to reduce the threat and eliminate the fear. While threat is the manifestation of a danger, fear is the state of uneasiness the individual feels in result to the threat.

The earliest fear research appeared to suggest that as the intensity of a fear appeal in advertising increases, its effectiveness in persuading audiences will decrease.[4] One explanation is that strong fear-evoking message components cause consumers to set up perceptual defense mechanisms to screen out the fearful aspects of the message. However in doing so, they also reject the rest of the message. The result of these and other early findings was that most advertisers became highly reluctant to use fear appeals for promoting their products or services.[5]

- - - - - - - - - - - - - - - - - -

[1] Madison Cathy, "Researchers Work Advertising into an Emotional State," Adweek, November 5, 1990, p. 30.

[2] Belch G. and Belch M., *op. cit.*, p. 184.

One well accepted view of the fear appeals is, psychologist Leventhal Howard's The Parallel Response Model that suggests a cognitive response.[6] The fear appeal not only evokes an emotional response, but also the belief that harm is likely to occur is evoked in addition. The audience reaction preferred by the advertiser is to have the audience comply with the communication and change attitudes and behaviour accordingly. But the audience may instead engage in defensive processes such as to deny vulnerability, counter-argue, become irritated at something in the advertisement or ignore it. For the preferred "comply" reaction to occur, the fear needs to be at just the right level.

According to a model by psychologist Thayer Robert, fear increased tension, which stimulates feelings of being active and energetic-up to a threshold point, after which the tension creates dysfunctional feelings of jitteriness and anxiety.[7] Thus, if the level of fear in the advertising is too low, the emotional response will not be forthcoming and the advertisement will not be successful at creating attention and interest in the basic problem.[8]

For several years other investigations began to uncover additional results. The conclusion then appeared to be summarised by what has become known as the "inverted-U" argument: low fear appeals are not effective because they generate little motivation for attitude change and high fear appeals also tend to yield little attitude change because, as said above, they activate defense mechanisms. Therefore moderate fear appeals, which provide sufficient motivation but do not activate perceptual defenses,

---

[3] Ruiter, Robert A. C., Abraham C. and Kok G., "Scary Warnings and Rational Precautions: A Review of the Psychology of Fear Appeals", Psychology and Health, Vol. 16, 2001, pp. 613- 630.

[4] Janis I. and Feshbach S., "Effects of Fear-Arousing Communications," Journal of Abnormal and Social Psychology, 48, 1953, pp. 78-92.

[5] Loudon David L. and Bitta Albert J. Della, *op. cit.*, p. 468.

[6] Rosen T. John, Terry Nathaniel S. and Leventhal Howard, "The Role of Esteem and Coping in Response to a Threat Communication," Journal of Research in Personality, 16 Spring 1983, pp. 90-110.

appeared most effective in generating attitude change. Chart 5.1 indicates this proposed inverted-U relationship between the intensity of fear appeals and amount of attitude change likely to be achieved.[9]

Chart 5.1

The relationship between intensity of fear appeal and resulting attitude change

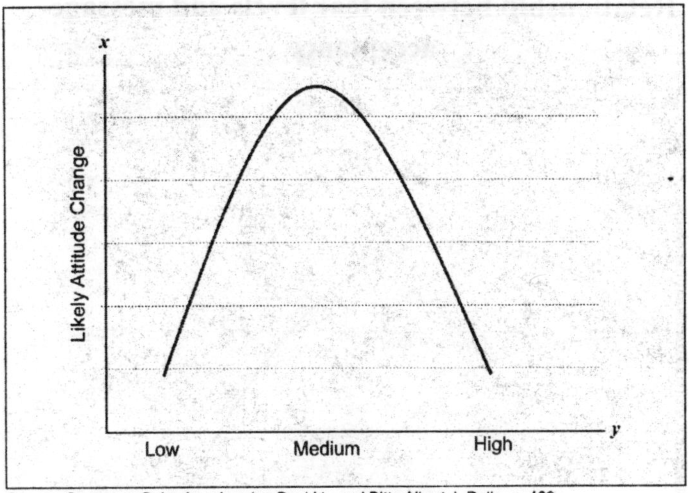

Source: Consumer Behaviour, Loudon David L. and Bitta Albert J. Della, p. 468.

According to the theory proposed by Ray Michael L. and Wilkie William L.,[10] the relationship between the intensity of fear in an advertising message and its persuasive impact on target audience is curvilinear such that as the amount of fear rises, the message

---

[7] Henthorne Tony L., LaTour Michael S. and Natarajan Rajan, "Fear Appeals in Print Advertising, An analysis of Arousal and Ad Response," Journal of Advertising, 22, No. 2, June 1983, pp. 59-69.

[8] Batra Rajeev, Myers John G. and Aaker David A., *op. cit.*, pp. 305-306.

[9] Loudon David L. and Bitta Albert J. Della, *op. cit.*, p. 468.

acceptance increases as shown in Chart 5.1. But this increase in message acceptance occurs only up to a point of fear intensity. Once this point is reached, any further increase in the amount of fear will fail to enhance message acceptance. On the contrary, the effect of increased fear beyond this point would increasingly decrease message acceptance.[11]

Chart 5.2
Relationship between fear levels and message acceptance

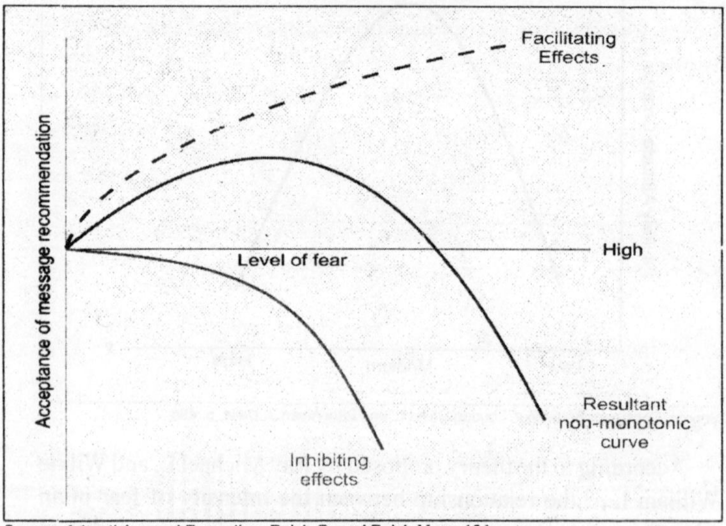

Source: Advertising and Promotion, Belch G. and Belch M., p. 184.

This relationship between fear and persuasion can be explained by the fact that fear appeal have both facilitating and inhibiting

---

[10] Ray Michael L. and Wilkie William L., "Fear: The Potential of an Appeal Neglected by Marketing," Journal of Marketing, 32, January 1970, pp. 54-62.
[11] Strenthal Brian and Craig Samuel C., "Fear Appeals Revisited and Revised," Journal of Consumer Research 1, December 1974, pp. 22-34.
Kazmi S. H. H. and Batra Satish K., *op. cit.*, pp. 116-118.

effects.[12] A low level of fear can have facilitating effects; it attracts attention and interest in the message and may motivate the receiver to act to resolve the threat. Thus, increasing the level of fear in a message from low to moderate can result in increased persuasion. High levels of fear, however, can produce inhibiting effects; the receiver may emotionally block the message by tuning it out, perceiving it selectively or denying its arguments outright. Chart 5.2 illustrates how these two counter effects operate to produce the curvilinear relationship between fear and persuasion.[13]

Another approach to the curvilinear explanation of fear is the protection motivation model by Rogers Ronald.[14] According to this theory, four cognitive appraisal processes mediate the individual's response to the threat.

Appraising the:

- information available regarding the severity of the perceived threat,
- perceived probability that the threat will occur,
- perceived ability of a coping behaviour to remove the threat and
- individual's perceived ability to carry out the coping behaviour.

This model suggests that both the cognitive appraisal of the information in a fear appeal message and the emotional response mediate persuasion. An audience is more likely to continue processing threat-related information, thereby increasing the likelihood that a coping behaviour will occur. The protection motivation model suggests that advertisement using fear appeals should give the target audience information about the severity of the threat, the probability of its occurrence, the effectiveness of a coping response and the ease with which the response can be implemented.

---

[12] Strenthal Brian and Craig Samuel C., "Fear Appeals Revisited and Revised," Journal of Consumer Research 1, December 1974, pp. 22-34.

However, Strenthal Brian, Craig Samuel and others have been arguing that perhaps it is inappropriate to draw general conclusions about any given level of fear appeal because numerous factors may influence how consumers will respond to the appeal.[15] The factors that may influence the persuasiveness of fear appeals include (1) source credibility, (2) audience characteristics, (3) the context of the message presentation and (4) the type of fear appeal used.

In reviewing research on fear appeals, Rotfeld Herbert has argued that some of the studies may be confusing different types of threats and the level of potential harm portrayed in the message with fear, which is an emotional response.[16] He concludes that the relationship between the emotional responses of fear or arousal and persuasion is not curvilinear but rather is monotonic and positive, meaning that higher levels of fear do result in greater persuasion. However, Rotfeld notes that not all fear messages are equally effective, because different people fear different things. Thus they will respond differently to the same threat, so the strongest threats are not always the most persuasive. This suggests that marketers using fear appeals must consider the emotional responses generated by the message and how they will affect reactions to the message.

In a nutshell, the models and theories presented here suggest that while using a fear appeal-based message strategy, the advertiser should consider how fear operates, what level to use and how different target audiences may respond. It is helpful to test the advertisement in advance to make sure the level of fear being depicted is not too high and that it is still likeable. It should

- - - - - - - - - - - - - - - - -

[13] Belch G. and Belch M., *op. cit.*, p. 184.

[14] Tanner John F., Hunt Jr., James B. and Eppright David R., "Protection Motivation Model: A Normative Mode of Fear Appeals," Journal of Marketing, 55, July 1991, pp. 36-45.

[15] Strenthal Brian and Craig Samuel C., *op. cit.*

also be noted that some studies have not found support for this idea that too much fear can backfire but studies instead have found that more fear is even better.[17] One more important essential of use of fear appeal is that threat generated in the advertisement should give full information of its severity and likelihood of its occurrence, suggest effective coping response and generate confidence that the coping response will essentially take care of the threat generated.

5.3 Study Two: Role of Fear Appeals in Social Advertising

Fear appeals in social advertising have played a significant role in many foreign countries for promoting various issues such as use of seat belts in cars, AIDS awareness and against smoking and drug abuse. In India too, there are host of social issues which can be effectively advertised by using fear appeals to bring about the desired change in the public. This study was conducted on a similar premise, to examine whether fear appeals have an impact on youth and whether they make any positive contribution towards the recall of social advertising.

The objective of the Study Two was to evaluate the effectiveness of fear appeals in social advertising. To achieve this, eight social advertisements were presented in the audio-video presentation. These eight social advertisements consisted of four social advertisements with fear appeals and four social advertisements with non-fear appeals that were pitched against each other. Table 5.1 gives the details of the social advertisements that were shown in the presentation:

- - - - - - - - - - - - - - - -

[16] Rotfeld Herbert J., "The Textbook Effect: Conventional Wisdom, Myth and Error in Marketing," Journal of Marketing 64, April 2000, pp. 122-27.
[17] Batra Rajeev, Myers John G. and Aaker David A., *op. cit.*, p. 306.

Table 5.1
Social advertisements presented in Study Two

Sr. No.	Social advertisements with fear appeals	Sr. No.	Social advertisements without fear appeal
1	Anti tobacco	1	AIDS awareness
2	Female feticide	2	Cleanliness awareness
3	Don't drink and drive	3	Spend time with elderly
4	Population control	4	Sex education for youth

Source: Compiled from primary data.

The responses to the questions based on the impact of fear appeals in the aided and unaided categories were carefully analysed in the following step-by-step manner:

[1] Number of social advertisements correctly recalled with fear appeals and with non-fear appeals in aided and unaided category were calculated.

[2] Means were calculated for number of social advertisements correctly recalled with fear appeals and with non-fear appeals in aided and unaided category.

[3] Paired samples T-test were conducted to compare recall of social advertisements with fear appeals and social advertisements without fear appeals under both aided and unaided conditions.

[4] Percentages of social advertisements recalled with fear appeals and without fear appeals under aided and unaided conditions were calculated.

[5] z-tests were performed to measure the significance of the difference between percentages of social advertisements with fear appeals and social advertisements without fear appeals recalled under aided and unaided conditions.

In the study specific questionnaire the subjects were required to recall the social advertisements that they had seen in the presentation. The responses were based on two categories, social advertisements with fear appeals and social advertisements without fear appeals. These two categories were further investigated under two conditions, viz. unaided and aided. Apart from this the subject's overall opinion about fear appeals and whether fear appeals contribute positively in social advertising was analysed.

5.3.1 Recall of social advertisements in unaided category

In the unaided recall category the subjects were supposed to recall and write the social advertisements that they had seen in the audio-video presentation. There was no clue or hint provided and they had to recall social advertisements on the basis of the issues addressed.

[1] Recall of social advertisements with fear appeals in unaided category

There were four social advertisements based on fear appeals. The advertisement on anti tobacco showed gory pictures of after-effects of smoking on different body organ/parts such as lungs, mouth and so on. The female feticide advertisement was an animated and intriguing story of a female fetus in the womb that is brutally stabbed to death.The 'don't drink and drive' advertisements was full of devastating pictures with young injured victims immediately after accidents. The fourth fear based advertisement dealt with the issue of population control that showed some disturbing consequences people have to bear if the population issue is not controlled.

Table 5.2
Recall of social advertisements with fear appeals in unaided category

Sr. No.	Social advertisements with fear appeal	Recall	% recall
1	Anti tobacco	104	**83.87**
2	Female Feticide	74	**59.68**
3	Don't drink and drive	66	**53.23**
4	Population control	65	**52.42**

Source: Compiled from primary data.

Graph 5.1
Recall of social advertisements with fear appeals in unaided category

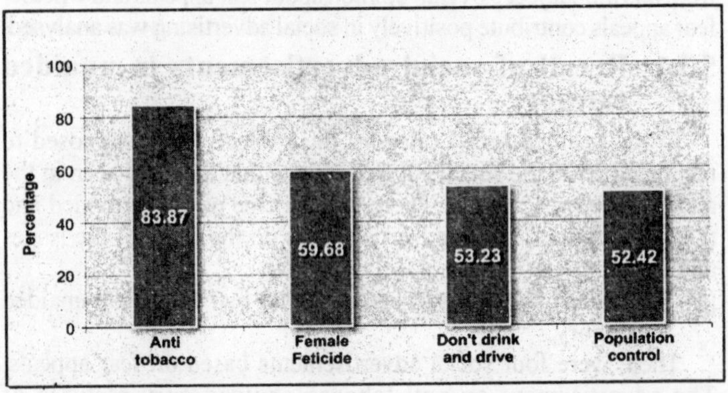

As indicated in Table 5.2 and Graph 5.1, within the fear appeal based social advertisements, the anti tobacco advertisement had a significantly high recall from 104 subjects (83.87 per cent) followed by female feticide advertisement which had a recall of 74 subjects (59.68 per cent) respectively. The advertisements based on awareness against drunken driving and population control were comparatively low in recall with 66 subjects (53.23 per cent) and 65 subjects (52.42 per cent) respectively.

[2] Recall of social advertisements with non-fear appeals in unaided category

There were four advertisements within the non-fear appeals social advertisements category. The issue of cleanliness was addressed through a celebrity based advertisement. The advertisement had eminent personalities including film actor Shahrukh Khan, former Chief Minister of Maharashtra, V. Deshmukh, former Mayor of Mumbai, Dutta Dalvi and Municipal Commissioner Johny Joseph. The comedian Navin Prabhakar addressed the issue of AIDS. The advertisement on sex education brought up the need for sex education amongst youth. 'Spend time with elderly' humorously addressed the issue of loneliness suffered by elderly in the city.

Table 5.3
Recall of social advertisements with non-fear appeals in unaided category

Sr. No.	Social advertisements with non-fear appeal	Recall	% recall
1	Cleanliness awareness	105	**84.68**
2	AIDS awareness	100	**80.65**
3	Spend time with elderly	43	**34.68**
4	Sex education for youth	24	**19.35**

Source: Compiled from primary data.

Graph 5.2
Recall of social advertisements with non-fear appeals in unaided category

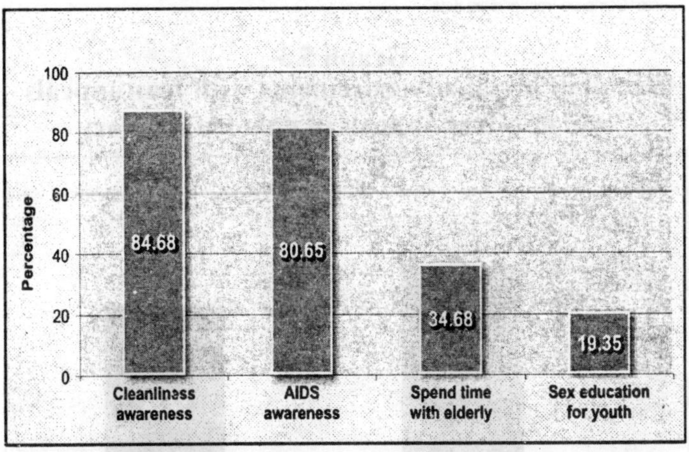

The responses, as revealed in Table 5.3 and Graph 5.2 indicate that social advertisement on cleanliness awareness had a significantly high recall from 105 subjects (84.68 per cent) closely followed by AIDS awareness advertisement which had a recall from 100 subjects (80.65 per cent). The advertisements on 'spend time with elderly' and sex education for youth were comparatively low in recall with 43 subjects (34.68 per cent) and 24 subjects (19.35 per cent) respectively.

[3] Comparison between recall of social advertisements with fear appeals and non-fear appeals in unaided category

The comparison of recall of social advertisements with fear appeals and social advertisements without fear appeals in the unaided category yielded the following results:

Table 5.4
Recall of social advertisements with fear appeals and non-fear appeals in unaided category

Sr. No.	Particulars	Total recall	% recall
1	Social advertisements with fear appeals	309	62.30
2	Social advertisements with non- fear appeals	272	54.84

Source: Compiled from primary data.

Graph 5.3
Recall of social advertisements with fear appeals and non-fear appeals in unaided category

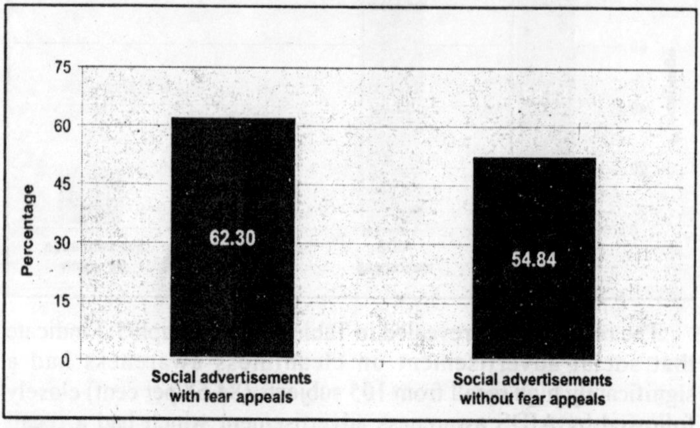

Table 5.4 and Graph 5.3 indicate that when the recall of social advertisements with fear appeals was compared with recall of

social advertisements with non-fear appeals in the unaided category it was found that the overall recall of the advertisements with fear appeals was higher (62.30 per cent) than that for the advertisements without fear appeals (54.84 per cent). The z-test revealed a significant difference ($z=2.29$), $p < 0.05$.

[4] Paired Sample T-test of recall in unaided category

The paired sample T-test comparing mean recall of social advertisements with fear appeals and without fear appeals showed the following results:

Table 5.5
Paired Sample T-test of recall in unaided category

Sr. No.	Paired sample	Mean	Df	Standard deviation	T
1	Recall of social advertisements with fear appeal	4.98	123	2.111	2.970*
2	Recall of social advertisements with non-fear appeal	4.39	123	1.724	

Source: Compiled from primary data.

* $p < 0.004$.

Graph 5.4
Mean scores of recall of social advertisements with fear appeals and non-fear appeals in unaided category

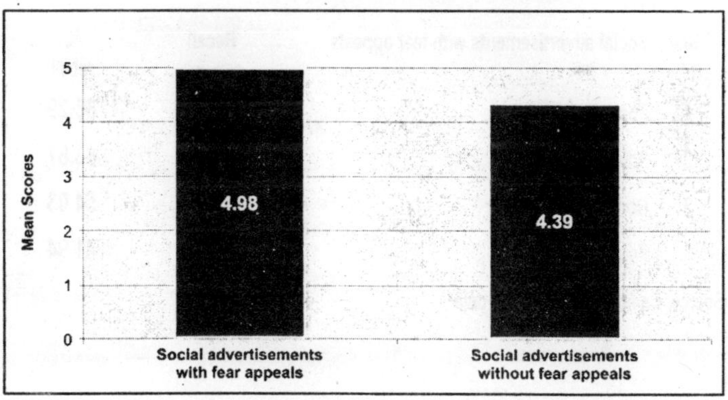

The paired sample T-test comparing mean recall of social advertisements with fear appeals and without fear appeals as indicated in Table 5.5 and Graph 5.4 showed a significant difference, (t = 2.970) at a probability < 0.004. The mean recall of the social advertisements with fear appeals (m = 4.98) was higher than the mean recall of social advertisements without fear appeals (m = 4.39) in unaided category.

5.3.2 Recall of social advertisements in aided category

In the aided category the subjects were supposed to recall the social advertisements with the help of some clues provided in the questionnaire for easy recall.

[1] Recall of social advertisements with fear appeals in aided category

The results of recall in the aided category for social advertisements with fear appeals where the subjects were provided with some clues for easy recall were as follows:

Table 5.6
Recall of social advertisements with fear appeals in aided category

Sr. No.	Social advertisements with fear appeals	Recall	% recall
1	Population control	107	**86.29**
2	Anti tobacco	104	**83.87**
3	Don't drink and drive	67	**54.03**
4	Female feticide	52	**41.94**

Source: Compiled from primary data.

Graph 5.5
Recall of social advertisements with fear appeals in aided category

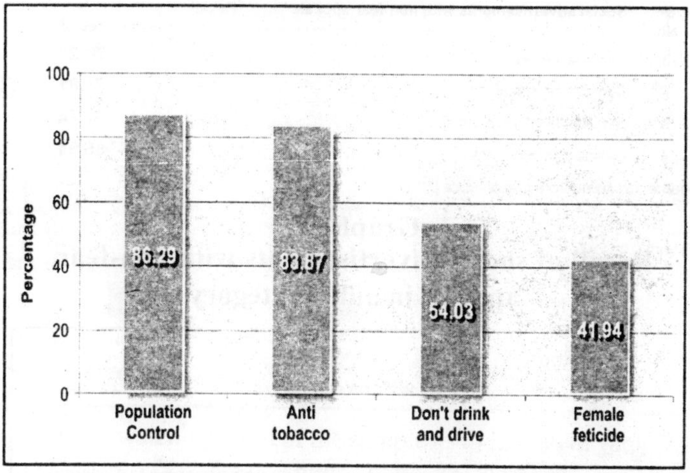

Table 5.6 and Graph 5.5 revealed that among the social advertisements with fear appeals the advertisement on population control had the highest recall of 107 subjects (86.29 per cent) closely followed by recall of 104 subjects (83.87 per cent) for the anti tobacco advertisement. The 'don't drink and drive' and female feticide campaigns registered a comparatively low recall from 67 subjects (54.03 per cent) and 52 subjects (41.94 per cent) respectively.

[2] Recall of social advertisements with non-fear appeals in aided category

The results of recall in the aided category for social advertisements without the use of fear appeals where the subjects were provided with some clues for easy recall were as follows:

Table 5.7
Recall of social advertisements with non-fear appeals in aided category

Sr. No.	Social advertisements with non-fear appeals	Recall	% recall
1	AIDS awareness	97	**78.23**
2	Spend time with elderly	94	**75.81**
3	Sex education for youth	84	**67.74**
4	Cleanliness awareness	83	**66.94**

Source: Compiled from primary data.

Graph 5.6
Recall of social advertisements with non-fear appeals in aided category

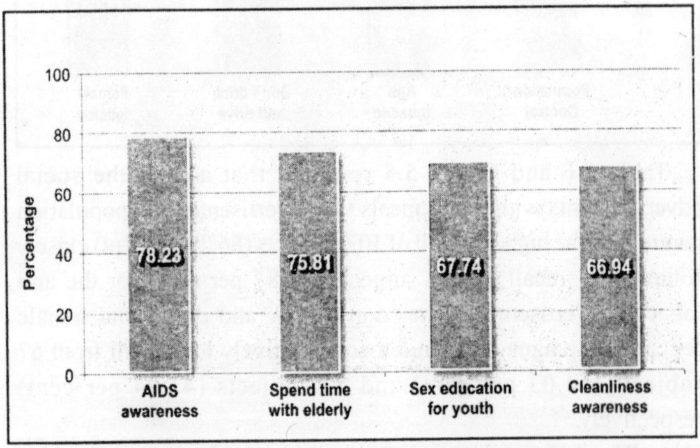

Table 5.7 and Graph 5.6 revealed that amongst the non-fear category social advertisement on AIDS awareness registered a recall from 97 subjects (78.23 per cent) followed by recall of 94 subjects (75.81 per cent) for the campaign 'spend time with elderly.' Advertisements on sex education for youth and cleanliness awareness had a recall of 84 subjects (67.74 per cent) and 83 subjects (66.94 per cent) respectively.

[3] Comparison between recall of social advertisements with fear appeals and non-fear appeals in aided category

Following is the result, when the recall of social advertisements with fear appeals was compared with recall of social advertisements with non-fear appeals in the aided category:

Table 5.8
Recall of social advertisements with fear appeals and non-fear appeals in aided category

Sr. No.	Particulars	Total recall	% recall
1	Social advertisements with fear appeal	330	66.53
2	Social advertisements without fear appeal	358	72.18

Source: Compiled from primary data.

Graph 5.7
Recall of social advertisements with fear appeals and non-fear appeals in aided category

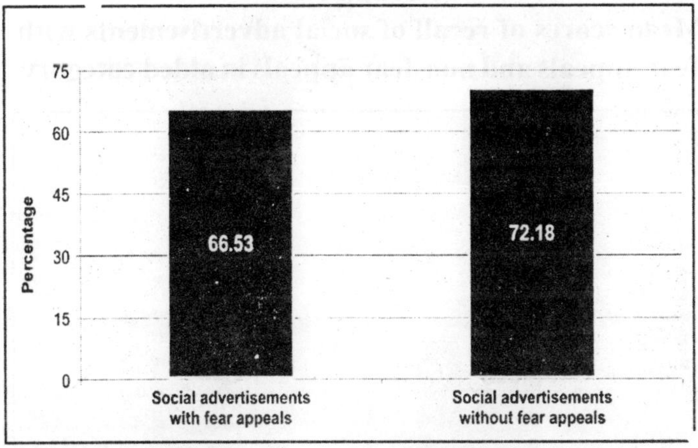

Table 5.8 and Graph 5.7 indicated that when the recall of social advertisements with fear appeals was compared with social

advertisements with non-fear appeals in the aided category it was found that the overall recall of social advertisements with fear appeals was lower (66.53 per cent) than the social advertisements without fear appeals (72.18 per cent). The z-test revealed a low significant difference ($z=1.87$) $p < 0.10$.

[4] Paired sample T-test of recall in aided category

The paired sample T-test comparing mean recall of social advertisements with fear appeals and social advertisements without fear appeals in aided category were as follows:

Table 5.9

Paired ample T-test in recall of aided category

Sr. No.	Paired sample	Mean	Df	Standard deviation	T
1	Recall of social advertisements with non-fear appeal	2.89	123	1.120	2.295*
2	Recall of social advertisements with fear appeal	2.66	123	1.066	

Source: Compiled from primary data.
* $p < 0.023$.

Graph 5.8

Mean scores of recall of social advertisements with fear appeals and non-fear appeals in aided category

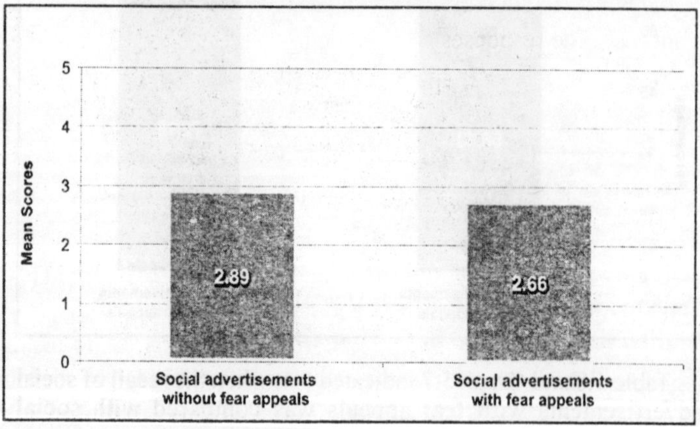

Table 5.9 and Graph 5.8 indicated that the paired sample T-test comparing mean recall of social advertisements with fear appeals and social advertisements without fear appeals in aided category did not show a significant difference (t = 2.295, probability < 0.023). The mean recall of the social advertisements without fear appeals (m = 2.89) is higher than the mean recall of social advertisements with fear appeals (m = 2.66).

5.3.3 Impact of Fear Appeals

Apart from the recall of social advertisements with and without fear appeals in the aided and unaided category the effectiveness of fear appeals was also judged by analysing whether there was any attitudinal change due to these social advertisements and what views subjects held about use of fear appeals in social advertising.

[1] *Opinion about social advertisements based on fear appeals*

In order to evaluate the effectiveness of fear appeals it was important to assess the subjects' views about use of fear appeals. To enable this, the subjects were provided with options to choose from. The options were based on the opinion about the information given in these advertisements ranging from absolutely genuine to not real. The responses were as under:

Table 5.10
Opinion about social advertisements with fear appeals

Sr. No.	Opinion about social advertisements	Subjects	%
1	Not real just to scare people	–	–
2	Exaggerated	5	**4.03**
3	Partially true	33	**26.61**
4	Absolutely genuine	86	**69.35**

Source: Compiled from primary data.

Graph 5.9
Opinion about social advertisements with fear appeals

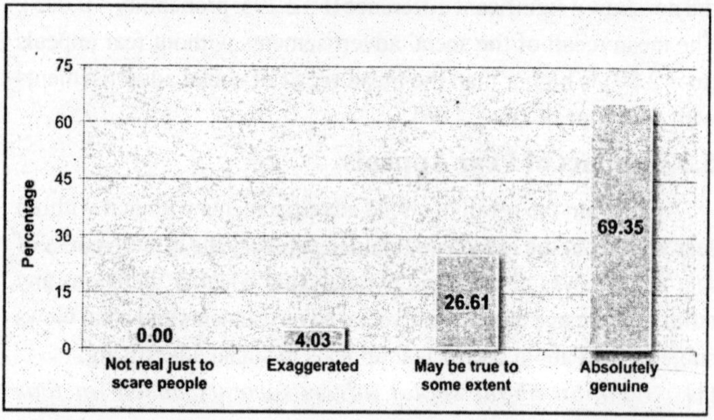

Table 5.10 and Graph 5.9 revealed that there were 86 subjects (69.35 per cent) who felt that the fear based advertisements were absolutely genuine and there were 33 subjects (26.61 per cent) who had doubts about absolute truth in the advertisements. There were 5 subjects (4.03 per cent) who found the information exaggerated but none of the subjects had doubts about the intentions of such social advertisement. Thus the responses of the subjects were more inclined towards information being real to partially true.

[2] Attitudinal change on subjects due to social advertisement

The impact of the anti tobacco advertisement on the subjects was analysed by providing them various options from which they were asked to choose the appropriate option or write any if it was not provided in the options. The tobacco advertisement was selected in particular for analysis because it had disturbing visuals of the after effects of regular tobacco consumption. The subjects were divided into smokers and non-smokers. Of the total 124 subjects five subjects accepted that they smoked cigarettes.

Table 5.11
Impact of social advertisements with fear appeals on smokers

Sr. No.	Opinion of smokers	Subjects	%
1	Try to give up smoking	2	40.00
2	Definitely give up smoking	3	60.00
3	Continue to smoke	–	–

Source: Compiled from primary data.

Graph 5.10
Impact of social advertisements with fear appeals on smokers

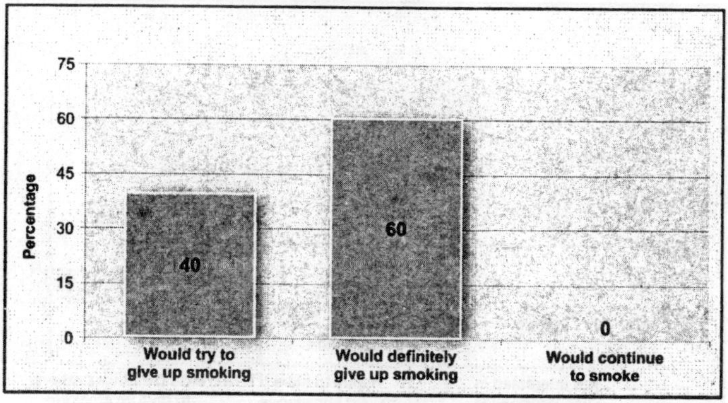

Table 5.11 and Graph 5.10 revealed that among the 5 subjects who admitted that they smoked cigarettes, 2 subjects (40 per cent) felt that they would like to try giving up smoking whereas the remaining 3 subjects (60 per cent) were more confident about giving up smoking after seeing the visuals. None of the smokers chose to continue smoking after seeing the advertisement which meant that there was a positive impact of the fear appeals.

The attitudinal change in the non-smokers was also measured. They were provided options to choose from, indicating the type of impact the advertisement had on them. Of the total sample 119 subjects stated they were not addicted to tobacco.

Table 5.12
Impact of social advertisements with fear appeals on non smokers

Sr. No.	Opinion of non-smokers	Subjects	%
1	Not interested in such information	22	**18.49**
2	Happy to have gained knowledge	13	**10.92**
3	Would motivate others to give up smoking	84	**70.59**

Source: Compiled from primary data.

Graph 5.11
Impact of social advertisements with fear appeals on non smokers

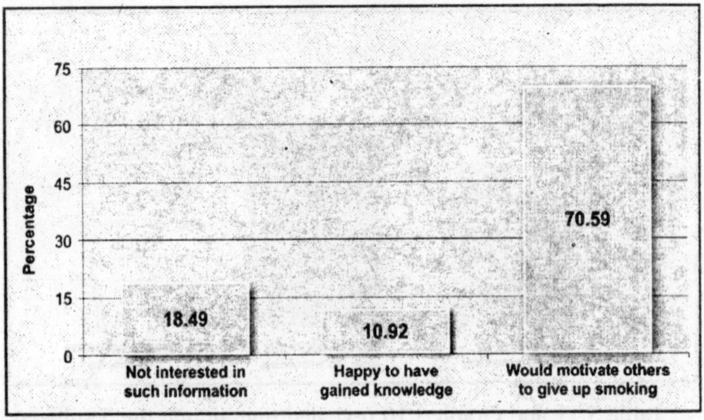

The responses of the non smokers were as indicated in Table 5.12 and Graph 5.11. Among the non smokers 22 subjects (18.49 per cent) were least interested in knowing about this issue since they were not addicted to tobacco. There were 13 subjects (10.92 per cent) who felt that though they do not smoke at least they got aware about the ill effects of cigarette smoking. There were 84 subjects (70.59 per cent) who in spite of being non-smokers themselves, showed keen interest in motivating others towards giving up smoking.

[3] Effectiveness of fear appeals in social advertising

The subject's views on effectiveness of fear appeals in social advertising were important to determine the feasibility of using fear or disturbing appeals in social advertisements. A simple dichotomous question based on opinion about effectiveness of fear appeal was asked to the subjects.

Table 5.13
Effectiveness of fear appeals in social advertising

Sr. No.	Opinion on use of fear appeals	Subjects	%
1	Fear appeals are effective	97	78.23
2	Fear appeals are not effective	27	21.77

Source: Compiled from primary data.

Graph 5.12
Effectiveness of fear appeals in social advertising

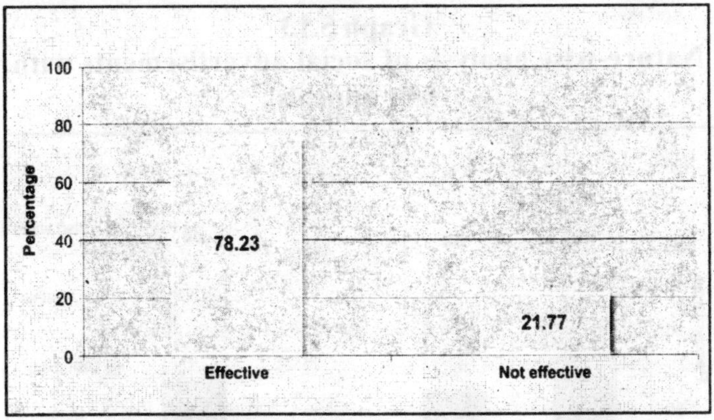

The responses as mentioned in Table 5.13 and Graph 5.12 revealed that 97 subjects (78.23 per cent) felt that frightening or disturbing advertisements would positively motivate the people and only 27 subjects (21.77 per cent) felt otherwise. This indicated that a majority of subjects felt fear appeals would achieve desired response.

[4] *Nature wise analysis of social advertisements with and without fear appeals*

In order to assess whether fear appeals were successful in generating the desired appeal, the subjects were provided with four options viz.frightening, disturbing, informative value and entertainment value. The subjects were supposed to select the most appropriate option for each of the eight social advertisements that best described the social advertisement.

Table 5.14
Nature-wise analysis of social advertisements with fear appeals

Sr. No.	Social advertisements	Frightening	Disturbing	Informative	Entertaining
1	Anti tobacco	45	29	49	1
2	Don't drink and drive	40	[illegible]	47	3
3	Population control	16	[illegible]	51	4
4	Female feticide	44	36	43	1

Source: Compiled from primary data.

Graph 5.13
Nature-wise analysis of social advertisements with fear appeals

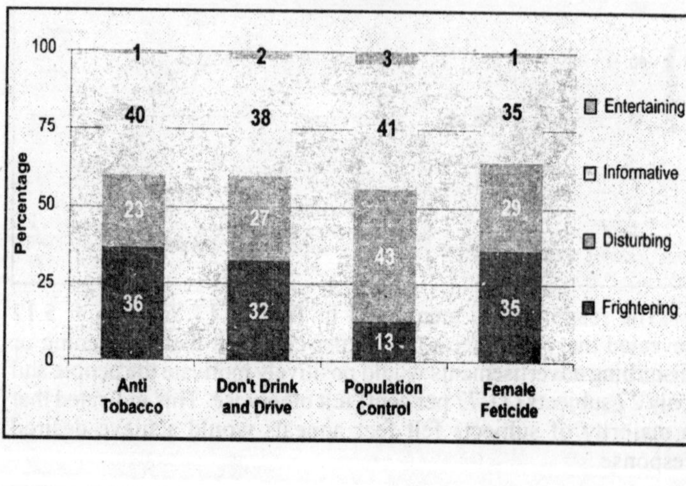

The frightening and disturbing options together dominated the responses as indicated in Table 5.14 and Graph 5.13, with 145 and 152 respectively. The social advertisements with fear appeals were also found to be informative with 190 responses. The responses for entertaining were the lowest.

Table 5.15
Nature-wise analysis of social advertisements with non fear appeals

Sr. No.	Social advertisements	Frightening	Disturbing	Informative	Entertaining
1	AIDS awareness	3	[illegible]	34	83
2	Cleanliness awareness	5	[illegible]	97	12
3	Spend time with elderly	6	[illegible]	67	25
4	Sex education for youth	6	[illegible]	113	1

Source: Compiled from primary data.

Graph 5.14
Nature-wise analysis of social advertisements with non fear appeals

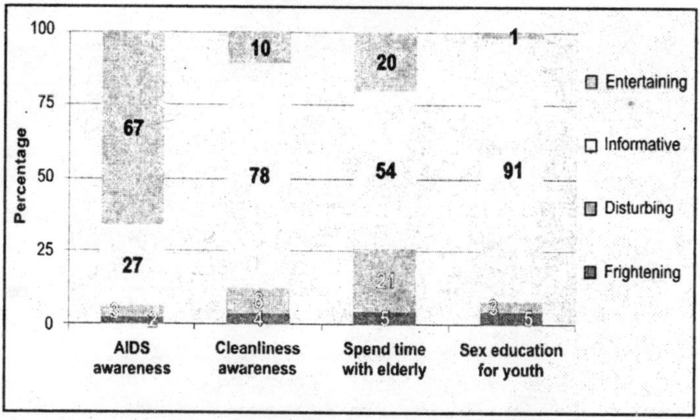

As per Table 5.15 and Graph 5.14 the responses for the social advertisements without fear appeals were considered informative and entertaining rather than frightening and disturbing.

5.4 Conclusion

In this research study, the impact of fear appeals was studied by comparing advertising with fear appeals with advertising without fear appeals. The social advertisements with fear appeals were higher on recall compared to social advertisements without fear appeals in the unaided category. In the aided category though, the recall of advertisements with non-fear appeals was higher than the advertisements with fear appeals. The subjects also felt that fear appeals used in social advertising contribute in motivating the target audience. As far as the recall of social advertising is concerned the fear appeals definitely made a positive contribution. The impact of fear appeals was evident from the higher recall of social advertising with such appeals compared to the recall of social advertising without fear appeals in the unaided category.

6
Barriers to Effective Social Communication

6.1 Introduction – Barriers to communication

Communication can be defined as transmitting, receiving and processing information. The communication process is part of any advertising program.The communication begins with the advertiser who is interested in gaining audience's attention for some messages. Encoding the messages is the second step in the communication process. The messages are constructed into attention getting advertisements designed for various media. The third stage is when the channel or medium delivers these messages. Decoding occurs when the messages reach to the intended receiver. The final component of the communication process is feedback. It is an indication that the message has reached and the receiver is responding. The response can take various forms such as purchases, inquiry and visit to the store and so on.

One obstacle that prevents the advertising messages from being efficient and effective is called noise. Noise is any factor that interferes with or distorts the delivery of the advertising message from the advertiser to the target audience. The noise can be physical or psychological and it can come from within or outside the intended communication effort. Psychological noise can occur for several reasons like inconsistent brand messages or when the source delivering the message is disliked or not trusted by the audience. The physical noise can occur when the selected channel does not deliver the message, like television or radio not reaching the audience due to poor transmission signals or newspaper advertisements not seeking attention due to poor quality of picture or copy. Noise from outside a communication process can take place due to various reasons like competitive messages, receiver being busy in variety of tasks and even by distracting sights and sounds in the environment.

The most common form of noise from outside a communication process affecting advertising communication is clutter. Clutter is the amount of advertising in a medium. Clutter exists when audience is exposed to numerous competitive marketing messages and most are tuned out. From the advertisers point of view it is a problem since the audience is exposed to loads of messages in various media. The chances of audience to respond in an intended manner are highly reduced when they are in a state of confusion or are unable to remember the products/brands advertised.

6.2 Clutter as a Barrier to Communication

Clearly, regardless of whether an advertisement is aiming at boosting recall, changing brand attitudes or inducing purchase action, there are two important prerequisites for any effect to occur.[1] First, an individual must be exposed to it and pay some attention to it. As gaining a consumer's attention is usually the first step in creating effective advertising. Getting such attention is rarely enough by itself, but an advertisement that fails to get attention is unlikely to achieve anything else. A consumer's attention is a necessary but not sufficient condition in creating effective advertising. In the second step, a consumer who does pay attention to an advertisement must interpret and comprehend it in the way the advertiser intended it to be interpreted. The communication must not be misinterpreted or miscomprehended; if this does happen, the

---

[1] Batra Rajeev, Myers John G. and Aaker David A., *op. cit.*, p. 220

[2] *Ibid.*, p. 223.

advertisement is unlikely to lead to the kind of attitude change that the advertiser seeks.

Attention can be viewed as an information filter - a screening mechanism that controls the quantity and nature of information any individual receives.[2] Getting a consumer's attention is not easy. An individual, overtly or accidentally, avoids exposure to stimuli. The advertising environment is truly "cluttered." People are inundated with innumerable commercial messages every day through different media. From indoor media options like television, radio and newspaper to outdoor media such as hoardings and billboards at railway stations and airports there is an overdose of commercial messages. Even personal devices like mobile phones and computers are not spared. Amid all this advertising "noise," it is not easy to create an advertisement that stands out enough to get noticed, processed and remembered.

The situation is especially made worse in the broadcast media, particularly television. When advertisers buy time on a television program, they are not purchasing guaranteed exposure but rather the opportunity to communicate a message to large numbers of consumers. But there is increasing evidence that the size of the viewing audience shrinks during a commercial break.[3] People leave the room to go to the bathroom or to get something to eat or drink or they are distracted in some other way during commercials.

Further there is clutter due to the use of shorter commercials and split-30s, 30-second spots in which the advertiser promotes two different products with separate messages. Clutter also results when the networks and individual stations run promotional announcements for their shows, make more time available for commercials and redistribute time to popular programs. The problems of fleeting messages and shorter commercials are compounded by the fact that the advertiser's message is only one

- - - - - - - - - - - - - - - - -

[3] Belch G and Belch M., *op. cit.*, p. 356.

[4] *Ibid.*

of many spots and other non programming material seen during a commercial break, so it may have trouble - being noticed. One of advertisers' greatest concerns with television advertising is the poten-tial decline in effectiveness because of such clutter. With all of these messages competing for attention, the viewer is confused or even annoyed and unable to remember or properly identify the product or service advertised.[4]

A major problem facing advertisers is the difficulty of gaining attention in the face of increasing advertising clutter. Research by Webb Peter and Ray Michael[5] has clearly shown that higher levels of clutter hurt the performance of individual advertisements, the more the clutter the lower are average levels of advertisement recall. Research shows that the effects of increased clutter do not affect all advertisements equally. Webb found that advertisements placed either at the beginning or at the end of a commercial break were less affected than were the advertisements in the middle of such breaks. This suggests that advertisers ought to negotiate the first or last position in a commercial break. High-involvement advertisements were also less affected than the lower involvement advertisements, suggesting that advertisements that evoke greater inherent involvement or succeed in creating enough "borrowed interest" might suffer less from clutter.[6]

One of the major concerns of television advertisers was to inhibit viewers from leaving the room during the commercials. However it is further compounded with more serious problem of commercials getting zapped with out leaving the room. Viewers have always had the freedom to do other things while a program is being shown, including leaving the room mentally or physically, but the use of remote control devices has made channel-switching

---

[5] Webb Peter H. and Ray Michael L., "Effects of TV Clutter," Journal of Advertising Research, 19, June 1979, pp. 7-12.

[6] Webb Peter H., *op. cit.*, pp. 225-236.

[7] Batra Rajeev, Myers John G. and Aaker David A., *op. cit.*, pp. 222-223.

endemic. Viewer can turn off the sound or change channels with a remote control tuner (zapping) or run fast-forward on a prerecorded program (zipping).[7] Zapping refers to changing channels to avoid commercials. Over three-quarters of homes in the United States have television sets with remote controls, which enable viewers to switch channels easily. An observational study conducted by Cronin John found as much as a third of program audiences may be lost to electronic zapping when commercials appear.[8] Probably, the incidence of zapping in India would not really be very different either.[9] Zipping refers to fast-forwarding through commercials as they appear when viewing a previously recorded movie or some other programme. Another study by Cronin found that most viewers watching previously recorded programmes fully or partially zipped commercials.

A Nielsen study found that most commercial zapping occurs at the beginning and to a lesser extent at the end of a program: Zapping at these points is likely to occur because commercial breaks are long and predictable. Viewers can switch over for a few news headlines, sports scores or a music video and then switch back to the program. Research shows that young adults zap more than older adults and that, men are more likely to zap than women. Meanwhile, according to proprietary studies by the scanner data company Information Resources, Inc. (IRI), zapping is higher among more media-savvy younger consumers, especially those who have

- - - - - - - - - - - - - - - - -

[8] Cronin John J., "In-home Observations of Commercial Zapping Behaviour," Journal of Current Issues and Research in Advertising, Vol. 17, No. 2, Fall 1995, pp. 69-75.

[9] Kazmi S. H. H. and Batra Satish K., *op. cit.*, p. 283.

[10] Heeter Carrie and Greenberg Bradley S., "Profiling the Zappers," Journal of Advertising Research, April/May 1985, pp. 9-15.

[11] Lex van Meurs, "Zapp ! A Study on Switching Behaviour During Commercial Breaks," Journal of Advertising Research, 38 (1), January/February 1998, pp. 43-53.

higher incomes and male. Zappers are less likely to plan their television viewing and more likely to flip television channels till they find something they like (sometimes called "channel grazing").[10]

A study on zapping among viewers of the five major commercial channels in Netherlands was conducted by Lex van Meurs.[11] He found that during commercial breaks 29 percent of the audience stopped watching television or switched away to another channel. This loss of viewers was partially compensated for by an average increase of seven percent of new viewers who zapped in from another channel. The study also found that people stop viewing television during a commercial break because they have a reason to stop watching television altogether or they want to find out what is being shown on other channels. The number of people zapping in and out during breaks was not caused by the type of products being advertised or by specific characteristics of the commercials.

The obvious approach to combating clutter is to create commercials that are so interesting that viewers will prefer to watch them rather than zap or zip them.[12] Research shows that zapping tend to occur most strongly during the first five seconds of a commercial, so that it is crucial to sustain the consumer's interest during these first few seconds. While making such advertisements, the "interesting" and "novel" elements appear to be more important than the "useful information" aspects, at least for casual, low-involvement viewers. Indeed, a study by Olney T. J., Holbrook

- - - - - - - - - - - - - - - - - - -

[12] Lacter Mark, "TV Commercial Industry Fights Back," San Francisco Chronicle, February 11, 1983, p. 50.

[13] Olney T. J., Holbrook Morris and Batra Rajeev, "Consumer Responses to Advertising: The Effects of Ad Content, Emotions and Attitude on Viewing Time," Journal of Consumer Research, March 1991.

[14] McSherry John, "The Current Scope of Channel Switching," Marketing and Media Decisions, June 1985.

[15] Business Week, November 23, 1987, p. 38.

Morris and Batra Rajeev found that viewers' tendency to zip and zap commercials was reduced to the extent they found the commercials pleasurable but increased for advertisements that were simply useful and utilitarian.[13] A study by the McCann-Erickson agency also found that zapping was reduced for advertisements that were more entertaining.[14] However, it must also be pointed out that getting and gaining attention is not enough. The executional elements that are used for making interesting advertisements must not detract and distract from the real, eventual purpose of the advertisement, such as changing attitudes. Ideally, advertisements should be so interesting that viewers would look for or wait for commercials to come on.

Overcoming clutter is a major challenge when creating an effective advertising campaign. In the print medium, several advertisers have tried to fight clutter by using devices as varied as three-dimensional pop-ups to musical microchips in their magazine advertisements.[15] One method advertisers use to overcome clutter in television advertising is by repetition of the commercial messages. Repeating an advertisement can increase brand and advertising recall. Mere repetition of an advertisement does not always work. Therefore, advertisers have begun to emphasise the principles present in variability theory.[16] The theory suggests that variable encoding occurs when a consumer sees the same advertisement in different environments. These varied environments increase an advertisement's recall and effectiveness by encoding it into the brain through various methods. Agency professionals can generate the effect by varying the situational context of a particular advertisement. At best, these approaches seem nothing

---

[16] Melton A. W., "The Situation with Respect to the Spacing of Repetitions and Memory," Journal of Verbal Learning and Verbal Behaviour, 9, 1970, pp. 596-606.

[17] Kazmi S. H. H. and Batra Satish K., *op. cit.*, p. 283.

more than wishful thinking, because an increasing number of audience members seem to be developing an aversion toward an ever-increasing onslaught of commercials. People primarily watch television because of its entertainment value and not because they wish to be bombarded by commercials.[17]

6.3 Study Three: Impact of Noise on Social Advertising

Social advertising in India takes all available routes to reach the audience as possible. The same media which are available for commercial advertising are used for social advertising too. In fact the social advertising is aired along with commercial advertisements in the same commercial breaks on television or radio. Therefore the issue of clutter is as much a problem for social advertising as it is for commercial advertising and it significantly impedes the reach of advertising.

With this consideration that noise and clutter in particular obstructs the reach of social advertising the present study was conducted to find out how it influences the recall of social messages. The effectiveness of noise/clutter was studied by analyzing the difference between recall of social advertisements shown along with commercial advertisements as they appear on all media in India and social advertisements shown exclusively without any commercial advertisements along with it. To assess the influence eight social advertisements were presented in the audio-video presentation. Of these eight social advertisements, four social advertisements were shown exclusively one after another and four social advertisements shown amidst commercial advertisements. The commercial advertisements were included to create the clutter as generally noticed on television in India. Table 6.1 gives the details of the social advertisements that were included in the presentation:

Table 6.1
Social advertisements presented in Study Three

Sr. No.	Social advertisements shown exclusively	Sr. No.	Social advertisements shown with commercial advertisements
1	Anti tobacco	1	Awareness against female feticide
2	Awareness against eve-teasing	2	Awareness about not using mobile phone while driving
3	Don't drink and drive	3	Be proud of yourself
4	Spend time with elderly	4	Sex education for youth

Source: Compiled from primary data.

The responses to the questions based on the impact of noise / clutter in the aided and unaided categories were carefully analysed in the following step-by-step manner:

[1] Number of social advertisements presented exclusively and presented with commercial advertisements correctly recalled in aided and unaided category were calculated.

[2] Means were calculated for number of social advertisements shown exclusively and shown amidst commercial advertisements correctly recalled in aided and unaided category.

[3] Paired samples T-test were conducted to compare recall of social advertisements shown exclusively and social advertisements shown amidst commercial advertisements under both aided and unaided conditions.

[4] Percentages of social advertisements recalled exclusively shown and shown amidst commercial advertisements under aided and unaided conditions were calculated.

[5] z-tests were performed to measure the significance of the difference between percentages of social advertisements recalled that were shown exclusively and social advertisements that were shown amidst commercial advertisements under aided and unaided conditions.

In the study specific questionnaire the subjects were required to recall the social advertisements that they had seen in the presentation in two categories, social advertisements seen along with the commercial advertisements and social advertisements seen exclusively. These two categories were further investigated under two conditions, viz. unaided and aided.

6.3.1 Recall of social advertisements in unaided category

In the unaided category the subjects were supposed to recall and write the social advertisements that they had seen in the audio-video presentation. There was no clue or hint provided and they had to recall social advertisements on the basis of the issues addressed.

[1] *Recall of social advertisements shown exclusively in unaided category*

In the presentation four social advertisements were exclusively shown back to back. The anti tobacco advertisement addressed the second hand smoke issue. The 'don't drink and drive' advertisement created awareness about drunk people driving the vehicles being threat to others. The spend time with elderly addressed the issue of loneliness suffered by aged people in our country. The eve-teasing advertisement was based on rising instances of eve-teasing and need to raise voice against it.

Table 6.2
Recall of social advertisements shown exclusively in unaided category

Sr. No.	Social advertisements shown exclusively	Recall	% recall
1	Anti tobacco	107	**90.68**
2	Don't drink and drive	106	**89.83**
3	Spend time with elderly	105	**88.98**
4	Awareness against eve-teasing	80	**67.80**

Source: Compiled from primary data.

Graph 6.1
Recall of social advertisements shown exclusively in unaided category

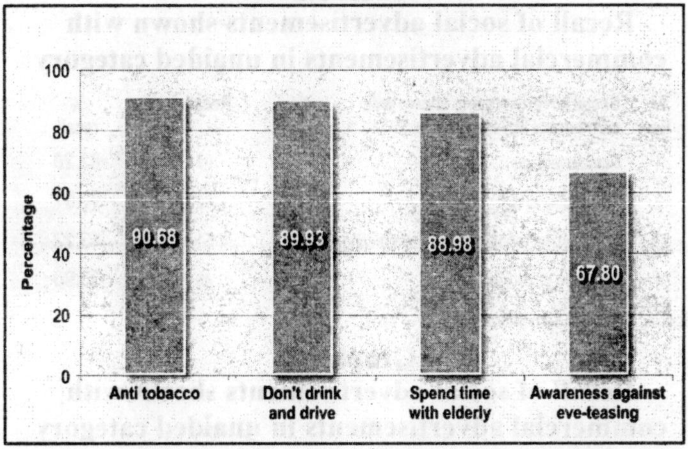

As indicated by Table 6.2 and Graph 6.1, within the exclusively shown social advertisements category the anti tobacco advertisement recorded the highest recall from 107 subjects (90.68 per cent) closely followed by 'don't drink and drive' advertisement which had a recall of 106 subjects (89.93 per cent). The advertisement 'spend time with elderly' registered a recall from 105 subjects (88.98 per cent) and the advertisement on awareness against eve-teasing registered the lowest recall from 80 subjects (67.80 per cent).

[2] *Recall of social advertisements shown with commercial advertisements in unaided category*

There were four social advertisements shown along with the clutter of commercial advertisements. The first social advertisement was an animated story of a female fetus that's stabbed in the womb. The second social advertisement dealt with creating awareness about disseminating sex education to youth. The third social advertisement addressed the issue of not talking on mobile phone while driving. The fourth social advertisement was based on anorexia, a problem on rise among young girls where they are obsessed with a perfect body figure.

Table 6.3
Recall of social advertisements shown with commercial advertisements in unaided category

Sr. No.	Social advertisements shown with commercial advertisements	Recall	% recall
1	Female feticide	97	82.20
2	Sex education for youth	92	77.97
3	Don't talk on mobile phone while driving	51	43.22
4	Be proud of yourself	40	33.90

Source: Compiled from primary data.

Graph 6.2
Recall of social advertisements shown with commercial advertisements in unaided category

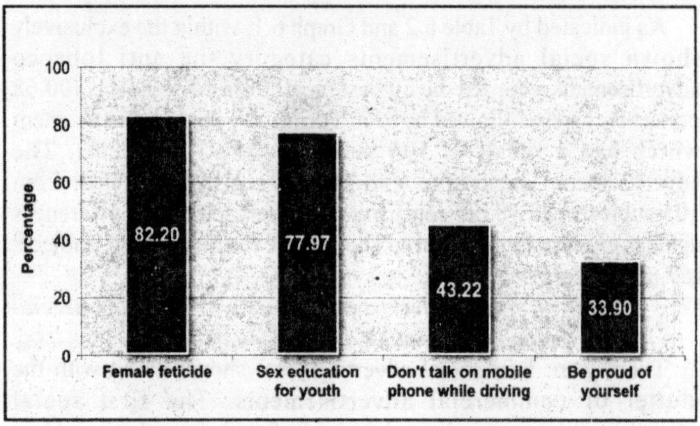

As revealed by Table 6.3 and Graph 6.2, the social advertisement on female feticide had the highest recall in this category with 97 subjects (82.20 per cent) followed by the advertisement on sex education for youth which had a recall from 92 subjects (77.97 per cent). The social advertisements on 'don't talk on mobile phone while driving' had a recall from 51 subjects (43.22 per cent) and the advertisement on 'be proud of yourself' which is rarely addressed in India registered the lowest recall from 40 subjects (33.90 per cent).

[3] *Comparison between recall of exclusively shown social advertisements and social advertisements shown along with commercial advertisements in unaided category*

The recall of social advertisements shown exclusively was compared with recall of social advertisements shown with commercial advertisements in the unaided category. The results were as follows:

Table 6.4

Recall of social advertisements in unaided category

Sr. No.	Particulars	Total recall	% recall
1	Social advertisements shown exclusively	398	84.32
2	Social advertisements shown with commercial advertisements	280	59.32

Source: Compiled from primary data.

Graph 6.3

Percentage recall of social advertisements in unaided category

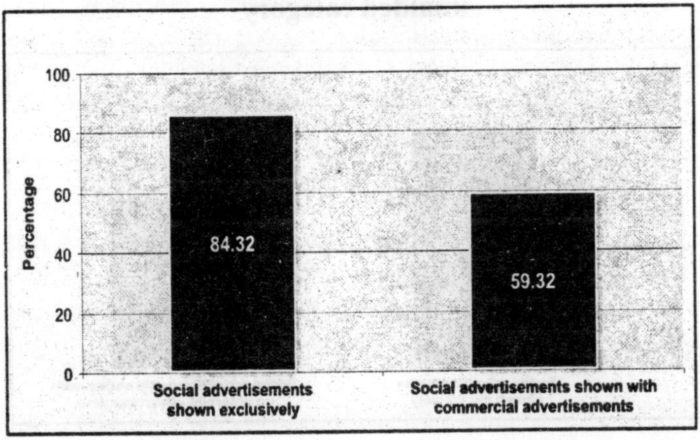

Table 6.4 and Graph 6.3 revealed that when the recall of social advertisements shown exclusively were compared with recall of social advertisements shown with commercial advertisements in the unaided category it was found that the overall recall of social advertisements shown exclusively was considerably higher (84.32 per cent) than that for the social advertisements shown amidst commercial advertisements (59.32 per cent). The z-test revealed a highly significant difference ($z = 8.99$), $p < 0.001$.

[4] Paired sample T-test of recall in unaided category

The paired sample T-test compared mean recall of social advertisements shown exclusively and shown with commercial advertisements in unaided category.

Table 6.5
Paired sample T-test of recall in unaided category

Sr. No.	Paired sample	Mean	Df	Standard deviation	T
1	Recall of social advertisements shown exclusively	6.75	117	1.770	9.065*
2	Recall of social advertisements shown with commercial advertisements	4.75	117	1.770	

Source: Compiled from primary data.

* $p < 0.000$.

Graph 6.4
Mean scores of recall of social advertisements in unaided category

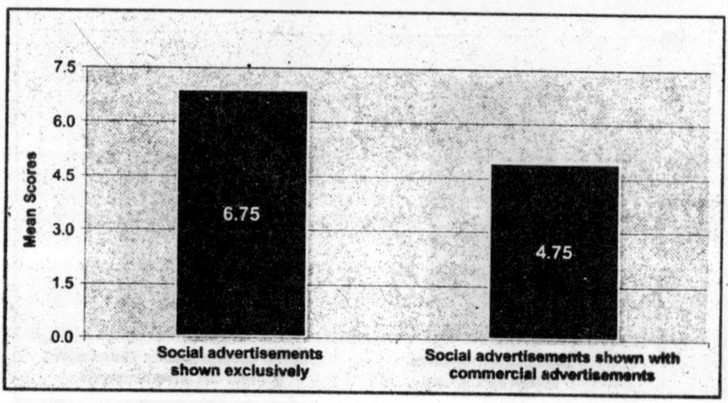

The paired sample T-test comparing mean recall of social advertisements shown exclusively and shown with commercial advertisements in unaided category as indicated in Table 6.5 and Graph 6.4 showed a significant difference, (t = 9.065) at a probability < 0.000. The mean recall of the social advertisements shown exclusively (m = 6.75) was higher than the mean recall of social advertisements shown with commercial advertisements (m = 4.75) in unaided category.

6.3.2 Recall of social advertisements in aided category

In the aided category the subjects were supposed to recall the social advertisements with the help of some clues provided in the questionnaire for easy recall.

[1] *Recall of social advertisements shown exclusively in aided category*

The recall of four social advertisements shown exclusively in aided category was analysed. The recall was as follows:

Table 6.6
Recall of social advertisements shown exclusively in aided category

Sr. No.	Social advertisements shown exclusively	Recall	% recall
1	Awareness against eve-teasing	233	98.73
2	Don't drink and drive	230	97.46
3	Anti tobacco	228	96.61
4	Spend time with elderly	224	94.92

Source: Compiled from primary data.

Graph 6.5
Recall of social advertisements shown exclusively in aided category

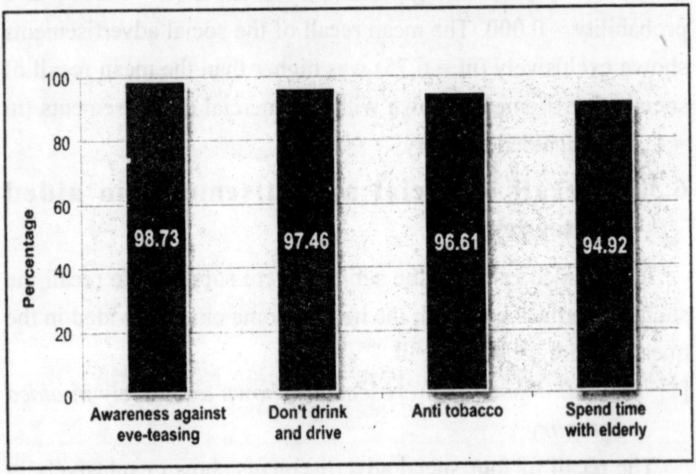

As per Table 6.6 and Graph 6.5, the recall in the aided category within the exclusively shown social advertisement category, the advertisement for awareness against eve-teasing recorded the highest recall of 233 (98.73 per cent) closely followed by 'don't drink and drive' advertisement which had a recall of 230 (97.46 per cent). The anti-tobacco advertisement registered a recall of 228 (96.61 per cent) and advertisement 'spend time with elderly' registered a recall of 224 (94.92 per cent).

[2] *Recall of social advertisements shown with commercial advertisements in aided category*

The recall of four social advertisements shown amongst the clutter of commercial advertisements in the aided category when analysed the recall was as follows:

Table 6.7
Recall of social advertisements shown with commercial advertisements in aided category

Sr. No.	Social advertisements shown with commercial advertisements	Recall	% recall
1	Don't talk on mobile phone while driving	217	**91.95**
2	Sex education for youth	206	**87.29**
3	Be proud of yourself	205	**86.86**
4	Female feticide	196	**83.05**

Source: Compiled from primary data.

Graph 6.6
Recall of social advertisements shown with commercial advertisements in aided category

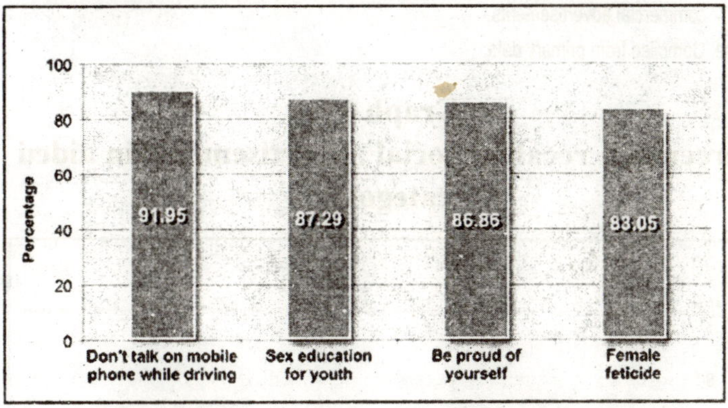

As per Table 6.7 and Graph 6.6, the social advertisement on 'don't talk on mobile phone while driving' had the highest recall in the aided category with 217 (91.95 per cent) followed by the advertisement on sex education for youth which had recall of 206 (87.29 per cent). 'Be proud of yourself' advertisement had recall of 205 (86.86 per cent) and the female feticide advertisement registered the lowest recall of 196 (83.05 per cent).

[3] *Comparison between recall of exclusively shown social advertisements and social advertisements shown along with commercial advertisements in aided category*

The recall of social advertisements shown exclusively was compared with recall of social advertisements shown with commercial advertisements in the aided category and the result was as follows:

Table 6.8

Recall of social advertisements in aided category

Sr. No.	Particulars	Total recall	% recall
1	Social advertisements shown exclusively	915	**96.93**
2	Social advertisements shown with commercial advertisements	824	**87.29**

Source: Compiled from primary data.

Graph 6.7

Percentage recall of social advertisements in aided category

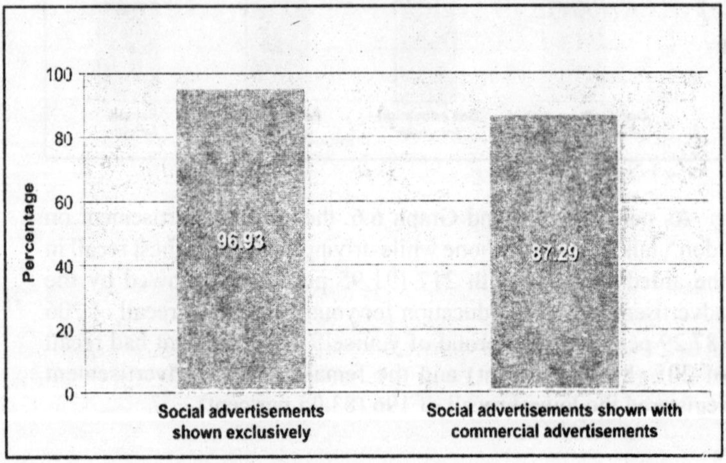

When the recall of social advertisements shown exclusively were compared with recall of social advertisements shown with commercial advertisements in the aided category, as indicated in Table 6.8 and Graph 6.7, it was found that the overall recall of social advertisements shown exclusively was higher (96.93 per cent) than that for the social advertisements shown amidst commercial advertisements (87.29 per cent). The z-test revealed a highly significant difference ($z = 8.07$), $p < 0.001$.

[4] *Paired sample T-test of recall in aided category*

The paired sample T-test compared the mean recall of social advertisements shown exclusively and social advertisements shown with commercial advertisements in aided category:

Table 6.9
Paired sample T-test of recall in aided category

Sr. No.	Paired sample	Mean	Df	Standard deviation	T
1	Recall of social advertisements shown exclusively	7.75	117	0.584	8.456*
2	Recall of social advertisements shown with commercial advertisements	6.98	117	1.046	

Source: Compiled from primary data.

* $p < 0.000$.

Graph 6.8
Mean scores of recall of social advertisements in aided category

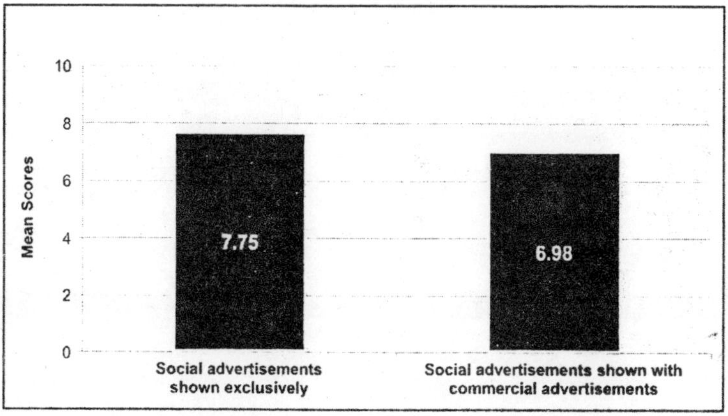

The paired sample T-test comparing mean recall of social advertisements shown exclusively and shown with commercial advertisements in aided category, as revealed in Table 6.9 and Graph 6.8 showed a significant difference, ($t = 8.456$) at a probability < 0.000. The mean recall of the social advertisements shown exclusively ($m = 7.75$) was higher than the mean recall of social advertisements shown with commercial advertisements ($m = 6.98$) in aided category.

6.4 Conclusion

In this research study, the impact of noise was studied by comparing social advertising shown exclusively with social advertising shown with other commercial advertisement. The social advertisements shown exclusively were higher on recall compared to social advertisements shown amidst the clutter of commercial advertisements. The recall of exclusively shown advertisements was higher in both categories, in the aided when the subjects were provided hints to recall the advertisements and in the unaided category when they had to recall the advertisements on their own without any clues. This was evident from the low recall of social advertising shown amidst clutter since the social advertisements that were affected by noise had comparatively lower recall compared to those social advertisements that were exclusively shown unaffected by noise / clutter.

7
Media Options for Targeting Youth

7.1 Introduction - Media for advertising

The basic process of communication includes two major participants, the sender and the receiver and another two major tools, message and channels. The media are the channels by which the communication travels from the source to the sender. All marketing communication messages are carried by some form of media. Channels can be further categorized in to personal and non personal channels. In personal channels there is inter-personal contact with target individuals or groups like personalized letters or telephone calls. Non personal channels are those that carry a message without interpersonal contact between sender and receiver. Generally television, radio, newspaper and magazine are non-personal channels referred to as mass media since the message is sent to too many individuals at one time. Further in case of broadcast media such as television or radio information cannot be processed at the audience's pace as it is externally paced and is controlled by the medium itself, whereas in case of newspaper and magazines the information processing is self-paced as the receiver can process the message at their convenience.

- - - - - - - - - - - - - - - - -

[1] Mcluhan Marshall, Understanding Media: The Extensions of Man, McGraw Hill, New York, 1966.

There are many choices of channels available for advertising. Effectively mixing these media is an important part of designing quality advertising. To do so, the advantages and disadvantages of each individual medium must be understood so that an advertising campaign features successful combinations. The media's job is not only to provide for media exposure, but media is also involved in adding values to messages by increasing their impact on attitudes and behaviours. Mcluhan Marshall aptly remarks "the medium is the message."[1] Though media are actually channel links between companies and their audience, people view them as sources. Some media are treated as more credible than others. And the reputation of the medium that carries the advertisement thus affects the credibility of the message. The reputation of the medium as to its honesty or objectivity also affects the credibility of the advertising. Further an advertising message is interpreted and influenced by the environment in which it is received and communicates an image that is independent of the message content. This effect is known as 'qualitative media effect.'

7.2 Assessing Youth's Media Exposure and Media Habits

Social advertising in India uses variety of media options. The various media used by advertisers to communicate with audiences are different in terms of several aspects such as the type and number of audience they reach, costs and qualitative factors. Also there are basic differences among media concerning the rate and the manner in which the information is communicated and can be processed by audiences.[2] So it was necessary to get acquainted with the youth's media exposure and their media viewing habits. This would enable the researcher to consider the appropriate

---

[2] Schiffman Leon G. and Kanuk Leslie Lazar, *op. cit.* p. 284.

media options for conducting the social advertising in India. With this view the media exposure of the sample to popular media options like television, radio, newspaper, magazine, cinema and Internet, along with their degree of exposure were analysed. Following are the results of the same with respect to individual media option:

7.2.1 Television

The exposure to television was analysed through the subject's daily viewing habit in terms of number of hours, the exact time slots at which they preferred to watch television on weekdays and weekends and the specific channels they watched the most.

a. *Daily exposure to television*

The subjects' exposure to television was accessed in detail in terms of number of hours watched on a daily basis. There were slots provided to choose from ranging between never to more than 6 hours a day. The responses were as follows:

Table 7.1
Sample's exposure to television on daily basis

Sr. No.	Daily exposure to television	Study One	Study Two	Study Three	Study Four	Study Five	Total	%
1	Never	5	5	1	7	6	24	**3.62**
2	0 - 2 hours a day	61	50	58	55	29	253	**38.16**
3	2 - 4 hours a day	50	52	40	53	54	249	**37.56**
4	4 - 6 hours a day	16	10	14	19	29	88	**13.27**
5	More than 6 hours a day	9	7	5	10	18	49	**7.39**
	Total	**141**	**124**	**118**	**144**	**136**	**663**	**100.00**

Source: Compiled from primary data.

Graph 7.1
Sample's exposure to television on daily basis

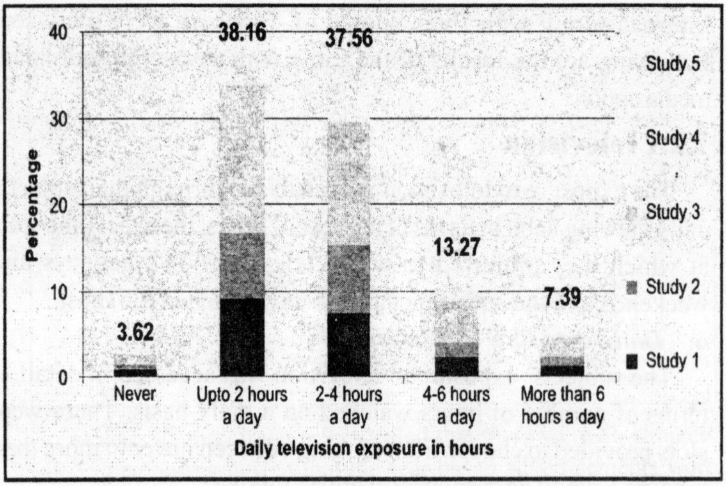

As indicated in Table 7.1 and Graph 7.1, the distribution of subjects based on their television viewing habit indicated 249 subjects (37.56 per cent) watched television 2 to 4 hours, 88 subjects (13.27 per cent) watched 4 to 6 hours and 49 subjects (7.39 per cent) watched for more than 6 hours a day. Out of the total sample, 253 subjects (38.16 per cent) watched television for less than 2 hours a day. Thus the subject's television viewing habit where 639 subjects (96.38 per cent) watched television on daily basis and the number of subjects not seeing television at all only being 24 subjects (3.62 per cent) was an indication of popularity of television.

b. Television viewing pattern on weekdays and weekends

The subjects' media viewing pattern was analysed for weekdays and weekends in order to assess whether there was any major difference in viewing pattern on weekdays and weekends.

This was important so as to enable the advertisers to effectively target the youth.

Table 7.2
Sample's exposure to television on weekly basis

Sr. No.	Daily exposure to television	Study One	Study Two	Study Three	Study Four	Study Five	Total	%
[1]	**On weekdays**							
1	Morning 6 a.m. -12 noon	3	9	1	8	0	21	**3.17**
2	Afternoon 12 noon -17 p.m.	52	54	39	62	58	265	**39.97**
3	Evening 17 p.m.- 20 p.m.	49	40	49	56	63	257	**38.76**
4	Night 20 p.m. - 0.hrs.	82	66	77	65	62	352	**53.09**
5	Late night 0 hrs – 6 a.m.	2	3	15	1	2	23	**3.47**
[2]	**On weekends**							
1	Morning 6 a.m. -12 noon	14	21	11	16	18	80	**12.07**
2	Afternoon 12 noon -17 p.m.	53	50	42	58	65	268	**40.42**
3	Evening 17 p.m.- 20 p.m.	41	47	38	41	56	223	**33.63**
4	Night 20 p.m. - 0 hrs.	87	71	70	62	61	351	**52.94**
5	Late night 0 hrs – 6 a.m.	2	3	24	7	4	40	**6.03**

Source: Compiled from primary data.

Graph 7.2
Sample's exposure to television on weekly basis

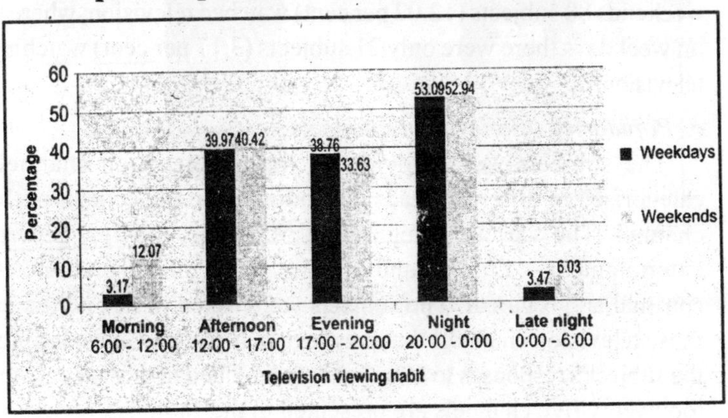

Table 7.2 and Graph 7.2 revealed that on weekdays 265 subjects (39.97 per cent) watched television in the afternoon slot between 12 noon to 5 p.m., 257 subjects (38.76 per cent) watched television in the evening slot of 5 p.m. to 8 p.m. and 352 subjects (53.09 per cent) watched television in the slot of 8 p.m. to 12 p.m. in the night. The viewership was very low in the morning slot between 6 a.m. and 12 noon when only 21 subjects (3.17 per cent) watched television and even in the late night slot of 12 p.m. to 6 a.m. only 23 subjects (3.47 per cent) watched television.

On weekends 268 subjects (40.42 per cent) watched television in the afternoon slot between 12 noon to 5 p.m., 223 subjects (33.63 per cent) watched television in the evening slot of 5 p.m. to 8 p.m. and 351 subjects (52.94 per cent) watched television in the slot of 8 p.m. to 12 p.m. in the night. The viewership was comparatively low in the morning slot between 6 a.m. and 12 noon when 80 subjects (12.07 per cent) watched the television and even in the late night slot of 12 p.m. to 6 a.m. when 40 subjects (6.03 per cent) watched television. Thus there was no major difference between weekdays and weekends, as far as the television viewing pattern is concerned. The viewing pattern on weekdays and weekends was marginally different in the morning slot between 6 a.m. to 12 noon, i.e. on weekends 80 subjects (12.07 per cent) watched television, whereas on weekdays there were only 21 subjects (3.17 per cent) watching television.

c. Popularity of television channels

The subjects were provided a list of television channels categorised in different heads depending upon the content of the channel. The various categories were music, movies, general entertainment – English and Hindi, sports, informative, news, spiritual and regional. The subjects were asked to tick across all those television channels that they regularly watch. On the basis of the subject's responses to 100 channels provided in the list, only the top twenty five channels are presented in the Table 7.3

Table 7.3
Most popular television channels

Sr. No.	Television Channels	Study One	Study Two	Study Three	Study Four	Study Five	Total	%
1	Aaj Tak	105	84	70	93	101	453	**68.33**
2	MTV	89	90	89	65	82	415	**62.59**
3	Discovery	89	83	59	82	84	397	**59.88**
4	Sony	72	62	58	76	75	343	**51.73**
5	Star Plus	73	57	51	73	89	343	**51.73**
6	Star News	77	78	42	70	71	338	**50.98**
7	Zee Cinema	72	64	47	74	76	333	**50.23**
8	Star One	54	53	70	71	70	318	**47.96**
9	Channel V	64	69	73	48	62	316	**47.66**
10	Star Gold	62	65	50	69	61	307	**46.30**
11	Ten Sports	62	65	55	62	57	301	**45.40**
12	9x m	53	53	45	67	77	295	**44.49**
13	B4U Music	59	65	42	54	61	281	**42.38**
14	Zoom	57	57	52	52	57	275	**41.48**
15	Star Sports	63	43	56	55	47	264	**39.82**
16	Zee tv	58	35	30	68	69	260	**39.22**
17	SET Max	57	52	41	56	51	257	**38.76**
18	Star Movies	53	44	66	44	47	254	**38.31**
19	9x	53	43	34	52	64	246	**37.10**
20	Pogo	48	56	38	49	53	244	**36.80**
21	Cartoon Network	42	48	42	45	62	239	**36.05**
22	Zee Music	47	57	29	49	50	232	**34.99**
23	NDTV India	40	51	44	44	52	231	**34.84**
24	ESPN	53	45	63	29	38	228	**34.39**
25	Animal Planet	45	52	28	49	53	227	**34.24**

Source: Compiled from primary data.

The analysis of the most watched television channels as revealed in Table 7.3 showed subjects watched variety of channels including news, sports, informative, music, films and general entertainment. This assortment of television channels regularly watched by youth is a clear indication that targeting youth is indeed a complex task.

7.2.1 Radio

The popularity of radio was analysed through the subject's daily listening habit in terms of number of hours and the radio stations they tuned in the most.

a. Daily exposure to radio

The exposure to radio was accessed in detail in terms of number of hours on a daily basis. There were slots provided to choose from, ranging between never to more than six hours a day. The responses were as follows:

Table 7.4

Sample's radio listening habit on daily basis

Sr. No.	Daily listenership of radio	Study One	Study Two	Study Three	Study Four	Study Five	Total	%
1	Never	7	6	6	5	5	29	**4.37**
2	0 – 2 hours a day	20	14	28	22	9	93	**14.03**
3	2 – 4 hours a day	67	71	41	86	74	339	**51.13**
4	4 – 6 hours a day	25	20	31	13	20	109	**16.44**
5	More than 6 hours a day	22	13	12	18	28	93	**14.03**
	Total	**141**	**124**	**118**	**144**	**136**	**663**	**100.00**

Source: Compiled from primary data.

Graph 7.3

Sample's radio listening habit on daily basis

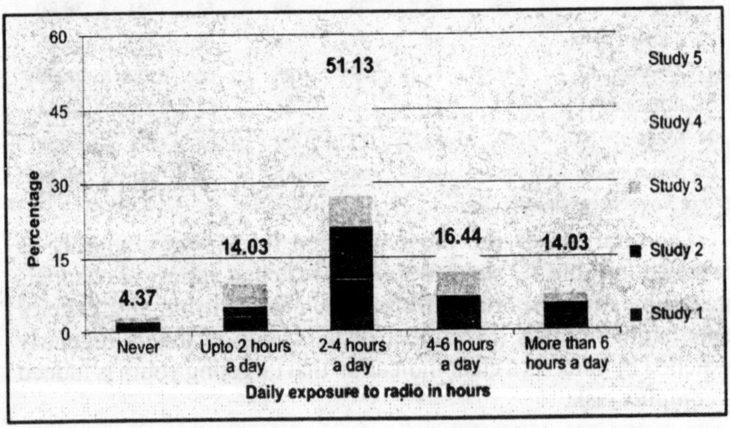

The distribution of subjects based on their radio listening habit as indicated in Table 7.4 and Graph 7.3, reveal that 339 subjects (51.13 per cent) listened to radio 2 to 4 hours, 109 subjects (16.44 per cent) listened for 4 to 6 hours and 93 subjects (14.03 per cent) listened for more than 6 hours a day. Out of the total sample, 93 subjects (14.03 per cent) listened to radio for less than 2 hours a day. The number of subjects not listening to radio only being 29 subjects (4.37 per cent) indicated the immense popularity of radio among the youth.

b. Popularity of radio stations

In Mumbai several FM and AM radio stations are available. But none of the subjects listen to the AM stations and their radio listening was restricted to the FM radio stations as indicated in Table 7.5.

Table 7.5
Most popular radio stations

Sr. No.	Radio stations	Study One	Study Two	Study Three	Study Four	Study Five	Total	%
1	Red FM 93.5	89	78	78	92	90	427	64.40
2	Radio Mirchi 98.3	82	64	64	84	68	362	54.60
3	Big FM 92.7	75	53	60	76	66	330	49.77
4	Radio City 91.1	63	39	59	57	72	290	43.74
5	Radio One 94.3	44	29	45	44	51	213	32.13
6	Fever 104	35	38	39	21	22	155	23.38
7	AIR FM Gold 100.7	19	14	8	27	44	112	16.89
8	AIR Rainbow 107.1	22	19	10	20	15	86	12.97

Source: Compiled from primary data.

Graph 7.4
Most popular radio stations

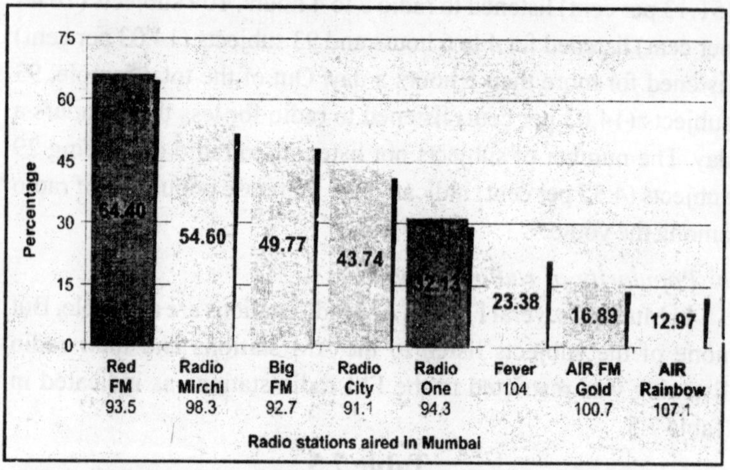

As revealed in Table 7.5 and Graph 7.4, among the radio stations Red FM 93.5 was the most tuned, leading the list with 427 subjects (64.40 per cent), closely followed by Radio Mirchi 98.3 with 362 subjects (54.60 per cent), Big FM 92.7 with 330 subjects (49.77 per cent) and Radio City 91.1 with 290 subjects (43.74 per cent). The radio stations Radio One 94.3 and Fever 104 followed with 213 subjects (32.13 per cent) and 155 subjects (23.38 per cent) respectively. Radio stations FM gold 100.7 and Air Rainbow 107.1 had comparatively limited popularity among 112 subjects (16.89 per cent) and 86 subjects (12.97 per cent) respectively.

7.2.2 Newspaper

The exposure to newspaper was analysed on the basis of whether the subjects read newspaper or not and if at all they did then which newspaper/s they preferred the most.

a. Newspaper readership

Newspaper is one of the most economical yet effective mass medium of reaching literate audience in urban setups. Social advertisers can use newspaper to add reminder value and keep the social campaigns in public eye. Therefore it was essential to gauge the newspaper reading habit among the target.

Table 7.6
Newspaper reading habit among sample

Sr. No.	Newspaper readership	Study One	Study Two	Study Three	Study Four	Study Five	Total	%
1	Regular readers	118	88	90	90	105	491	**74.06**
2	Non readers	23	36	28	54	31	172	**25.94**
	Total	**141**	**124**	**118**	**144**	**136**	**663**	**100.00**

Source: Compiled from primary data.

Graph 7.5
Newspaper reading habit among sample

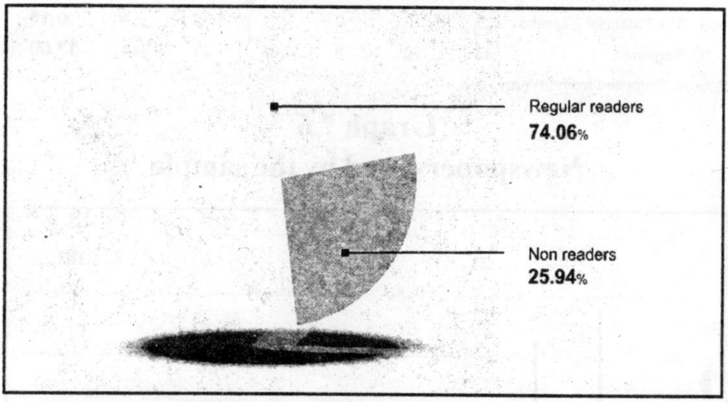

As indicated in Table 7.6 and Graph 7.5, out of the sample, 491 subjects (74.06 per cent) read newspaper regularly and the remaining 172 subjects (25.94 per cent) did not read any newspaper at all. This indicated a high prevalence of newspaper reading habit among the subjects.

b. Popularity of newspapers

To assess what type of newspaper and exactly which newspapers are generally read by subjects, a list of some popular newspapers was provided and subjects were required to tick across which all newspapers they read.

Table 7.7
Newspapers read by the sample

Sr. No.	Newspapers	Study One	Study Two	Study Three	Study Four	Study Five	Total	%
1	Times of India	58	40	68	38	54	258	**38.91**
2	Mumbai Mirror	63	30	60	34	37	224	**33.79**
3	Mid Day	13	24	14	19	28	98	**14.78**
4	DNA	24	20	21	16	13	94	**14.18**
5	The Economic Times	3	6	22	5	3	39	**5.88**
6	Hindustan Times	9	10	7	5	4	35	**5.28**
7	Indian Express	0	1	5	2	1	9	**1.36**
8	Business Standard	1	1	3	2	1	8	**1.21**
9	The Financial Express	0	0	0	1	0	1	**0.15**
10	Regional	33	20	5	35	23	116	**17.50**

Source: Compiled from primary data.

Graph 7.6
Newspapers read by the sample

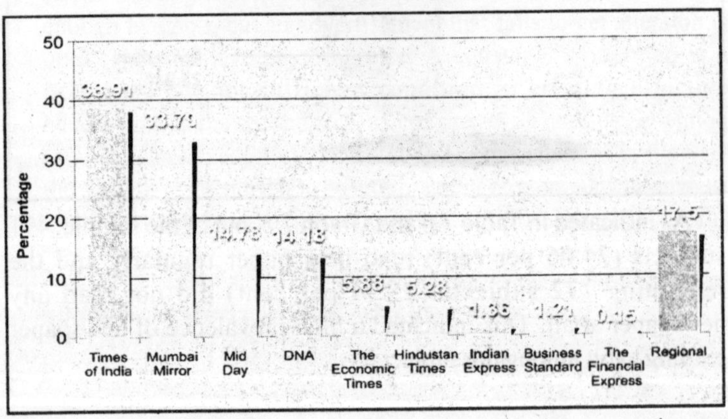

As indicated by Table 7.7 and Graph 7.6, among the newspapers Times of India was the most read leading the list with 258 subjects (38.91 per cent), followed by Mumbai Mirror with 224 subjects (33.79 per cent). The newspapers Mid Day and DNA followed with 98 subjects (14.78 per cent) and 94 subjects (14.18 per cent) respectively. Newspaper, The Economic Times was read by 39 subjects (5.88 per cent), Hindustan Times by 35 subjects (5.28 per cent) and Indian Express by 9 subjects (1.36 per cent). Business newspapers, Business Standard and The Financial Express had limited readership with 8 subjects (1.21 per cent) and 1 subject (0.15 per cent) respectively. The various regional newspapers were read by 116 subjects (17.50 per cent).

7.2.1 Magazines

While assessing the sample's exposure to magazines it was found that the sample had a very limited access to magazines.

a. Exposure to magazines

Magazines offer high demographic and geographic selectivity and can be effective to reach out to a selective audience. To assess the popularity of magazines among subjects, they were provided with a simple dichotomous question and they were supposed to mention whether they read any magazines or not. The responses were as follows:

Table 7.8

Popularity of magazines among the sample

Sr. No.	Magazine readership	Study One	Study Two	Study Three	Study Four	Study Five	Total	%
1	Non-readers	106	90	69	118	104	487	**73.45**
2	Regular readers	35	34	49	26	32	176	**26.55**
	Total	**141**	**124**	**118**	**144**	**136**	**663**	**100.00**

Source: Compiled from primary data.

Graph 7.7

Popularity of magazines among the sample

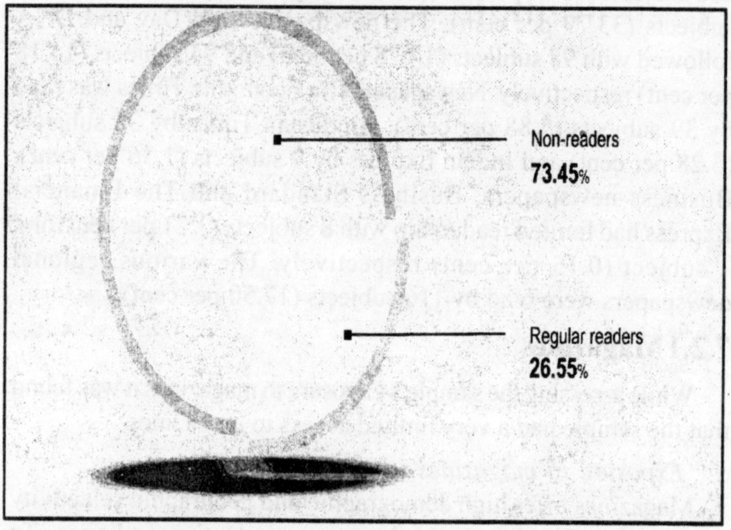

As revealed in Table 7.8 and Graph 7.7, 176 subjects (26.55 per cent) responded positively to reading magazines regularly while the remaining 487 subjects (73.45 per cent) did not read any magazine on regular basis. This is an indication that magazines are not a very popular medium for reaching to youth.

b. Types of magazines read by the sample

To assess the popularity of magazines the subjects were asked to write the names of the magazines they read regularly. On the basis of the names provided by the subjects the magazines were classified into various categories. After categorising the magazines on the basis of content following list emerged:

Table 7.9
Magazines read by the sample

Sr. No.	Types of magazines	Study One	Study Two	Study Three	Study Four	Study Five	Total	%
1	Women	9	13	17	23	14	76	**11.46**
2	General	16	13	13	5	13	60	**9.05**
3	Film	3	3	12	6	2	26	**3.92**
4	Automobile	4	2	9	–	1	16	**2.41**
5	Business	1	–	11	–	–	12	**1.81**
6	Regional	1	–	–	–	11	12	**1.81**
7	Sports	4	3	1	3	–	11	**1.66**
8	Computer	–	1	8	–	–	9	**1.36**
9	Health	1	1	–	–	1	3	**0.45**
10	Travel	–	1	–	–	1	2	**0.30**
11	Children	–	1	–	–	–	1	**0.15**
	Total	**39**	**38**	**71**	**37**	**43**	**228**	**34.39**

Source: Compiled from primary data.

Graph 7.8
Magazines read by the sample

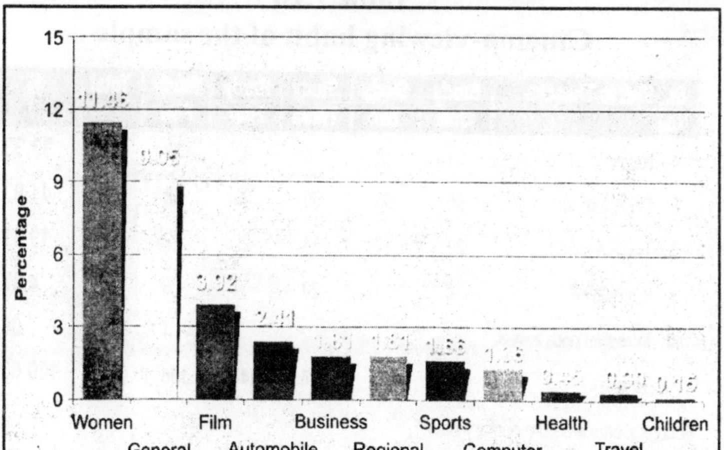

As indicated in Table 7.9 and Graph 7.8, the most popular category was the women's magazines that was read by 76 subjects (11.46 per cent), followed by general magazines category that was read by 60 subjects (9.05 per cent). Film based magazines were read by 26 subjects (3.92 per cent) and automobile related magazines by 16 subjects (2.41 per cent). Business and regional magazines were read by 12 subjects (1.81 per cent) each. Sports magazines were read by 11 subjects (1.66 per cent) and computer related magazines were read by 9 subjects (1.36 per cent). There were 3 subjects (0.45 per cent) reading health magazines, 2 subjects (0.30 per cent) reading travel magazines and 1 subject (0.15 per cent) reading children's magazine.

7.2.2 Cinema

Cinema is an interesting media option for targeting youth considering the popularity of films in India. To assess the popularity of cinema among the subjects their cinema watching habit was investigated on a monthly basis. The subjects were to choose from a list which had frequency of visit to theatres for watching cinema from never to more than once a week.

Table 7.10

Cinema-viewing habit of the sample

Sr. No.	Visit to Theaters	Study One	Study Two	Study Three	Study Four	Study Five	Total	%
1	Never	51	40	8	83	39	221	33.33
2	Once a month	65	56	50	39	68	278	41.93
3	Twice a month	21	27	38	20	22	128	19.31
4	Every Week	4	1	20	1	3	29	4.37
5	More than once a week	–	–	2	1	4	7	1.06
	Total	**141**	**124**	**118**	**144**	**136**	**663**	**100.00**

Source: Compiled from primary data.

Graph 7.9
Cinema-viewing habit of the sample

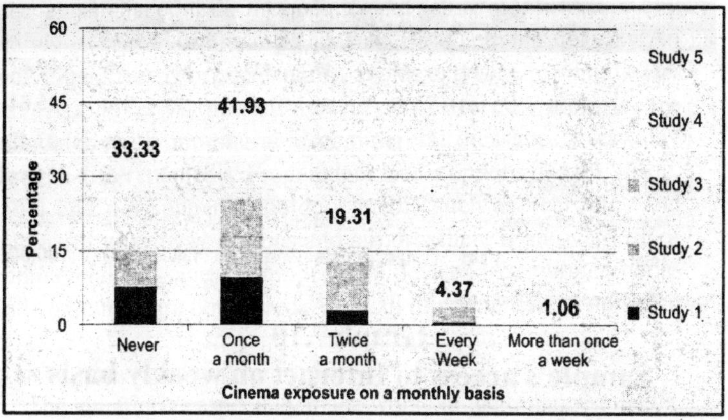

Cinema watching habit of the sample as indicated in Table 7.10 and Graph 7.9 revealed that 278 subjects (41.93 per cent) watched cinema in theatres once a month, 128 subjects (19.31 per cent) watched twice a month and 29 subjects (4.37 per cent) watched every week. There were 221 subjects (33.33 per cent) who never watched cinema in theatres and there were 7 subjects (1.06 per cent) watching cinema in theatre for more than once a week. Thus the subjects did not exhibit a high exposure to cinema especially by visiting theatres.

7.2.3 Internet

From a marketing perspective Internet is one of the most inexpensive and interactive communication medium. Considering the popularity of Internet among youth worldwide, the exposure to Internet among the sample was analysed. The subjects were provided with options to choose from on the basis of how often they accessed Internet in terms of number of hours in a week.

Table 7.11
Sample's access to Internet on weekly basis

Sr. No.	Internet exposure	Study One	Study Two	Study Three	Study Four	Study Five	Total	%
1	Never	61	63	10	110	84	328	**49.47**
2	0 – 4 hrs a week	49	38	20	26	37	170	**25.64**
3	4 – 10 hrs a week	21	18	35	5	10	89	**13.42**
4	10 – 18 hrs a week	4	2	25	1	2	34	**5.13**
5	More than 18 hrs a week	6	3	28	2	3	42	**6.33**
	Total	**141**	**124**	**118**	**144**	**136**	**663**	**100.00**

Source: Compiled from primary data.

Graph 7.10
Sample's access to Internet on weekly basis

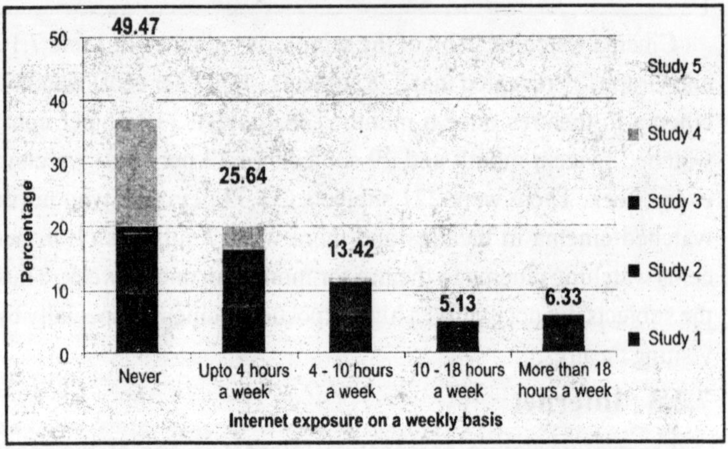

The Internet surfing habit as indicated in Table 7.11 and Graph 7.10 revealed that of the entire sample, 328 subjects (49.47 per cent) did not access Internet at all. There were 170 subjects (25.64 per cent) who accessed Internet up to 4 hours a week, 89 subjects (13.42 per cent) accessed for 4 to 10 hours a week and 34 subjects (5.13 per cent) accessed for 10 to 18 hours a week. There were 42 subjects (6.33 per cent) who accessed Internet for more than 18 hours a week. The sample's Internet surfing habit was a clear indication that Internet was not a popular option among the subjects.

7.2.4 Inter-Media Comparison on the Basis of the Sample's Preferences

Sample's media viewing habit, media popularity and preference was analysed. Sample's media viewing preferences were compiled together and following was the result:

Table 7.12
Inter-media comparison on the basis of sample's preferences

Sr. No.	Media	Subjects regularly exposed	% regularly exposed	Subjects not exposed	% not exposed
1	Television	639	**96.38**	24	**3.62**
2	Radio	634	**95.63**	29	**4.37**
3	Newspaper	491	**74.06**	172	**25.94**
4	Cinema	442	**66.67**	221	**33.33**
5	Internet	335	**50.53**	328	**49.47**
6	Magazines	176	**26.55**	487	**73.45**

Source: Compiled from primary data.

Graph 7.11
Inter-media comparison on the basis of sample's preferences

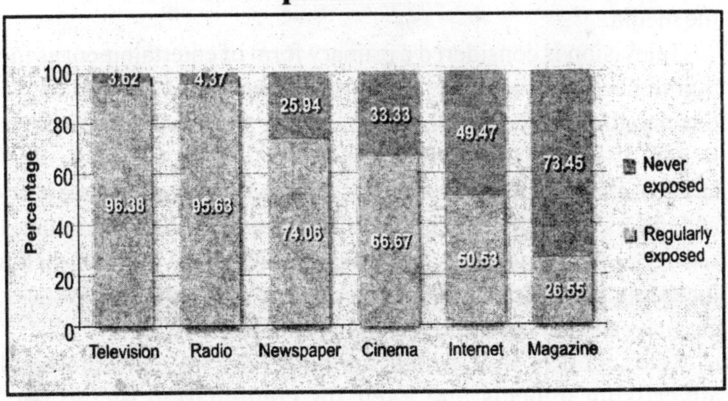

Table 7.12 and Graph 7.11 revealed that on the basis of the sample's exposure television emerged as the most popular medium with 639 subjects (96.38 per cent) exposed to it, followed by radio with 634 subjects (95.63 per cent). The next popular media option was newspaper with 491 subjects (74.06 per cent) reading it on a regular basis and this was followed by Cinema with 442 subjects (66.67 per cent) regularly watching it in theatres. The Internet was accessed only by 335 subjects (50.53 per cent) regularly. Magazine was the least preferred media option with only 176 subjects (26.55 per cent) reading it regularly.

7.3 Assessing Effectiveness of Television

Television is a great medium of news and entertainment. Television is a type of broadcast media that contains the elements of sight, sound and motion. It is the most powerful and dominant source of information. Television has influenced the lives of people and increased their awareness manifold. People generally rate television as one of the most credible source of information. Advertisers that advertise on television gain a qualitative edge and a prestigious reputation because television enjoys the most positive image of all media. For years television has enjoyed the reputation of being the most glamorous advertising medium. Television is believed to be the most authoritative, influential and exciting of all the media.

Television is considered a primary form of entertainment as the quintessential advertising medium. Television has the ability to develop the most creative and imaginative appeals of any medium. It has often been said that the television is the most ideal advertising medium since it offers tremendous creative flexibility and makes possible dramatic, lifelike representations of products / services.[3] Television has numerous advantages over other media including creativity and impact, coverage and cost effectiveness, captivity and attention and selectivity and flexibility.

Television is well suited for both rational and emotional advertising appeals and even for combination of the two.

Television is particularly well suited to drama; no other advertising medium can touch emotions as well. Various emotional appeals such as humor, fear and fantasy work well on television. As people learn through their senses the combined power of sight, sound, motion and emotion creates a synergistic effect that is more effective than individually stimulated senses. Television is essentially an entertainment medium and many advertisers recognise that their commercials are most successful when they entertain as well as inform. Television can be used to convey a mood or image for a brand that help make a dull product appear interesting. One of the advantages of television is its ability to present the advertising messages in the most unique way. In general television is considered as an indispensable part of modern society. Television has become more of a necessity than a luxury.[4]

In television unlike print, the viewer does not control the rate at which the message is presented, so there is no opportunity to review points of interest or revisit things that are not communicated clearly. Television has the advantage of intrusion value, in a way that commercials impose themselves on viewers while the viewers are watching their favourite programmes. Unless the viewers make a special effort to avoid commercials, most of them are exposed to thousands of them each year. Further the low-involvement nature of consumer learning and response processes may mean television advertising have an impact on consumers simply through heavy repetition and exposure to catchy slogans and jingles.[5]

Television is basically a non-selective medium as it is difficult for it to reach a precisely-defined market segment, yet some selectivity is possible due to variations in the composition of audiences as a result of regional coverage, channel / programme content, broadcast time and geographical coverage. A number of

---

[3] Kazmi S. H. H. and Batra Satish K., *op. cit.*, p. 280.

[4] Nath Sirisha P., "Television and Its Impact on Children," Advertising Express, The ICFAI University Press, January 2008. pp. 52-58.

options are available to advertisers using television as part of their media mix. They can purchase time in a variety of program formats that appeal to various types and sizes of audiences. They can purchase time on a national, regional or local basis. They can sponsor an entire program, participate in the sponsorship or use spot announcements between programs.

Television commercials have several components. The video element of a commercial is what is seen on the television screen. The visual portion generally dominates the commercial, so it must attract viewers' atten-tion and communicate an idea, message and/or image. The audio portion of a commercial includes voices, music and sound effects that are used in different ways in commercials. The video and audio must work together to create the right impact and communicate the advertiser's message.[6]

Audio and visual elements can be combined to produce several types of television commercials, just as a story can be told in many different ways. Emphasis can be placed on the story itself, on the problem to be solved, on the central character such as in a testimonial or on special human emotions or storytelling techniques such as satire, humor, fantasy and so on.[7] Book Albert and Cary Norman[8] provide a useful classification of the possible alternatives, based on the point of emphasis, focus or style adopted. Each is referred to as a particular kind of commercial structure to emphasise that a commercial is other than an unrelated jumble of ideas and techniques. The thirteen types of structure identified by them are as follows:

1. *Story line*: a commercial that tells a story; a clear step-by-step unfolding of a message that has a definite beginning, middle and end.
2. *Problem-solution*: presents the viewer with a problem to be solved and the sponsor's product as the solution to that problem.

- - - - - - - - - - - - - - - - - -

[5] Sharma S. and Singh R., *op. cit.*, pp. 351- 357.

3. *Chronology*: delivers the message through a series of related scenes, each one growing out of the one before. Facts and events are presented sequentially as they occur.
4. *Special effects*: no strong structural pattern; strives for and often achieves memorability through the use of some striking device. For example, an unusual musical sound or pictorial technique.
5. *Testimonial*: also called word-of-mouth advertising; it uses well-known figures or an unknown "man in the street" to provide product testimonials.
6. *Satire*: a commercial that uses sophisticated wit to point out human foible generally produced in an exaggerated style.
7. *Spokesperson*: the use of an on-camera announcer who, basically "talks." Talk may be fast and hard sell or more personal and intimate sell.
8. *Demonstration*: uses some physical apparatus to demonstrate a product's effectiveness.
9. *Suspense*: somewhat similar to story-line or problem-solution structures, but the buildup of curiosity and suspense to the final resolution is given a heightened sense of drama.
10. *Slice-of-life*: a variation on problem solution; begins with a person at the point of and just before the discovery of, an answer to a problem.
11. *Analogy*: offers an extraneous example and attempts to relate it to the product message. Instead of delivering a message simply and directly, an analogy uses one example to explain another by comparison or implication.

---

[6] Kazmi S. H. H. and Batra Satish K., *op. cit.*, pp. 280-290.
[7] Batra Rajeev, Myers John G. and Aaker David A., *op. cit.*, p. 437.
[8] Book Albert C. and Cary Norman D., The Television Commercial: Creativity and Craftsmanship, Decker Communication, New York, 1970

12. *Fantasy*: uses caricatures or special effects to create fantasy surrounding product and product use.
13. *Personality*: a technical variation of the spokesperson or announcer-on-camera, straight-sell structure, relies on an actor or actress rather than an announcer to deliver the message and uses a setting rather than the background of a studio. The actor plays a character and talks about the product, reacts to its use or demonstrates its use or enjoyment di-rectly to the camera.

However, to many critics of advertising television commercials personify everything that is wrong with the industry. Critics often single out television commercials because of their pervasiveness and the intrusive nature of the medium. Consumers are seen as defenseless against the barrage of television advertisements since they cannot control the transmission of the message and what appears on their screens. According to Alwitt Linda F. and Prabhakar Parul R., audiences dislike television advertising when they believe it to be offensive, uninformative or shown too frequently or when they do not like its content.[9] Studies have shown that of the various forms of advertising, distrust is generally the highest for television commer-cials.[10] Also concern has been raised about the effects of television advertising on specific groups, such as children or the elderly.

A number of researches have been conducted to find out the impact of television and there are both positive and negative impacts. There are surfeit of channels that offer both good and deplorable quality programs. Select viewing of television can help

---

[9]Alwitt Linda F. and Prabhakar Parul R., "Identifying Who Dislikes Television Advertising: Not by Demographics Alone," Journal of Advertising Research, Vol. 32, No. 5, 1992, pp. 30-42.

[10] Mittal Banwari, "Public Assessment of TV Advertising: Faint Praise and Harsh Criticism," Journal of Advertising Research, Vol. 34, No. 1, 1994, pp. 35-53.

in cognitive development of children, while watching without any discretion results in aggressiveness. Shared television viewing creates an opportunity for families to spend time together and increase family bond. Television can incorporate important values and life lessons.[11]

A survey conducted by the Kaiser Family Foundation found that more than 60 percent of the teens thought of entertainment media as their top source of information on sexuality and sex health. Television is the main source of information related to sex. Though television can be a powerful tool for educating youth about the responsibilities and risks of sexual behaviour, these issues are rarely dealt with in a meaningful way in programs having sexual content. Young children get affected easily by watching television.

7.4 Television an Aptmedia for Social Advertising in India

Television in India is a home and family entertainment medium. Regardless of location, income, age, sex or educational level significant number of people watch television programmes on a regular basis. Television appeals to the audiences' senses more than any other medium. Television can create a powerful and emotional connect with its audiences and create high impact by offering dynamic and visual messages. It has an aura of importance and is a popular medium. Television is a very useful medium because of the enormous range it has and the interest that it generates amongst its viewers. In India television has been used as a source of educative information as well as entertainment. Doordarshan, the national channel had been playing a pivotal role through entertaining programmes and advertisements and educating at the same time. Many educative programmes for different segments of society living in rural and urban India have been regular features of television advertising. It takes care of

[11] Nath Sirisha P., op. cit. pp. 52-58

illiteracy problems in India and can reach to regional audience in regional languages. Just like television, films another audio-video medium has been very popular in India. Different film-makers have used films also as a platform for social awareness. Various issues like AIDS, plight of women, poverty, national integration and terrorism have been sensitively canvassed through films in India.

Television offers advertisers the most extensive coverage and highest reach of any of the media after radio in India. A single advertisement can reach millions of viewers simultaneously. Even though total cost of running the advertisements is high the cost per contact is relatively low. In India television is one of the most suitable media for social advertising since it has the highest daily and weekly reach among all the media. Doordarshan claims to have largest terrestrial networks in the world, with 1400 terrestrial transmitters covering more than 90.7 percent of India.[12] According to Indian Readership Survey TV Report 2006 (Round 2) there are 212.7 million television homes in the country. About 56 per cent television homes in the country have cable connections. The corresponding percentage in urban and rural areas is 70 and 42 respectively. Some 230 millions individuals watch television every week. It is estimated that at least 250 to 300 television channels in different languages are available in India, although some are confined to certain states or regions only.[13] Television is credited as being the single biggest factor in opening up the huge rural market to a variety of consumer products. Television has been instrumental in raising the level of aspirations of the Indian middle class.

With respect to the current sample television dominated the scene as far as household product consumption was concerned. The electronic productwise consumption of the sample is as follows:

---

[12] www.ddindia.gov.in.

[13] www.infochangeindia.org.

Table 7.13
Household product consumption wise composition of the sample

Sr. No.	Products in the house	Study One	Study Two	Study Three	Study Four	Study Five	Total	%
1	Television	137	110	118	120	129	**614**	**92.61**
2	Music system	97	82	106	94	97	**476**	**71.79**
3	Washing machine	60	51	101	55	46	**313**	**47.21**
4	Computer/ laptop	70	54	93	41	41	**299**	**45.10**
5	Video-camera	20	38	73	14	27	**172**	**25.94**
6	Air conditioner/cooler	25	18	79	17	19	**158**	**23.83**
7	Micro-wave oven	22	18	76	19	15	**150**	**22.62**

Source: Compiled from primary data.

Graph 7.12
Household product consumption wise composition of the sample

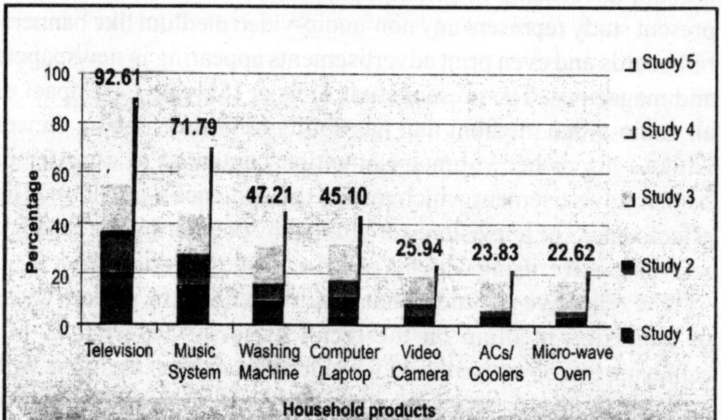

The household product wise consumption of the sample as revealed in Table 7.13 and Graph 7.12 indicated that television was the most common products owned by 614 subjects (92.61 per cent) followed by music systems that was possessed by 476 subjects (71.79 per cent). There were 313 subjects (47.21 per cent) who had washing machines, 299 subjects (45.10 per cent) who had computer / laptop and 172 subjects (25.94 per cent) had video-camera in their houses. The products like air conditioner or cooler was owned by 158 subjects (23.83 per cent) and micro-wave oven by 150 subjects (22.62 per cent).

7.5 Study Four: Assessing Effectiveness of Television in Social Advertising

The present study is not a comparison between television advertising and poster advertising. Rather television in this study symbolises audio-video medium and stands for all those options which have the capacity to transform the advertising messages with the same strength and power that can combine visual images, sound, motion and colour, such as films, computer and even mobile phones. Similarly since it was practically difficult to manipulate outdoor advertising in general, posters were used. Posters in the present study represent any non-audio-video medium like banners, bill boards and even print advertisements appearing in newspapers and magazines. The present study aims at studying the impact of an audio-video medium that has ability to intrude upon a viewer without his or her voluntary attention compared to a poster or banner advertisement which awaits the audience's attention. The effectiveness of television was studied by comparing the recall of television advertising with the recall of poster advertising.

The objective of Study Four was to evaluate the effectiveness of television medium on the recall of social advertising. For achieving this objective the audio-video presentation was done with eight social advertisements of which four social advertisements were presented on television and four social advertisements were shown through posters. Table 7.14 gives details of the social advertisements shown in the presentation:

Table 7.14
Social advertisements presented in Study Four

Sr. No.	Social advertisements presented on television	Sr. No.	Social advertisements on posters
1	Don't talk on mobile phone while driving	1	Anti tobacco
2	Awareness against eve-teasing	2	Awareness against domestic violence
3	Don't drink and drive	3	Female feticide
4	Spend time with elderly	4	Awareness against poverty

Source: Compiled from primary data.

The responses to the questions based on television advertisements and poster advertisements in the aided and unaided categories were carefully analysed in the following step-by-step manner:

[1] Number of social advertisements correctly recalled that were presented on television and shown through posters in aided and unaided category were calculated.

[2] Means were calculated for number of social advertisements correctly recalled that were presented on television and that were shown on posters in aided and unaided category.

[3] Paired samples T-test were conducted to compare recall of social advertisements presented on television and shown through posters under both aided and unaided conditions.

[4] Percentages of social advertisements presented on television and shown on posters recalled under aided and unaided conditions were calculated.

[5] z-tests were performed to measure the significance of the difference between percentages of social advertisements presented on television and shown on posters under aided and unaided conditions.

In the study specific questionnaire the subjects were required to recall the social advertisements that they had seen in the presentation in two categories, social advertisements seen on television and social advertisements seen on posters. These two categories were further investigated under two conditions, viz. unaided and aided.

7.5.1 Recall of Social Advertisements in Unaided Category

In the unaided category the subjects were supposed to recall and write the social advertisements that they had seen in the audio-video presentation. There was no clue or hint provided and they had to recall social advertisements on the basis of the issues presented on television and social advertisements seen through posters.

[1] *Recall of social advertisements presented on television in unaided category*

There were four social advertisements presented on television. The first social advertisement was issue of not driving when drunk. The second social advertisement created awareness about not talking on mobile phone while driving. The third social advertisement was based on spending time with elderly. The last social advertisement was based on rising instances of eve-teasing.

Table 7.15

Recall of social advertisements presented on television in unaided category

Sr. No.	Social advertisements presented on television	Recall	% recall
1	Don't drink and drive	78	**57.35**
2	Don't talk on mobile phone while driving	69	**50.74**
3	Spend time with elderly	64	**47.06**
4	Awareness against eve-teasing	42	**30.88**

Source: Compiled from primary data.

Graph 7.13
Recall of social advertisements presented on television in unaided category

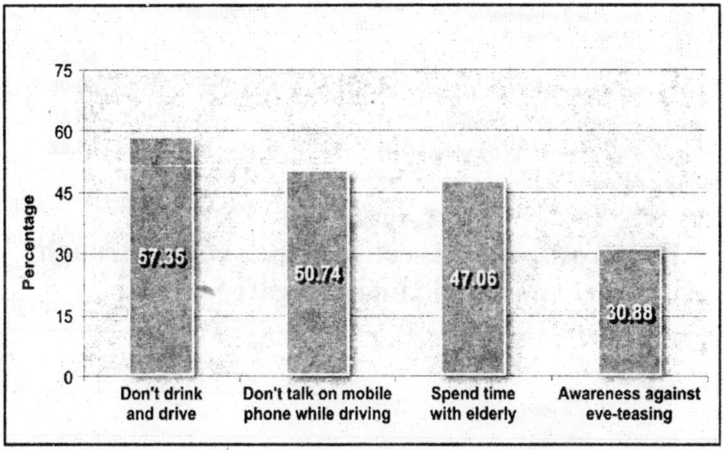

From Table 7.15 and Graph 7.12 it was revealed that the social advertisement on 'don't drink and drive' had the highest recall in this category with 78 subjects (57.35 per cent) followed by the advertisement on 'don't talk on mobile phone while driving' which had a recall from 69 subjects (50.74 per cent). The social advertisement on 'spend time with elderly' had a recall from 64 subjects (47.06 per cent) and the advertisement against eve-teasing registered the lowest recall from 42 subjects (30.88 per cent).

[2] *Recall of social advertisements shown through posters in unaided category*

There were four social advertisements shown through posters. The first issue addressed through posters was about female feticide. The second social advertisement was based on cigarette smoking causing oral cancer. The third social advertisement dealt with issue of poverty and the last social advertisement created awareness against domestic violence.

Table 7.16
Recall of social advertisements shown through posters in unaided category

Sr. No.	Social advertisements shown on posters	Recall	% recall
1	Female feticide	68	**50.00**
2	Anti-tobacco	68	**50.00**
3	Awareness against poverty	50	**36.76**
4	Awareness against domestic violence	12	**8.82**

Source: Compiled from primary data.

Graph 7.14
Recall of social advertisements shown through posters in unaided category

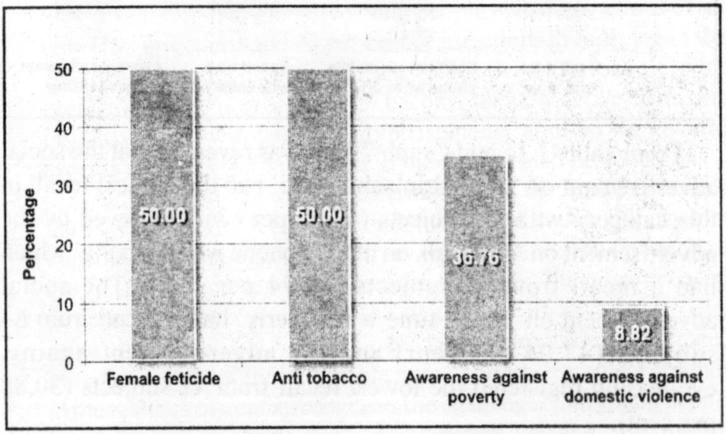

As Table 7.16 and Graph 7.13 indicate, within the social advertisements shown through posters anti-tobacco advertisement and female feticide advertisements both recorded a recall from 68 subjects (50 per cent) each followed by advertisement creating awareness against poverty which had a recall of 50 subjects (36.76 per cent). The advertisement against domestic violence registered the lowest recall from 12 subjects (8.82 per cent).

[3] *Comparison between recall of television and poster social advertisements in unaided category*

The recall of social advertisements shown on television was compared with recall of social advertisements shown on posters in the unaided category. The responses were as follows:

Table 7.17
Recall of social advertisements in unaided category

Sr. No.	Particulars	Total recall	% recall
1	Social advertisements shown on television	253	**46.51**
2	Social advertisements shown through posters	198	**36.40**

Source: Compiled from primary data.

Graph 7.15
Percentage recall of social advertisements in unaided category

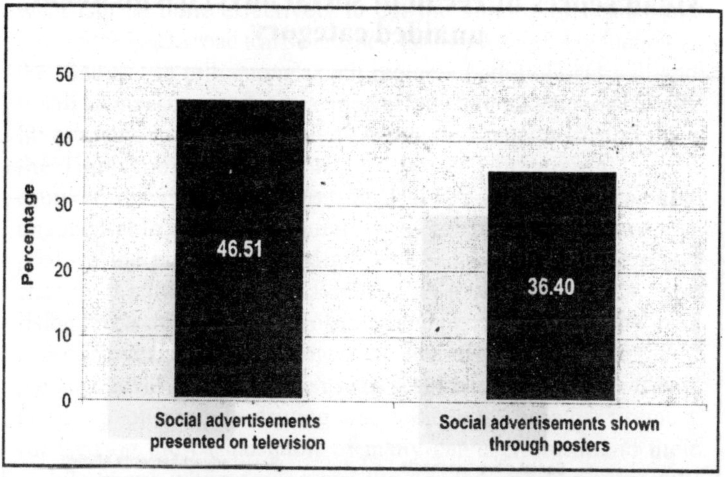

When the recall of social advertisements shown on television were compared with recall of social advertisements shown on posters in the unaided category, as indicated in Table 7.17 and Graph 7.14, it was found that the overall recall of social advertisements presented on television was higher (46.51 per cent) than that for the social advertisements shown through posters (36.40 per cent). The z-test revealed a significant difference ($z = 3.41$), $p < 0.001$.

[4] *Paired sample T-test of recall in unaided category*

The paired sample T-test compared the mean recall of social advertisements presented on television and shown through posters in unaided category.

Table 7.18

Paired sample T-test of recall in unaided category

Sr. No.	Paired sample	Mean	Df	Standard deviation	T
1	Recall of social advertisements presented on television	3.72	135	2.139	3.447*
2	Recall of social advertisements shown through posters	2.91	135	1.976	

Source: Compiled from primary data.
* $p < 0.001$.

Graph 7.16

Mean scores of recall of social advertisements in unaided category

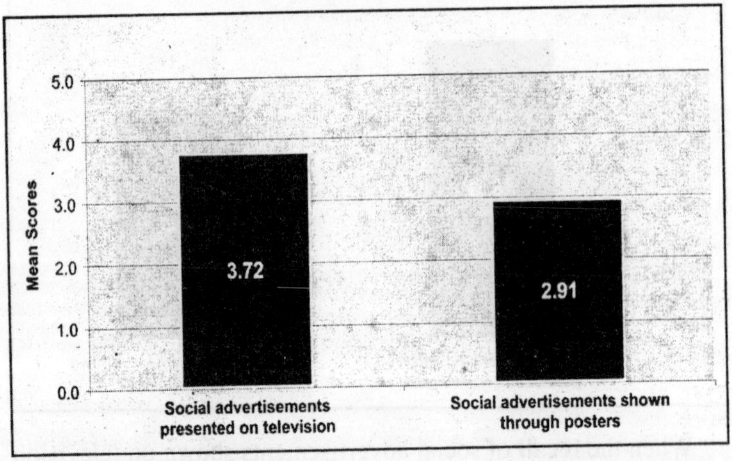

The paired sample T-test comparing mean recall of social advertisements presented on television and shown through posters in unaided category as revealed by Table 7.18 and Graph 7.15, showed a significant difference, ($t = 3.447$) at a probability < 0.001.

The mean recall of the social advertisements presented on television (m = 3.72) was higher than the mean recall of social advertisements shown through posters (m = 2.91) in unaided category.

7.5.2 Recall of Social Advertisements in Aided Category

In the aided category the subjects were supposed to recall the social advertisements with the help of some clues provided in the questionnaire for easy recall.

[1] *Recall of social advertisements presented on television in aided category*

The result of the recall of four social advertisements presented on television in the aided category was as follows:

Table 7.19

Recall of social advertisements presented on television in aided category

Sr. No.	Social advertisements presented on television	Recall	% recall
1	Don't drink and drive	247	**90.81**
2	Spend time with elderly	231	**84.93**
3	Don't talk on mobile phone while driving	226	**83.09**
4	Awareness against eve-teasing	215	**79.04**

Source: Compiled from primary data.

Graph 7.17

Recall of social advertisements presented on television in aided category

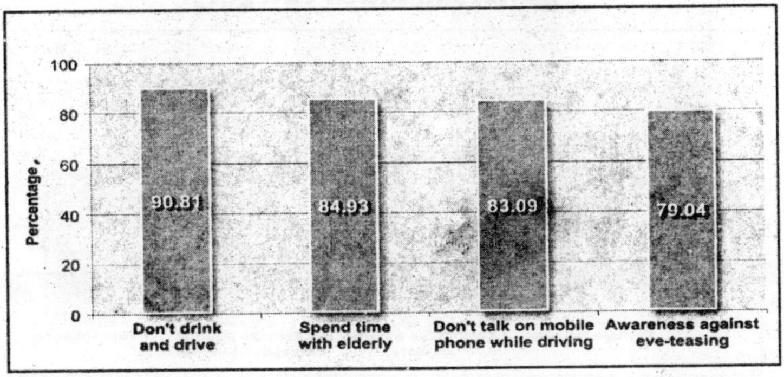

Table 7.19 and Graph 7.16 indicated that in the aided category within the social advertisements presented on television category, the social advertisement on 'don't drink and drive' had the highest recall in this category with 247 (90.81 per cent) followed by the advertisement on 'spend time with elderly' which had a recall of 231 (84.93 per cent). Advertisement 'don't talk on mobile phone while driving' had a recall of 226 (83.09 per cent) and the advertisement against eve-teasing registered the lowest recall of 215 (79.04 per cent).

[2] *Recall of social advertisements shown through posters in aided category*

The responses to four social advertisements shown through posters in aided category were analysed and following results were found:

Table 7.20
Recall of social advertisements shown through posters in aided category

Sr. No.	Social advertisements shown on posters	Recall	% recall
1	Female feticide	216	79.41
2	Awareness against poverty	209	76.84
3	Awareness against domestic violence	196	72.06
4	Anti-tobacco	174	63.97

Source: Compiled from primary data.

Graph 7.18
Recall of social advertisements shown through posters in aided category

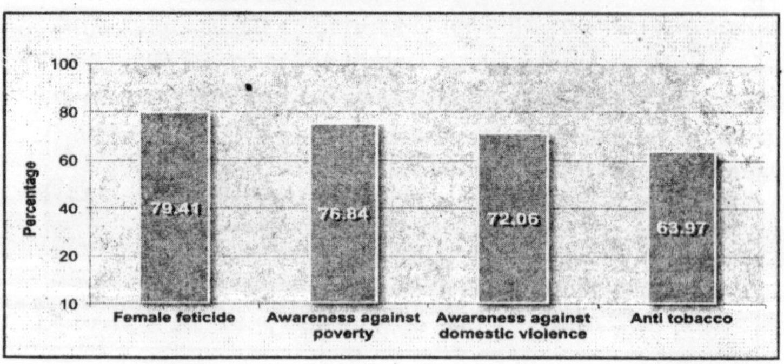

Table 7.20 and Graph 7.17 revealed that in the aided category, within the social advertisements shown through posters the female feticide advertisement recorded the highest recall of 216 (79.41 per cent) closely followed by awareness against poverty which had a recall of 209 (76.84 per cent). The advertisement 'awareness against domestic violence' registered a recall of 196 (72.06 per cent) and anti-tobacco advertisement registered the lowest recall of 174 (63.97 per cent).

[3] *Comparison between recall of social advertisements presented on television and shown through posters in aided category*

The recall of social advertisements presented on television was compared with recall of social advertisements shown through posters in the aided category. The result was as follows:

Table 7.21
Recall of social advertisements in aided category

Sr. No.	Particulars	Total recall	% recall
1	Social advertisements presented on television	919	**84.47**
2	Social advertisements shown through posters	795	**73.07**

Source: Compiled from primary data.

Graph 7.19
Percentage recall of social advertisements in aided category

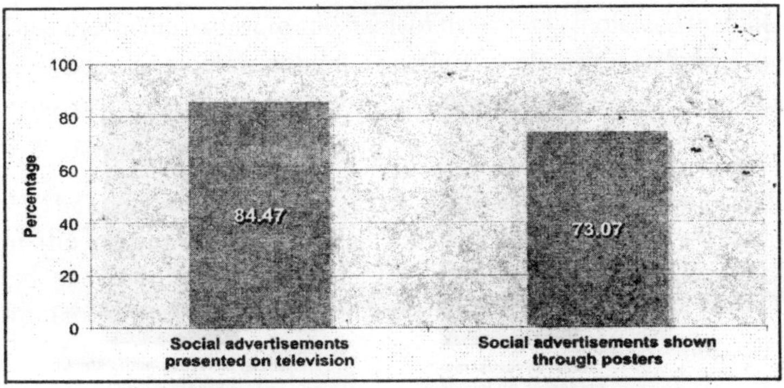

When the recall of social advertisements presented on television were compared with recall of social advertisements shown through posters in the aided category as indicated in Table 7.21 and Graph 7.18, it was found that the overall recall of television social advertisements was higher (84.47 per cent) than that for the social advertisements shown through posters (73.07 per cent). The z-test revealed a highly significant difference ($z = 6.59$), $p < 0.001$.

[4] *Paired sample T-test of recall in aided category*

The paired sample T-test compared mean recall of social advertisements presented on television and shown through posters in aided category.

Table 7.22
Paired sample T-test of recall in aided category

Sr. No.	Paired sample	Mean	Df	Standard deviation	T
1	Recall of social advertisements presented on television	6.76	135	1.358	6.652*
2	Recall of social advertisements shown through posters	5.85	135	1.366	

Source: Compiled from primary data.
* $p < 0.000$.

Graph 7.20
Mean scores of recall of social advertisements in aided category

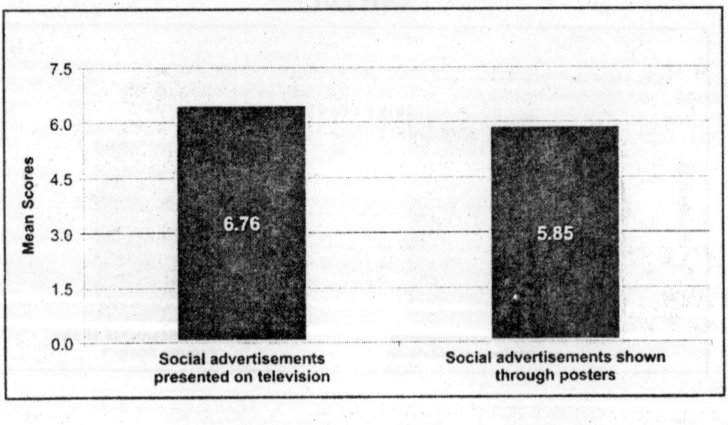

The paired sample T-test comparing mean recall of social advertisements presented on television and shown through posters in aided category as revealed in Table 7.22 and Graph 7.19, showed a difference, ($t = 6.652$) at a probability < 0.000. The mean recall of the television social advertisements ($m = 6.76$) was higher than the mean recall of poster social advertisements ($m = 5.85$) in aided category.

7.6 Conclusion

In this research study, the impact of audio-video medium like television was studied by comparing social advertising presented on television with advertising shown on non-audio-video medium like posters. The social advertisements presented on television were higher on recall compared to social advertisements shown through posters. This was reported in the unaided category where the subjects had to recall the social advertisements seen in the presentation on their own without any clues and even in the aided category when the subjects were provided hints to recall the social advertisements.

This study gave a valuable insight about the youth with respect to their media exposure and media habits. The study of the media exposure of the sample indicated that television was the most popular media, followed by radio, print, cinema and Internet respectively. The study four also highlighted the effectiveness of an audio-video medium over non intriguing medium such as posters. The responses clearly indicate the supremacy of television over other media. To conclude television is certainly the most effective and appropriate medium for reaching youth through social advertising is concerned.

8

Influence of Repetition in Social Advertising on Youth

8.1 Introduction - Role of Repetition in Advertising

Advertisement like any programme on television or news item in a newspaper cannot be just exposed once. Especially in the era where the audience is exposed to hundreds of media options indoor and outdoor it is very likely for any advertising communication to get neglected. Since the aim of advertising is not only to make the audience aware of the product but also prompt them to buy it, one exposure of the advertisement cannot be enough. In fact advertiser cannot boast of reaching the target audience by just picking up one media vehicle and advertising just once. The more often the audiences are exposed to the same advertisement the more likely they are to understand and remember the message. Repeated exposure to an advertising message can help surmount clutter and thus facilitate message reception and to raise awareness and comprehension. Adequate repetition is certainly required to be noticed and remain in the minds of the audience. Repetition is particularly required in marketing when new products are introduced, new campaigns are started and when brand attitudes are to be formed. That is the reason one comes across the same advertising messages repeated over television channels, radio stations, newspapers and magazines.

However any advertising message cannot be just repeated aimlessly. It is very important to determine the effective frequency, the number of times a target audience must be exposed to a particular advertisement in a given medium to communicate the message and stimulate action. Although experts agree that one exposure is not enough, there is no agreement on the optimal number of exposures needed to stimulate a response. Providing too few exposures means that, audience may not hear or see the message often enough to be aware of the company's communication. However providing too many exposures wastes money and can lead to wear out, as this may lead to the audience turning away from the advertisements or respond negatively after repeated exposures. According to the study conducted by Naples Michael J. in general around three exposures in a four week cycle are about adequate to lead or to maintain the desired level of brand awareness or brand attitudes. First exposure elicits 'what is it?' type of response where the audience exposed to the message will try to understand the nature of the communication. The second exposure might be the extension of understanding the communication better and it will elicit an evaluative response. The audience will attempt to determine the relevance of the message or the brand advertised. The third and last exposure is basically a reminder so as to make the audience to act upon the message. The three or maximum four exposures per-four-week is just an average. When the consumer is less involved or less knowledgeable higher levels of repetitions are warranted since they lead to increasing attitudes. The complexity and size of the communication and persuasion task will also affect the repetitions needed. High frequencies are advised when the message is complicated so as to aid the audience to understand and retain the message.

The role of repetition is as crucial in social advertising as it is in commercial advertising. In case of social advertising in specific situations like where the objectives may be as difficult as making the audience to change their deep-rooted habit of giving up smoking or changing their attitude towards AIDS patients then just three or four exposures may not be certainly enough. To ensure that the audience is involved and they connect with the messages presented in social advertising frequent repetitions of the messages are very crucial. In India it is often observed that the repetition of social advertising is very limited. This is because social advertising is done arbitrarily and lacks professionalism. There are companies without real commitment to the social cause, making social advertisements just to boast their corporate philanthropy. Such companies often expect media to contribute their bit towards the cause by providing free space or air time. Requests for free air time is an unwarranted burden on media as airing such advertisements repeatedly in peak hours in place of paid up commercial advertisements means huge financial loss for media. As a result one finds good social advertisements aired scantily on media and lost in the clutter of commercial messages. This half heartedness from everyone involved in social advertising ultimately leads to failure of social advertising in reaching the audience and bringing about the desired effect in the society at large.

Since repetition plays an important role in the reach and success of social advertising campaigns the present chapter is based on the study that attempts to analyse the effect of repetition on recall of social advertising. This test was conducted to study whether the repetition has an impact on the audience and whether they make any positive contribution towards the recall of social advertising. While some social advertisements were repeatedly presented, some social advertisements were presented just once and the recall in both these cases, repeated and non-repeated were studied.

8.2 Assessing the Literature on Repetition

There is some general agreement on how peo-ple learn, regardless of whether what they are learning is a concept, a message, information about a brand or even such things as typing and bicycle riding. Learning is slow at first, but with repetition it increases rapidly until a plateau is reached, after which it slows down again. With more repetition, a new plateau may be reached.[1]

Repetition is considered an important requisite for effective learning.

From the consumers' point of view advertising is considered as a source of information. The consumer in their purchase related decision-making, cognitively process this information. Their attitudes towards brands and ultimately their decisions to purchase or not, are largely based on this process of learning. Nonetheless people also have a tendency to forget. Considering the number of sources and media through which information is bombarded at audience, chances of confusions are often high. So in a cluttered environment and availability of multiple media options one aid for retention is repetition. Repetition can facilitate the learning process to take place since it ensures that the audience is exposed to the advertising. Also one more rational for repetition of advertising messages is that just one exposure might be inadequate for audience to process information.

Repetition is believed to work by strengthening the bond of association and thus slowing the process of forgetting.[2] Learning follows a pattern which is known as learning curve. In Chart 8.1 "*x*" axis shows the number of repetitions and '*y*' axis represents the amount of learning. In a typical case, the rate of learning is quite rapid in the early stages. In later stages, as the amount learned accumulates, the rate of learning per repetition decreases. This shows that there is a limit to the amount of repetition that will aid learning and beyond a limit the attention and the rate of learning will decline. And the advertiser beyond a point pays only for fractional increases in consumer learning. Another implication is the effect known as 'advertising wear-out' which is the result of over-exposure because of much advertising leading to individuals' boredom, disinterest and decreased attention and retention of the message.

- - - - - - - - - - - - - - - - -

[1] Kassarjian Harold H., "Applications of Consumer Behaviour to the Field of Advertising," Journal of Advertising, Vol. 3, No. 3, 1974, p. 11.

Chart 8.1
A Typical Learning Curve

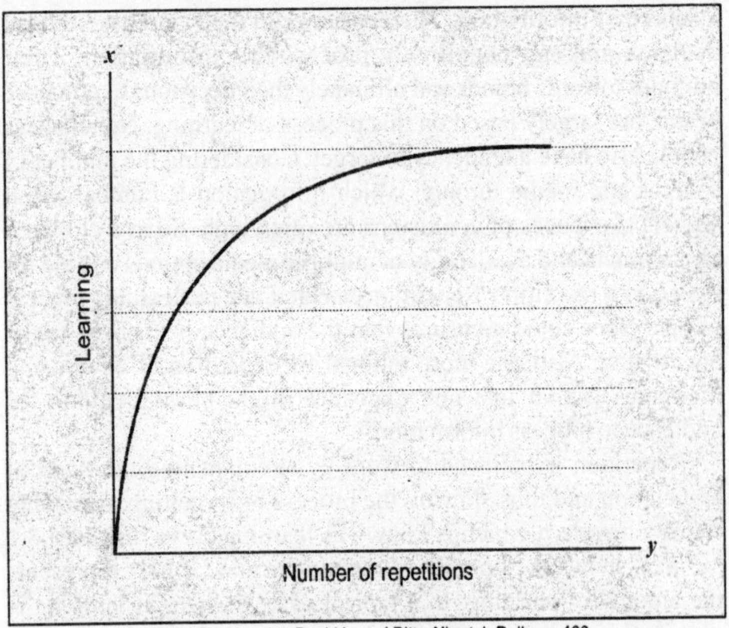

Source: Consumer Behaviour, Loudon David L. and Bitta Albert J. Della, p. 468.

If a message is not repeated, consumers tend to forget most of it rapidly and repetition becomes necessary just to maintain consumers' level of learning. Advertisers are convinced about the principles of repetition.[3] But an important question for the media planner is how many exposures the target audience should receive. There is no agreement on the optimal number of exposures needed to stimulate a response.[4] There is a general agreement on one exposure isn't enough to make the audience aware of the product or to prompt them to buy it: the more often they are exposed to advertisements the more likely they are to

---

[2] Kazmi S. H. H. and Batra Satish K., *op. cit.*, pp. 144-145.

understand and remember the message. But certain situations demand special consideration with respect to repetition such as when a new product is introduced, a new campaign is started or while breaking through clutter to raise awareness and comprehension.[5] Similarly high frequencies are advised when the message is complicated so as to aid the audience to understand and retain the message. It is very important to determine the effective frequency, the number of times a target audience must be exposed to a particular advertisement in a given medium to communicate the message and stimulate action. Although experts agree that one exposure is not enough, providing too few exposures means that audience may not hear or see the message often enough to be aware of the company's communication. However providing too many exposures wastes money and can lead to wear out, which happens when your audience turns away from the advertisements or responds negatively after repeated exposures.[6]

Research is inconclusive, but Kassarjian believes that the massive repetition of an advertisement may be sufficient to induce the consumer to buy the product advertised.[7] Several other researchers consider three advertisement exposures as the optimum number, known as three-hit theory. The first exposure is needed to make consumers aware and second exposure shows consumer the relevance of the product. The third exposure is needed to remind the consumers. The opinion of other researchers is that an average exposure frequency of eleven to twelve is needed to increase the probability that audiences will be actually exposed three times. Most advertisers seem to have settled on three exposures as the least number since less than that is assumed to give insufficient exposure and more than ten exposures are considered overexposure.

Some advertisements have very low information content and

- - - - - - - - - - - - - - - - -

[3] *Ibid.*

[4] Bogart Leo, Strategy in Advertising, 2nd ed.. NTC Business Books, Lincolnwood, Illinois, 1990.

yet seem to be effective at affecting attitudes, particularly with repetition. The premise here being is that repeated exposure to an advertised brand can, by itself, create a liking.

The most extreme and controversial version of this mere exposure effect was initially offered in the late 1960s by a prominent psychologist, Zajonc R. B., who hypothesised that preference is created simply from repeated exposure, with no as-sociated cognitive activity.[8] In one study, for example, researchers presented subjects with a series of polygons, at different levels of repetition.[9] They then exposed the subjects to pairs of polygons, asking which one they had seen previously and which one was new and which they preferred. The previously exposed polygons were preferred even though there was no recognition above chance levels as to which they had actually seen previously. This implies that the exposure effect occurred at some preconscious level and not simply because subjects preferred those polygons they thought they had seen earlier.

Clearly, applicability of research on polygons for making decisions about advertising processing is not fully conclusive, because advertisements (unlike polygons) contain meaningful information and can therefore be cognitively processed. Nevertheless, these studies suggest that advertising repetition may in some situations itself lead to preference, even if consumers don't absorb information on product benefits and so on. It is therefore clear that keeping brand awareness at a high level should often be considered as a possible advertising objective.

A related view of the exposure effect suggests that repeated exposure creates a conscious sense of familiarity with the brand,

---

[5] Kaatz Ron, Advertising and Marketing Checklists, 2nd Edition Lincolnwood, Illinois, NTC Business Books, 1992, pp. 127-128.

[6] Surmanek Jim, Media Planning: A Practical Guide, NTC Business Books, Lincolnwood, Illinois, 1986.

[7] Kassarjian Harold H., *op. cit.*

which then causes liking. The concept here is that familiar, known objects are evaluated more highly than arc unknown objects with associated uncertainty. Perhaps uncertainty creates tension which is undesirable and conversely familiarity may create positive feelings of comfort, security, ownership or intimacy. As the advertising researcher Krugman H. E. has pointed out, a product is often preferred not because it is indeed better but because of "the pleasure of its recognition. . . sheer familiarity."[10]

This familiarity model would explain why people develop positive attitudes toward brands and advertisements that are recognisable, even if these people cannot provide any facts about the brands. Although the familiarity model, like the mere exposure model, may not involve any indepth cognitive activity, there is evidence proving that people can actually perceive objects faster if they are familiar with them, a phenomenon called perceptual fluency. Such perceptual fluency is believed to lead to the feeling of familiarity people experience when they encounter these previously repeated objects.

Hawkins Scott A. and Hoch Stephen J.[11] found that when consumers processed advertisements under low-involvement conditions they began to believe statements about a brand to be more true simply as a function of how often those statements were repeated to them in advertising. In other words, those assertions were felt to be "more true" simply because they were repeated more frequently. These effects emerged even though the consumers were not processing the advertising information evaluatively.

Relatedly, research by Kirmani Amna and Wright Peter[12] also suggests that con-sumers sometimes use the perceived amount of

- - - - - - - - - - - - - - - - -

[8] Zajonc R. B., "Feeling and Thinking: Preferences Need No Inferences," American Psychologist, 35, 1980, pp. 151-175.

[9] Kunst-Wilson W. R. and Zajonc R. B., "Affective Discrimination of Stimuli That Can Not Be Recognised," Science, 207, February 1980, pp. 557-558.

advertising (judged by advertisement size, advertisement frequency etc.) they see for a brand as an indicator of the brand's quality and of the advertiser's willingness to back that high quality with a high degree of marketing effort. The implication here is that building a sense of familiarity may be especially important if the company is new and needs to overcome doubts about its reliability. Such a signaling effect, however, works only as long as the consumer cannot find some other justification or explanation for the high spending level such as a belief that the company is spending so much because it is desperate to move merchandise; such negative beliefs may arise especially when the perceived level of advertising spending appears excessive to consumers.

In a study comparing consumer thoughts in response to television advertisements versus print advertisements Krugman[13] observed that despite their apparent inability to communicate much information, television advertisements appeared to increase brand preference after repetition. This was found in low-involvement situations with a low involvement medium such as television particularly because of repetitive advertising.

Further work on such low-involvement learning was reported by Ray Michael L. and colleagues in a series of repetition studies done at Stanford University in the early 1970s.[14] In essence they argued that when the products involved were of low risk and low interest (and thus of low involvement) to the consumer and when the advertisements involved were television advertisements,

- - - - - - - - - - - - - - - - -

[10] Krugman H. E., "The Learning of Consumer Likes, Preferences and Choices," in Bass, King and Pessemier (eds.), Applications of the Sciences in Marketing Management, New York, Wiley, 1968.

[11] Hawkins Scott A. and Hoch Stephen J., "Low Involvement Learning: Memory Without Involvement," Journal of Consumer Research, 19, September 1990, pp. 160-171.

[12] Kirmani Amna and Wright Peter, "Money Talks: Perceived Advertising Expense and Expected Product Quality," Journal of Consumer Research, 16, December 1989, pp. 344-53.

advertising did not lead to an information-based attitude change, which then led to trial. Instead, the advertisements appeared to lead to trial simply because of greater top-of-mind awareness; this trial then led to attitude change.

Together the research reviewed above seems to suggest that a high level of advertising repetition is especially important when consumers don't process advertisements with a view to extracting much information from them. When advertisements are likely to be processed in such a shallow manner, a high level of advertising repetition can lead to brand preference simply because that brand is now top-of-mind, feels familiar and comfortable, is preconscious liked, is perceived to be more believable and feels safer and more trusted. Research on repetition by Sawyer[15] suggests the following:

1 Repetition can result in increased liking for the repeated stimulus.
2 Increases in the number of outside cues available to a subject and in the monotony of the repeated exposure are likely to lead to zero or negative effects on attitudes.
3 The effects of repetition seem to be less on measures of behaviour, such as purchasing action, than on measures of affect such as brand evaluation or intention to purchase.
4 The effects of repetition in advertising depend upon the given advertising situation. The effects are likely to be influenced by factors such as the type of product or brand, the appeal and for-mat of the advertisement and the media frequency schedule.

Thus repetition is an important pre-requisite for cognitive processing of advertising messages. Repetition aids memory and helps message retention. In a cluttered environment repetition helps breaking the clutter and facilitates reach of the advertising

- - - - - - - - - - - - - - - - -

[13] Krugman H. E., op. cit., pp. 353.

[14] Ray Michael L. et al., "Marketing Communications and the Hierarchy of Effects," in P. Clarke (ed.), New Models for Communications Research, Sage Publications, Beverly Hills, CA, 1973.

message. Repetition is found particularly effective in low involvement situation where it leads to brand preference due to high top of mind awareness.

8.2 Study Five: Impact of Repetition on Recall of Social Advertising

The researcher's Study Five was an attempt to analyse the impact of repetition as an aid to memory in social advertising. The objective of Study Five was to evaluate the impact of repetition on the recall of social advertising. In this study audio-video presentation was done with eight social advertisements, of which four social advertisements were repeated several times and four social advertisements were presented only once. Table 8.1 gives details of the social advertisements used in the presentation:

Table 8.1

Social advertisements presented in Study Five

Sr. No.	Social advertisements shown repeatedly	Sr. No.	Social advertisements shown once
1	Don't talk on mobile phone while driving	1	Anti tobacco
2	Female feticide	2	Awareness against eve-teasing
3	Be proud of yourself	3	Don't drink and drive
4	Sex education for youth	4	Spend time with elderly

Source: Compiled from primary data.

The responses to the questions based on the impact of repetition in the aided and unaided categories were carefully analysed in the following step-by-step manner:

[1] Number of social advertisements shown repeatedly and shown only once correctly recalled in aided and unaided category were calculated.

[2] Means were calculated for number of social advertisements shown repeatedly and shown only once correctly recalled in aided and unaided category.

[3] Paired samples T-test were conducted to compare recall of social advertisements shown repeatedly and social advertisements shown only once under both aided and unaided conditions.

[4] Percentages of social advertisements recalled were calculated that were repeatedly shown and that were shown only once under aided and unaided conditions.

[5] z-tests were performed to measure the significance of the difference between percentages of social advertisements that were shown repeatedly and social advertisements that were shown only once recalled under aided and unaided conditions.

In the study specific questionnaire the subjects were required to recall the social advertisements that they had seen in the presentation in two categories, social advertisements seen repeatedly and social advertisements seen only once. These two categories were further investigated under two conditions, viz. unaided and aided.

8.2.1 Recall of Social Advertisements in Unaided Category

In the unaided category the subjects were supposed to recall and write the social advertisements that they had seen in the audio-video presentation. There was no clue or hint provided and they had to recall social advertisements on the basis of the issues addressed and the celebrities involved.

[1] *Recall of social advertisements shown repeatedly in unaided category*

There were four social advertisements shown in the unaided category repeatedly. The responses to these social advertisements when analysed the result was as follows:

- - - - - - - - - - - - - - - - - -

[15] Sawyer Alan G., "The Effects of Repetitions: Conclusions and Suggestions About Experimental Laboratory Research," in G. David Hughes and Michael L. Ray (eds.). Buyer/Consumer Information Processing, The University of North Carolina Press. Chapel Hill, 1974

Table 8.2
Recall of social advertisements shown repeatedly in unaided category

Sr. No.	Social advertisements shown repeatedly	Recall	% recall
1	Sex education for youth	124	**86.11**
2	Female feticide	120	**83.33**
3	Don't talk on mobile phone while driving	76	**52.78**
4	Be proud of yourself	17	**11.81**

Source: Compiled from primary data.

Graph 8.1
Recall of social advertisements shown repeatedly in unaided category

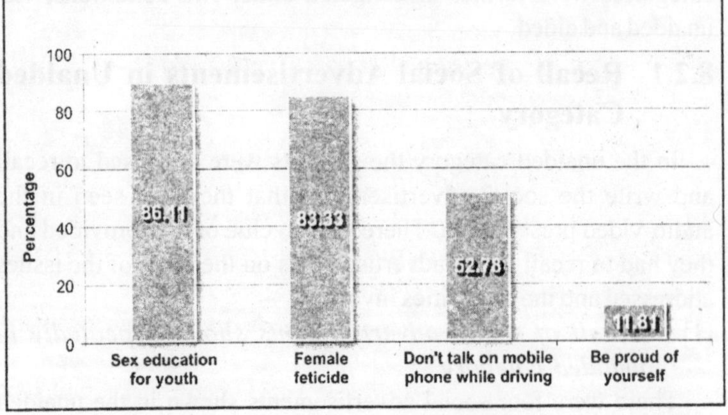

There were four social advertisements shown repeatedly as shown in Table 8.2 and Graph 8.1. The social advertisement on sex education for youth had the highest recall in this category with 124 subjects (86.11 per cent) closely followed by the advertisement on female feticide which had a recall from 120 subjects (83.33 per cent). The social advertisements on 'don't talk on mobile phone while driving' had a recall from 76 subjects (52.78 per cent) and the advertisement on 'be proud of yourself' registered the lowest recall from 17 subjects (11.81 per cent).

[2] *Recall of social advertisements shown only once in unaided category*

There were four social advertisements shown in the unaided category. These social advertisements were not repeated. The responses to these social advertisements when analysed the result was as follows:

Table 8.3
Recall of social advertisements shown only once in unaided category

Sr. No.	Social advertisements shown only once	Recall	% recall
1	Anti tobacco	110	**76.39**
2	Don't drink and drive	46	**31.94**
3	Spend time with elderly	19	**13.19**
4	Awareness against eve-teasing	7	**4.86**

Source: Compiled from primary data.

Graph 8.2
Recall of social advertisements shown only once in unaided category

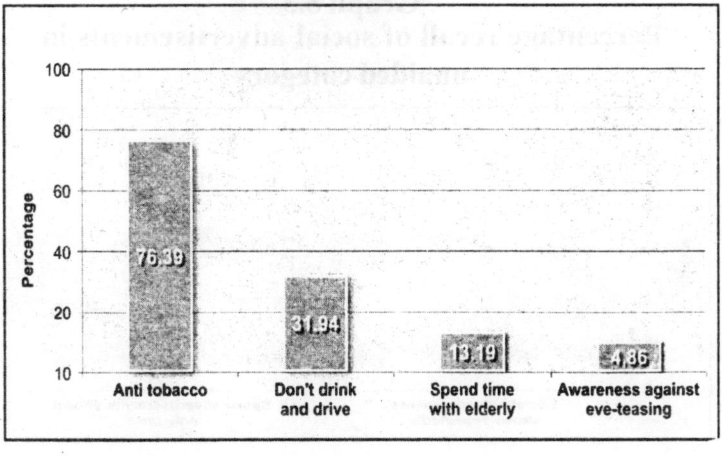

As indicated in Table 8.3 and Graph 8.2, among the social advertisements shown only once, the anti tobacco advertisement recorded the highest recall from 110 subjects (76.39 per cent) followed by 'don't drink and drive' advertisement which had a recall of 46 subjects (31.94 per cent). The advertisement 'spend time with elderly' registered a recall from 19 subjects (13.19 per cent) and the advertisement 'awareness against eve-teasing' had the lowest recall from only 7 subjects (4.86 per cent).

[3] *Comparison between recall of repeatedly shown social advertisements and social advertisements shown only once in unaided category*

The recall of social advertisements shown repeatedly was compared with recall of social advertisements shown only once in the audio-video presentation in the unaided category to analyse the impact of repetition on recall. The result of the comparison was as follows:

Table 8.4
Recall of social advertisements in unaided category

Sr. No.	Particulars	Total recall	% recall
1	Social advertisements shown repeatedly	337	**58.51**
2	Social advertisements shown only once	182	**31.60**

Source: Compiled from primary data.

Graph 8.3
Percentage recall of social advertisements in unaided category

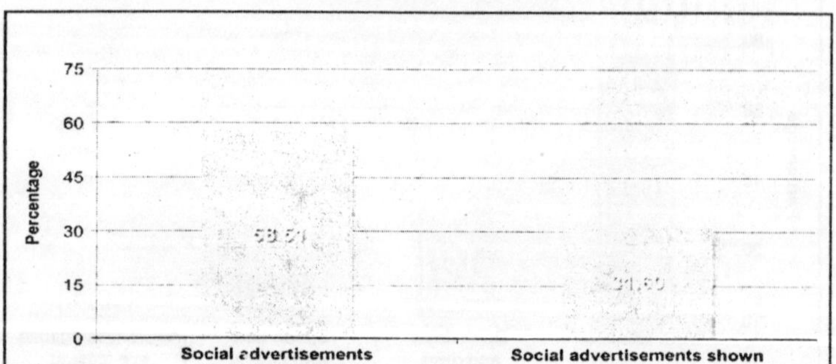

As revealed in Table 8.4 and Graph 8.3, when the recall of social advertisements shown repeatedly were compared with recall of social advertisements shown only once in the audio-video presentation in the unaided category it was found that the overall recall of social advertisements shown repeatedly was higher (58.51 per cent) than that for the social advertisements shown only once (31.60 per cent). The z-test revealed a significant difference ($z = 9.53$), $p < 0.001$.

[4] *Paired sample T-test of recall in unaided category*

The paired sample T-test compared mean recall of social advertisements shown repeatedly and shown only once in unaided category.

Table 8.5
Paired sample T-test of recall in unaided category

Sr. No.	Paired sample	Mean	Df	Standard deviation	T
1	Recall of social advertisements shown repeatedly	4.68	143	1.708	10.97
2	Recall of social advertisements shown only once	2.53	143	1.551	

Source: Compiled from primary data.

* $p < 0.000$.

Graph 8.4
Mean scores of recall of social advertisements in unaided category

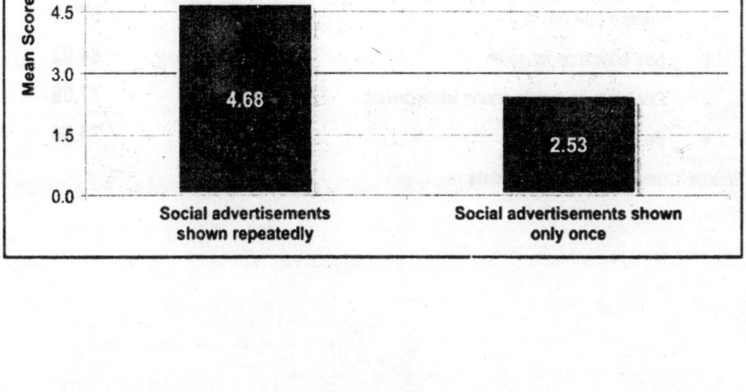

The paired sample T-test comparing mean recall of social advertisements shown repeatedly and shown only once in unaided category showed a significant difference as indicated in Table 8.5 and Graph 8.4, (t = 10.973) at a probability < 0.000. The mean recall of the social advertisements shown repeatedly (m = 4.68) was higher than the mean recall of social advertisements shown only once with (m = 2.53) in unaided category.

8.2.2 Recall of Social Advertisements in Aided Category

In the aided category the subjects were supposed to recall the social advertisements with the help of some clues provided in the questionnaire for easy recall.

[1] *Recall of social advertisements shown repeatedly in aided category*

The responses to social advertisements shown repeatedly were analysed and result was as follows:

Table 8.6

Recall of social advertisements shown repeatedly in aided category

Sr. No.	Social advertisements shown repeatedly	Recall	% recall
1	Female feticide	253	**87.85**
2	Sex education for youth	242	**84.03**
3	Don't talk on mobile phone while driving	222	**77.08**
4	Be proud of yourself	218	**75.69**

Source: Compiled from primary data.

Graph 8.5
Recall of social advertisements shown repeatedly in aided category

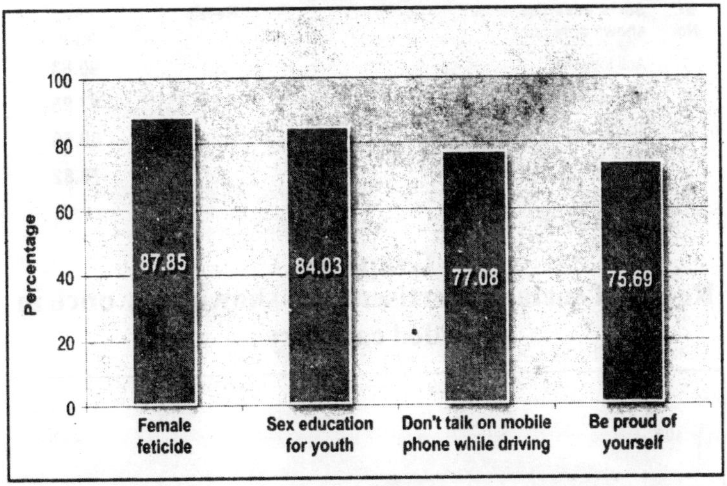

The responses as revealed by Table 8.6 and Graph 8.5, indicated that social advertisements on female feticide had the highest recall in this category with 253 (87.85 per cent) followed by the advertisement on sex education for youth which had a recall of 242 (84.03 per cent). Advertisement 'don't talk on mobile phone while driving' had a recall of 222 (77.08 per cent) and the advertisement 'Be proud of yourself' registered the lowest recall of 218 (75.69 per cent).

[2] *Recall of social advertisements shown only once in aided category*

In the aided category, the responses to social advertisements shown only once were analysed and result was as follows:

Table 8.7
Recall of social advertisements shown only once in aided category

Sr. No.	Social advertisements shown only once	Recall	% recall
1	Anti tobacco	261	90.63
2	Spend time with elderly	253	87.85
3	Awareness against eve-teasing	232	80.56
4	Don't drink and drive	227	78.82

Source: Compiled from primary data.

Graph 8.6
Recall of social advertisements shown only once in aided category

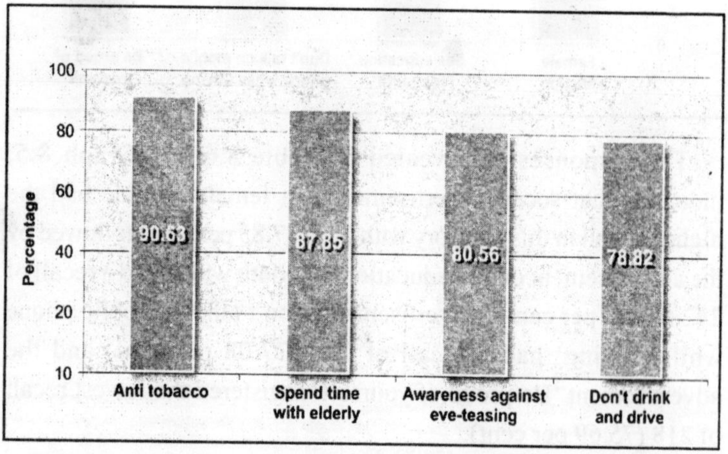

Table 8.7 and Graph 8.6 revealed that in the aided category, within the social advertisements shown only once category, the anti tobacco advertisement recorded the highest recall of 261 (90.63 per cent) closely followed by 'spend time with elderly' which had a recall of 253 (87.85 per cent). The advertisement 'awareness against eve-teasing' registered a recall of 232 (80.56 per cent) and

advertisement 'don't drink and drive' registered a recall of 227 (78.82 per cent).

[3] *Comparison between recall of social advertisements shown repeatedly and social advertisements shown only once in aided category*

The recall of social advertisements shown repeatedly were compared with recall of social advertisements shown only once in the audio-video presentation in the aided category. The result was as follows:

Table 8.8
Recall of social advertisements in aided category

Sr. No.	Particulars	Total recall	% recall
1	Social advertisements shown repeatedly	935	**81.16**
2	Social advertisements shown only once	973	**84.46**

Source: Compiled from primary data.

Graph 8.7
Percentage recall of social advertisements in aided category

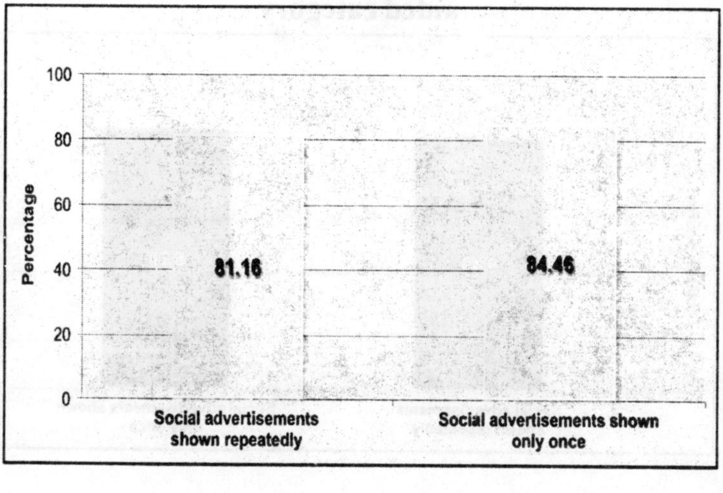

When the recall of social advertisements shown repeatedly were compared with recall of social advertisements shown only once in the audio-video presentation in the aided category as indicated in Table 8.8 and Graph 8.7, it was found that the overall recall of social advertisements shown repeatedly was lower (81.16 per cent) than that for the social advertisements shown only once (84.46 per cent). The z-test revealed a difference at lower significance ($z = 2.20$), $p < 0.05$.

[4] *Paired sample T-test of recall in aided category*

The paired sample T-test compared the mean recall of social advertisements shown repeatedly and shown only once in aided category and the result was as follows:

Table 8.9

Paired sample T-test of recall in aided category

Sr. No.	Paired sample	Mean	Df	Standard deviation	T
1	Recall of social advertisements shown repeatedly	6.49	143	1.177	[illegible]
2	Recall of social advertisements shown only once	6.76	143	1.313	

Source: Compiled from primary data.

* $p < 0.016$.

Graph 8.8

Mean scores of recall of social advertisements in aided category

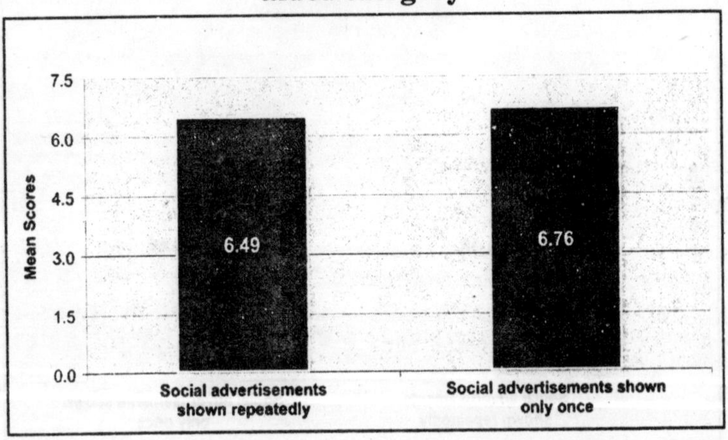

The paired sample T-test comparing mean recall of social advertisements shown repeatedly and shown only once in aided category, as indicated in Table 8.9 and Graph 8.8 did not show any significant difference ($t = 2.444$, at a probability < 0.016). The mean recall of the social advertisements shown repeatedly ($m = 6.49$) was lower than the mean recall of social advertisements shown only once ($m = 6.76$) in aided category.

8.3 Conclusion

In this research study, the impact of repetition as an aid to memory was studied by comparing recall of social advertising shown repeatedly with recall of social advertising shown only once. The social advertisements shown repeatedly were higher on recall compared to social advertisements shown only once in the audio-video presentation. This was reported in the unaided category where the subjects had to recall the social advertisements seen in the presentation on their own without any clues. However in the aided category when the subjects were provided hints to recall the social advertisements the recall of social advertisements shown once was found to be higher than that of social advertisements shown repeatedly though the difference was not significant.

9

Synthesis of the Study of Social Advertising

9.1 Introduction

The final outcome and, hence the value of a research project lies in its findings.[1]The purpose of research itself is not well served unless the findings are made known to others.[2] This chapter presents the conclusions developed on the basis of the data gathered, statistically analysed and interpreted in detail in the earlier chapters. The chapter is categorised into general conclusions and specific conclusions. Since the whole research was divided in five studies the specific conclusions are based on these studies, whereas the general conclusions are concerned with the awareness of social advertising and the general attitude of youth towards social advertising that is being done in India.

9.2 General Conclusions

The conclusions discussed here are derived from the sample's views on different aspects of social advertising.

9.2.1 The findings with respect to recall of social advertisements in India led to a conclusion that subjects were high on awareness as far as social advertising in India was concerned.

- - - - - - - - - - - - - - - - -

[1]Das D. K. Lal, Designs of Social Research, Rawat Publications, Jaipur. 2005, p. 296.

[2] Kothari C. R., Research Methodology Methods and Techniques, 2nd ed., New Age International Publishers, New Delhi, 2004.

The subjects responded with positive recall for all issues presented to them in the general questionnaire indicating high exposure level. The social messages advertised on television and radio were generally higher in recall as compared to the social messages advertised on media such as newspaper and outdoor. The recall was exceptionally high on those social advertisements which enjoyed overall high media coverage. Pulse Polio and AIDS awareness campaigns which are heavily advertised in India were high in recall too.

9.2.2 Recall of celebrities indicated that film personalities were generally well received by the subjects. With reference to celebrities that feature in social advertising in India, the findings indicated that subjects recalled around 75 celebrities from various fields like films, television serials, sports and music. Amitabh Bachchan and Shahrukh Khan the popular film stars were significantly high on recall compared to the other film stars, television actors and sports personalities who have lend their support to the social causes. In fact out of the top ten celebrities recalled seven belonged to film fraternity indicating the immense impact that film stars have on youth. These findings from the general questionnaire correspond to the study specific findings with respect to film based and television based celebrities where too the film based celebrity's recall was higher than the television based celebrities. The subjects not only recalled the names of the celebrities seen in social advertisements but also remembered the slogans of these advertisements.

9.2.3 The subject's opinion on celebrities supporting social issues led to a conclusion that celebrities are an important requisite of social advertising in India and they must be used regularly to persuade the audience. As many as 473 subjects (71.34 per cent) indicated a strong preference towards use of celebrities in social advertising while only 190 subjects (28.66 per cent) had their reservations for using celebrities in social advertising. as per the findings in genral questionnair. The celebrities were effective in spite of the fact that subjects felt celebrity's involvement in social advertising is mainly for monetary reasons. Majority of the subjects felt celebrities were effective because they provide the required publicity to the social issues, whereas a small number of subjects felt they were effective because of their trustworthiness. The subjects who felt celebrities were not effective felt so because celebrities were involved at superficial level only and were not genuinely concerned about the society.

9.2.4 The subjects indicated varying degree of attitudinal change in response to the exposure of social advertisements shown in the audio-video presentation. A considerable number of them gained knowledge and some of them showed willingness to fight for the issues given an opportunity. There were only few subjects (just above two percent) who did not gain anything from the social advertisements, rest all indicated some positive change. Considering the favourable response towards social advertising it can be implied that social advertisement had strong positive influence on the sample.

9.2.5 With regards to social advertisements shown in the audio-video presentation in comparison to the commercial advertisements, most of the subjects found social advertisements to be better than the commercial advertisements. It indicated subjects do not make any comparison between commercial and social advertisements. And if done effectively social advertisements can even score over commercial advertisements.

9.2.6 The findings with respect to the overall social advertising carried in India, suggested that the sample was dissatisfied with it. They felt social advertising must be done more frequently in India and more issues should be covered. The sample suggested number of social issues on which either there was no social advertising in India or which was inadequately done.

9.2.7 The sample's responses in all the five studies was an indication that subjects look up to social advertising as a source of information and therefore according to them information is the most essential element of social advertising which was rated over emotions, straightforwardness, simplicity and even celebrities.

9.2.8 According to the sample, sponsoring social advertising in India is the prime responsibility of the government and its various ministries. Other entities such as media, NGOs and corporate had a limited responsibility with regards to social advertising.

9.2.9 Subjects unanimously felt television was the most effective medium, when asked to suggest most appropriate medium for social advertising. Other media options suggested were films, radio and mobile phones for social advertising in the respective order. Print medium was least effective according to them for social advertising in spite of the fact that almost 74 per cent of the sample read newspapers regularly.

9.2.10 The study of sample's media exposure also indicated that television was the most popular media. Compared to all other electronic or consumer durables such as washing machine, music system and computer, television was the most common product owned by the subjects. Television was owned by almost 93 per cent of the subjects. Majority of the subjects (above 96 per cent) were exposed to television regularly for some time in the day considering the daily viewing habit in terms of number of hours. The viewing pattern on weekdays and weekends did not reveal any major difference, apart from the fact that on weekends subjects watched television in the morning slots too.

9.2.11 The analysis of most preferred television channels indicated that the subjects watched variety of channels from all categories such as music, movies, general entertainment (English and Hindi), sports, informative, news, spiritual and regional. But the most preferred channel was a Hindi news channel 'Aaj Tak' followed by a youth centric music channel 'MTV' which was followed by an informative channel 'Discovery'.

9.2.12 The radio listening habit of the sample indicated, that barring four per cent of the subjects, all of them listened to radio on a daily basis. This indicated that radio is one of the most popular media option among the youth. The popular radio stations were among the FM radio stations and none of the subjects had heard of AM stations. The three most popular radio stations in the order of their preference were Red FM, Radio Mirchi and Big FM.

9.2.13 The newspaper reading habit was prevalent among almost two third of the sample indicating a considerable newspaper exposure among the subjects. The most read newspaper was an English daily The Times of India, followed by English tabloids Mumbai Mirror and Mid Day. The subjects indicated a low readership towards specialised newspapers like The Financial Times or Business Standard that catered to business, economic and financial news. There was a small segment of the sample that read regional newspapers on a regular basis. The high prevalence of newspaper reading habit could be the result of high rate of literacy among the subject's parents.

9.2.14 Magazines were not so popular among the subjects and only one fourth of the sample responded to reading magazines on a regular basis. Women, general and film based magazines were the most popular magazine categories among the subjects.

9.2.15 The popularity of cinema among the subjects was analysed by studying their monthly exposure to cinema in theatres.

The findings indicated tnat two third of the subjects visited theatres on a regular basis in a month, of course the frequency ranged from once a month to even more than once a week for different subjects. The low cinema watching trend in theatres could be either because of availability of many television channels that show latest films or because of general low standard of living of the subjects that they couldn't afford watching cinema in theatres.

9.2.16 Internet surfing was not very popular among the subjects. Around half of the sample did not access Internet or used computer at all. Computer or laptops was not a household product and was owned by only 45 per cent of the sample, this could be probably because of the low standard of living of the sample.

Thus a detail analysis of media exposure and habit based on the responses of the sample of all the five studies indicated that television emerged as the most popular medium with 639 subjects (96.38 per cent) exposed to it, followed by radio with 634 subjects (95.63 per cent). The next popular media option was newspaper with 491 subjects (74.06 per cent) reading it on a regular basis and this was followed by Cinema where 442 subjects (66.67 per cent) regularly watching it in theatres and Internet was accessed by 335 subjects (50.53 per cent). Magazine was the least preferred media option with only 176 subjects (26.55 per cent) reading it regularly. Thus the media exposure and habit of the sample indicated that the most popular media among the youth was television followed by radio, print, cinema and Internet respectively.

9.3 Specific Conclusions

The specific conclusions are based on the five studies conducted in the present research. Each of the studies deal with an independent variable and accordingly the conclusions are derived from the observations and findings of that respective study.

9.3.1 Study One

Study One was an attempt to find out the role of celebrity in social advertising. From the findings of this study following conclusions were deduced:

1. In the unaided category, the recall of the social advertisements with celebrities was higher than social advertisements without celebrities. The overall recall of advertisements with celebrities was higher (61.35 per cent) than that for the advertisements without celebrities (54.08 per cent). The z-test revealed a significant difference ($z = 2.47$), $p < 0.02$. The paired sample T-test comparing mean recall of social advertisements with celebrities and without celebrities showed a significant difference, ($t = 3.105$) at a probability < 0.002. The mean recall of the social advertisements with celebrity ($m = 4.91$) was higher than the mean recall of social advertisements without celebrity ($m = 4.33$). It can be therefore deduced that celebrities have considerable impact on the subjects. The principal findings derived by applying various statistical tools proved that celebrities contribute positively towards social advertising. This could be because the celebrities had generated interest in the advertisement and subjects perhaps remembered the social advertisement only because of the celebrity factor. The findings of this study were consistent with the findings of a study conducted by Murphy Claire in Great Britain[1] that indicated celebrities held a greater appeal for the 15 to 24-year-old age bracket, where 62 percent of that group stated that a famous person in an advertisement would get their

---

[1] Murphy Claire, "Stars Brought Down to Earth in Television Ads Research," Marketing, January 22, 1998, pp. 1.

[2] Atkin Charles and Block Martin, "Effectiveness of Celebrity Endorsers," Journal of Advertising Research 23, February-March, 1983, pp. 57-61.

[3] Keller Kevin L., Strategic Brand Management, 2nd ed., Pearson Education Inc., Delhi, 2007

attention. Another study by Atkins and Block too found that college-age students were more likely to have a positive attitude towards a product endorsed by a celebrity than were older consumers.[2]

2. It was also deduced, in contrast that in the aided category social advertisements without celebrities had higher recall compared to social advertisements with celebrities. The overall recall of the celebrity social advertisements was lower (68.09 per cent) than the social advertisements without celebrities (74.82 per cent). The z-test revealed a difference ($z=2.51$), $p < 0.02$. The paired sample T-test comparing mean recall of social advertisements with celebrities and without celebrities showed a significant difference, ($t = 3.136$) at a probability < 0.002. The mean recall of the social advertisements without celebrities ($m = 2.99$) was higher than the mean recall of social advertisements with celebrities ($m = 2.72$). The difference in the recall of this category however was less significant than the difference in the unaided category. It can be an indication that celebrities were influential only up to generating initial interest, but as far as the content of the message was concerned they could not make any impact. This could be perhaps a result of vampire effect, a peril associated with celebrity endorsement where the celebrity distracts attention from the advertised message such that audience notices or remembers the celebrity but has trouble remembering the message.[3]

3. Among the celebrities featuring in social advertisements that were shown in the audio-video presentation, the recall of celebrities from films was higher compared to the television celebrities. The popularity of film based celebrities such as Ajay Devgan and Shahrukh Khan was higher than the television based celebrities such as Rohit Roy, Manasi Roy and Ehsaan Qureshi. There could be several reasons for this. Firstly film celebrities live larger than life characters in films

and represent an idealisation of life that most people imagine that they would love to live. Film stars are more universal in their appeal compared to the television actors whose life is restricted to the serials in which they feature. The film actors are considered to be stars and therefore more glamorous compared to television actors who generally resemble the target audience through the various characters they portray in their serials. The film stars have a much bigger fan following compared to television actors perhaps because Indian films generally get international exposure whereas the reach of television serials is comparatively restricted. Youngsters exhibit their loyalty towards their favourite celebrities by emulating their dressing style, hairstyle and other attributes as film stars are considered as role models and trendsetters.

4. The findings revealed that number of subjects who felt that celebrities are desirable in social advertising was higher than those subjects who felt celebrities were ineffective in social advertising. The subjects at large felt celebrities play a positive role in influencing target audience through social advertising. The opinion on underlying reasons as to why celebrities make their appearances in social advertising garnered a divided response. The subjects felt either the celebrities are paid for it or because celebrities want to enhance their image. Very few subjects felt that celebrities might be genuinely concerned about the society. In fact though the subjects felt celebrities contribute positively in social advertising none of them actually felt celebrities are trustworthy. The responses to important element in social advertising, also revealed celebrities was a last choice after emotions, informative value, simplicity and entertainment value. When social advertisements were judged on different criteria such as entertaining, informative, genuineness and boring, the response was more for informative value and

genuineness. The celebrities thus were not entertaining at all in social advertising. The responses clearly indicated that the subjects were not smitten by celebrities and chose to apply their brain and not heart when it comes to celebrities. It was also obvious that the subjects were not very keen on seeing celebrities in advertisements or may not be themselves aware about celebrity's effectiveness. But their responses when carefully analysed under different conditions in the study clearly indicated that the recall was higher wherever celebrities were involved compared to non-celebrity social advertisements. So to conclude celebrities are effective as a source in social advertising though the subjects were not aware, at the sub-conscious level the celebrities did influence the recall positively.

9.3.2 Study Two

The objective of Study Two was to find out the role of appeals and particularly the fear appeals on the recall of social advertising among the youth. The findings of the Study Two lead to following conclusions:

1. Fear appeals contribute positively towards recall of social advertising since the recall of the social advertisements with fear appeals was significantly higher than social advertisements without fear appeals in the unaided category. The recall of the advertisements with fear appeals was (62.30 per cent) as compared to the advertisements without fear appeals (54.84 per cent). The z-test revealed a significant difference ($z=2.29$), $p < 0.05$. The findings of the paired sample T-test comparing mean recall of social advertisements witl fear appeals and without fear appeals indicated a significant difference, ($t = 2.970$) at a probability < 0.004. The mean recall of the social advertisements with fear appeals ($m = 4.98$) was higher than the mean recall of social advertisements without fear appeals ($m = 4.39$).

The findings of this study were identical to the findings of a study conducted by Michele Dion[4] where it was found that fear appeal had an influence on the reception of the message by the audience and it plays a role in directing attention to the issue for a target group of young adults.

2. The recall of social advertisements with fear appeals when compared with social advertisements with non-fear appeals it was found that the overall recall of social advertisements with fear appeals was lower (66.53 per cent) than the social advertisements without fear appeals (72.18 per cent). The difference was not significant as z-test revealed a low significant difference ($z=1.87$), $p < 0.10$. The paired sample T-test comparing mean recall of social advertisements with fear appeals and social advertisements without fear appeals in aided category indicated there was no significant difference ($t = 2.295$, probability < 0.023). The mean recall of the social advertisements without fear appeals ($m = 2.89$) was higher than the mean recall of social advertisements with fear appeals ($m = 2.66$).
3. The general attitude of youth towards use of fear or disturbing appeals in social advertising in India was positive. The findings led to a conclusion that most of the subjects found such advertisements to be genuine or partially true but did not find them unreal.
4. The subjects who were addicted to cigarette smoking admitted a positive attitudinal change of either quitting altogether or at least trying to give up smoking after seeing the social advertisements. The subjects, who were not addicted to tobacco, also indicated a positive change. They were keen in motivating their friends or relatives who were

---

[4] Michèle Dion, 'Is Fear Really Persuasive, The Case of Antismoking Advertisement for Young Adults,' Communication Studies, Roskilde University, Spring 2005.

addicted to tobacco, to give up the habit. So to conclude, the immediate reaction of the subjects after the audio-video presentation indicated a significant attitudinal change.

5. The findings also led to a conclusion that fear factor in social advertisements make social advertising effective, since majority of felt fear or disturbing appeals in social advertising can positively influence the target audience and only few of them (21.77 per cent) felt otherwise. However the fear based social advertisements were largely perceived as informative rather than scary or disturbing and were found to be least entertaining.

9.3.3 Study Three

Study Three was aimed at finding out the role of noise / clutter and how it affects the recall of social advertising.

1. The findings indicated that recall of the recall of social advertisements shown exclusively was considerably higher (84.32 per cent) than that for the social advertisements shown amidst commercial advertisements (59.32 per cent) in the unaided category. The z-test revealed a highly significant difference ($z = 8.99$), $p < 0.001$. The paired sample T-test comparing mean recall showed a significant difference, ($t = 9.065$) at a probability < 0.000. The mean recall of the social advertisements shown exclusively ($m = 6.75$) was higher than the mean recall of social advertisements shown with commercial advertisements ($m = 4.75$).

   In the aided category too, the recall of social advertisements shown exclusively was higher (96.93 per cent) than that for the social advertisements shown amidst commercial advertisements (87.29 per cent). The z-test revealed a highly significant difference ($z = 8.07$), $p < 0.001$. The paired sample T-test comparing mean recall of social advertisements shown exclusively and shown with commercial advertisements showed a significant difference, ($t = 8.456$) at a probability < 0.000. The mean recall of the social advertisements shown exclusively (m = 7.75) was higher than the mean recall of social advertisements shown with commercial advertisements (m = 6.98). This was an indication that noise /clutter negatively influences social advertising as far as the recall of social advertising is concerned.

The findings of this study where the clutter affected the recall negatively are consistent with the findings of research by Webb Peter and Ray Michael[5] that had concluded that higher levels of clutter hurt the performance of individual advertisements - the more the clutter, the lower are average levels of advertisement recall.

9.3.4 Study Four

The objective of Study Four was to find out the effect of audio-video medium like television in comparison to non-audio-video advertising medium like posters for social advertising.

1. The recall of social advertisements shown on television were compared with recall of social advertisements shown on posters in the unaided category and it was found that the overall recall of social advertisements presented on television was higher (46.51 per cent) than that for the social advertisements shown through posters (36.40 per cent). The z-test revealed a significant difference (z = 3.41), $p < 0.001$.The paired sample T-test comparing mean recall of social advertisements presented on television and shown through posters in unaided category showed a significant difference, (t = 3.447) at a probability < 0.001. The mean recall of the social advertisements presented on television (m = 3.72) was higher than the mean recall of social advertisements shown through posters (m = 2.91).

In the aided category too the recall of social advertisements presented on television were compared with recall of social advertisements shown through posters and it was found that the

[5] Webb Pe-ter H. and Ray Michael L., "Effects of TV Clutter," Journal of Advertising Research, 19 June 1979, pp. 7-12.

overall recall of television social advertisements was higher (84.47 per cent) than that for the social advertisements shown on posters (73.07 per cent). The z-test revealed a highly significant difference ($z = 6.59$), $p < 0.001$. The paired sample T-test comparing mean recall of social advertisements presented on television and shown through posters showed a difference, ($t = 6.652$) at a probability < 0.000. The mean recall of the television social advertisements ($m = 6.76$) was higher than the mean recall of poster social advertisements ($m = 5.85$).

A significantly high recall in the aided as well as the unaided category indicated that the audio-video medium is more powerful compared to non audio-video medium. To conclude television contributes positively to the recall compared to a non-audio-video medium like posters.

Similar results where television advertising appeared to be more effective than print advertising were found in a study conducted by Krugman.[6] In a study comparing consumer thoughts in response to television advertisements versus print advertisements, Krugman[7] observed that despite their apparent inability to communicate much information, television advertisements appeared to increase brand preference. Krugman concluded that the findings were a result of repetition rather than television's audio-video ability over print medium, yet it cannot be denied that the option of repetition was available in print too but still television advertising seem to have a better impact compared to print.

9.3.5 Study Five

Study Five was aimed at finding how repeatedly shown social advertisements affect the recall of social advertising. The study was an attempt to analyse the impact of repetition as an aid to memory in social advertising.

---

[6] Krugman H. E., "The Impact of Television Advertising: Learning Without Involvement," Public Opinion Quarterly, 29, 1965, pp. 353.

[7] *Ibid.*

1 When the recall of social advertisements shown repeatedly were compared with recall of social advertisements shown only once in the audio-video presentation it was found that the overall recall of social advertisements shown repeatedly was higher (58.51 per cent) than that for the social advertisements shown only once (31.60 per cent). The z-test revealed a significant difference ($z = 9.53$), $p < 0.001$. The paired sample T-test comparing mean recall of social advertisements shown repeatedly and shown only once showed a significant difference, ($t = 10.973$) at a probability < 0.000. The mean recall of the social advertisements shown repeatedly ($m = 4.68$) was higher than the mean recall of social advertisements shown only once with ($m = 2.53$). This was an indication that repetition aids memory and contributes positively towards recall.

A similar conclusion was derived by Ray Michael and colleagues in a series of repetition studies done at Stanford University in the early 1970s.[8] However their studies indicated that repetition works when the products involved were of low risk and when the advertisements involved were television advertisements. The advertisements appeared to lead to product trial sim-ply because of greater top-of-mind awareness; this trial then led to attitude change.

When the recall of social advertisements shown repeatedly were compared with recall of social advertisements shown only once in the audio-video presentation in the aided category it was found that the overall recall of social advertisements shown repeatedly was lower (81.16 per cent) than that for the social advertisements shown only once (84.46 per cent). The z-test revealed a difference at lower significance ($z = 2.20$), $p < 0.05$. The paired sample T-test comparing mean recall of social advertisements shown repeatedly

---

[8] Ray Michael L. et al., "Marketing Communications and the Hierarchy of Effects," in P. Clarke (ed.), New Models for Communications Research, Sage Publications, Beverly Hills, CA, 1973

and shown only once did not show any significant difference ($t = 2.444$, $p < 0.016$). The mean recall of the social advertisements shown repeatedly ($m = 6.49$) was lower than the mean recall of social advertisements shown only once ($m = 6.76$). Though the recall of social advertisements not repeated in the aided category was higher than the social advertisements repeatedly presented the difference was not significant. Thus it can be concluded that social advertisements repeatedly presented positively contribute towards recall.

9.2 Conclusion

This chapter presented the conclusions deduced by the researcher on the basis of the collected data and its interpretation. The specific conclusions exclusively dealt with the five studies conducted. The general conclusions dealt with awareness of social advertising and the general attitude of youth towards social advertising that is being done in India. The conclusions of the youth's media habits and media exposure were also presented to facilitate effective media planning and scheduling for targeting youth.

10
Suggestions and Recommendations

10.1 Introduction

This chapter presents the suggestions and recommendations that the authors have developed on the basis of the findings and its interpretations. The chapter has five major modules namely, general suggestions, specific suggestions, general recommendations, specific suggestions and scope for future research. The entire research was conducted, arranged and presented on the basis of five separate studies. To maintain this order the specific suggestions and specific recommendations are also presented study wise.

10.2 General Suggestions

10.2.1 The first and the most important finding of the study with reference to social advertising is that the social advertising does not go unnoticed - it is seen, recalled and liked. The overall response of the subjects towards social advertising which was more than fifty per cent in all the four categories viz. aided-celebrity, aided non-celebrity, unaided celebrity and unaided non-celebrity, indicated that social advertising was recalled. The impact of the social advertisements was not limited to the recall since some of the social issues shown in the presentation were also influential in bringing some attitudinal change. Barring a negligible number of subjects who were indifferent, most of them were keen in knowing more about some of the issues or were willing to lend their support towards the social causes. Even in the general questionnaire when subjects were asked to recall social advertising that they have heard or seen earlier, they recalled many social advertisements which are run regularly in India. Not only they remembered the general ideas behind these social advertisements but also recalled the slogans and the celebrities that were a part of it. This indicates that social advertising is noticed and remembered. So definitely for youth social advertising works and therefore it is strongly suggested, social advertising must be done regularly.

10.2.2 During the research it was found that, youth was looking up to social advertising as a source of information and they consider social advertising as genuine. The subjects believed that the most important element of social advertising was information. In fact for youth the informative value of social advertising scored over use of celebrities and humour. Therefore any social advertising must be informative. In India there are hardly any authentic sources available to youth or children that provide information and guidance on various matters crucial to them. Many developed countries have health centers and NGOs that disseminate information via their centers at different locations, help-lines and websites. Such effort is missing in India in general and in fact social advertising can fill in this gap to some extent.

10.3 Specific Suggestions

10.3.1 Study One

The findings clearly support the use of celebrities for social advertising. Celebrities are instrumental in bringing the social issues to forefront. Celebrities ensure the social issues get due publicity. The celebrities are influential in motivating the youth towards the desired aim. Therefore while conducting social advertising it is suggested that celebrities must be prominently used.

Several specific suggestions with reference to use of celebrities in social advertising are as follows:

a) Celebrities selected must be popular and preferably be belonging to films. The findings indicated that celebrities from films are much better remembered than celebrities from television.

b) The credibility of a celebrity is an important factor to look out for while selecting a celebrity. Credibility of the presenter is an important determinant of the acceptance of the advertised message. Also credible sources are more persuasive. If some event happens that affects the reputation of the celebrity, the negative publicity could backfire on the associated social issue as well. Though the behaviour of the celebrity cannot be predicted at least past performance can be an indicator while selecting a celebrity for social advertising.

c) Overly exposed celebrity, specially the one doing multiple social advertisements must be avoided. A single celebrity addressing too many social issues can lead to a fair degree of confusion among the audience and little room for credibility.

d) It is equally important that there is an appropriate fit between the celebrity and the target audience. The celebrities that can be influential for social advertising directed at youth may not be equally persuasive while advertising for elderly. So while selecting celebrity the target audience's preferences must be considered for greater impact.

10.3.2 Study Two

Fear appeals are designed to stir up some negative emotions. Further these aroused emotions are those mental agitations or excited states of feelings which actually motivate interest and prompt the audience to behave in the desired manner. Therefore fear appeals can be effectively used in social advertising to bring about the preferred change. However while using fear appeals in social advertising certain suggestions are worth considering:

a) An advertisement in which the level of fear is too low will not generate the necessary emotional response, thereby failing to create attention and interest in the basic problem.. High fear appeals also tend to yield little attitude change because they activate defense mechanisms. Therefore moderate fear appeals, which provide sufficient motivation but do not activate perceptual defenses, can be used for generating attitudinal change.

b) It is often noticed consumers counter argue to protect themselves from fear generating advertising messages. However this can be avoided if the source used in the advertisement is highly credible, one such that he/she can influence audience attitudes. This will ensure that the consumers refrain from counter arguing.

c) The audience for whom the advertising message is designed has to be properly known since the audience's characteristic determines the degree to which they will be persuaded by fear appeals. For example fear appeals are more effective when the message recipient is self-confident and prefers to cope with dangers rather than avoid them.

d) There is some evidence suggesting that fear of social disapproval may be more effective in influencing actual behaviour than the fear of physical harm. So social advertising exploiting fear appeals must try to focus on social ramifications that the audience may have to suffer in case they do not accept the advertised proposition.

e) Fear appeals are effective when the advertisement provides information about the seriousness of the threat, suggest the probability of its occurrence and advise practical steps to avoid the fearful consequences in the advertisement.

Messages not suggesting a solution to the audience are less likely to be persuasive.

10.3.3 Study Three

Since noise affects the receipt, attention and recall of social advertising it is suggested that social advertisements have to be treated differently to avoid the impact of clutter. Various ways to minimise the impact of clutter can be used such as:

a) Designing exclusive breaks on television and radio between programmes that are fully dedicated to social advertising. This would avoid the chances of social advertisements losing in the clutter of general advertising in the commercial breaks. Also it`is important the breaks meant for social advertising should not have too many social advertisements because that would again lead to clutter. Similarly in print media, full page can be exclusively used for social advertisements so that it is not disturbed by other commercial advertisements.

b) Research shows that the effects of increased clutter do not affect all advertisements equally. Advertisements placed either at the beginning or at the end of a commercial break are less affected than the advertisements in the middle of such breaks. This suggests that social advertisers ought to negotiate the first or last position in a commercial break.

c) One more way to zap-proof television advertisements is to produce creative advertising messages that will attract and hold viewers' attention. When the commercials are interesting as well as entertaining viewers will prefer to watch them rather than zap or zip them. Research shows that zapping tends to occur most strongly during the first five seconds of an advertisement, so it is crucial to sustain the consumer's interest during these first few seconds.

10.3.4 Study Four

The recall of advertising presented on audio-video medium such as television was higher than non-audio-video medium such as posters. Therefore it is suggested that social advertisers must dedicate more of their advertising budget for audio-video media option such as television. The impact of sight, sound and motion definitely commands better recall compared to the other media options where all of the features of television are not available. Television can be best suited for almost all type of advertisements; be it providing demonstrations, featuring testimonials and celebrities or creating drama. The radio, print and outdoor can be considered for playing the role of supportive media. There are several other audio-video media options that can be effectively used, such as:

a) Mobile phones are an interesting advertising media option for the advertisers, at one end they can be seen as an extension of mass medium such as radio as they are usually loaded with radio connectivity. Secondly mobile phones are extremely selective advertising medium where the advertiser can decide to exactly whom to reach out in terms of demographics as well as geographic location. Thirdly mobile phones especially the high end ones are enabled with audio-video facility and provide almost all other amenities of a computer.

b) Similarly social advertisers can make use of computers. Creating their websites on Internet and having all related information available on it is one effective way of reaching, at least to the educated and urban audience. Internet can provide all benefits of an audio-video medium such as television and further provide advantages of interactivity and round the clock exposure. Internet can also render additional benefits that television does not provide, for e.g. target audience can get their queries sorted by securing their anonymity. One more advantage of computers over television is that it is not intrusive like television and target audience can choose to be exposed to the advertising message on their own at their convenience.

c) Films present one more effective audio-video option for social advertising. Cinema has unique characteristics that set it apart from other forms such as television and radio, where the viewer has the opportunity to avoid advertisements in myriad of ways. However, the cinema prevents this ease of avoidance due to the viewing context of the advertisement. There are two film related advertising options. One is targeting the audience going to watch cinema in theatres by presenting social advertising either before the movie begins or in the intervals. Second is more effective where social advertisements are a part of the movie itself. This type of commercial advertising promoted through films is called as product placement. Similar concept can be used to promote social issues, where the characters from the films promote some social cause as if it is a part of the film.

10.1.1 Study Five

Study five indicated social advertisements presented repeatedly contribute positively towards the recall of social advertising. It is important that social advertisements are repeated over the same media for better recall. To ensure that the audience is involved and they connect with the messages presented in social advertising, frequent and adequate repetitions of the messages are very crucial.

Though research is inconclusive about exact number of repetitions for attitudinal change, in general minimum three and maximum ten repetitions have been suggested to avoid the wear out effect by different researchers. However buying slot on television or radio does not guarantee that the target audience is definitely going to be exposed to the advertised messages. Issues such as clutter, zipping and zapping are further multiplied due to availability of variety of television channels or radio stations that narrow down the chances of reaching a specific audience. So it is suggested that advertisers repeat the messages sufficient times.

Mere repetition may not always work so the same messages can be presented by emphasising on the principle of variability theory. This theory suggests that variable encoding occurs when the audience sees the same advertisement in different environments. These varied environments increase an advertisement's recall and effectiveness by encoding it into the brain through various methods.

10.2 General Recommendations

10.2.1 There are several recommendations for the government that's supposed to be the prime social advertiser in India:

a) It has been noticed that the Government in India is using advertising as a strategy just around the time of the elections to enhance their image. The supposed to be social advertisements are more of political advertisements highlighting the achievements of the government in power and their ministries. So it is recommended the funds allocated for social advertising be distinctly used for social advertising only.

b) Its observed that in India social advertisements focus on limited issues. A developing country like India is confronted with many serious and pressing issues which need immediate attention and action. Issues such as eve-teasing, dowry deaths, female feticide, increasing instances of drug and cigarette addiction, ragging, domestic violence and rash and drunken driving to name the few are barely advertised. Not that these issues could be tackled only through social campaigns, but social advertising can bring to light many aspects pertaining to these issues and at least lead to social consciousness. Such advertising can bring about public awareness with respect to legal protection available for the victims (in case of domestic violence or ragging), medical aid for the patients (in case of tuberculosis, leprosy), assistance available from NGOs and so on.

c) Governments are also recommended to pump in adequate funds for social advertising. The funds can be used for various purposes such as to sponsor social research, book different media options and rope-in popular celebrities in social advertisements. Adequate funds would make possible for social advertisements to be aired during prime time slots or to be published in best of the publications thereby leading to better reach and overall impact of social advertising.

d) The governments are recommended to create an environment conducive for successful social campaigns. With this regard three conditions laid down by Lazarsfield and Merton[1] for the effectiveness of mass media for propaganda purposes are worth considering. The first condition is real or psychological monopolisation by the media; that is a condition marked by the absence of counterpropaganda. The second condition required for effective mass propaganda is canalisation, the presence of an existing attitudinal base for the feelings that the social communicators are striving to shape. The third condition is supplementation by which they mean the effort to follow up mass communication campaigns with programs of face to face contacts. Many a time social campaigns fail because social advertising is practiced rather than social marketing. The inherent difference between the two is that a social advertising approach contrives only the event of mass media communication and leaves the response to natural social processes. Social marketing however arranges for a step-down communication process. The message is passed on and discussed in more familiar surroundings to increase its memorability, penetration and action consequences.

10.2.2 The responsibility of social welfare primarily lies on the government but media can also contribute in multiple ways such as:

a) Media can provide free spaces or slots for promoting social advertisements to various social advertisers. If free slots are not possible during prime time slots, at least a special rate card can be devised for social advertisements.

b) Many media owners have established their own award functions to recognise the work that's been done on their media. Such award functions can also recognise the efforts of different social advertisers by way of felicitations or rewards for their worthwhile contributions.

c) Media can also acquire the role of social advertisers. In India television channel Aaj Tak promoted the issue of second hand smoke and eve-teasing, DNA an English newspaper addressed the issue of terrorism and radio station Radio Mirchi addressed the issues of piracy and car pooling. The other media can also take a clue and support social issues they identify with.

d) Media can run such movies and serials that address social issues. To motivate the producers such serials can be given some preferential treatments in terms of rates, timing or slots.

10.2.3 Similarly advertising agencies over the years have taken a sort of liking for social advertising. Social advertising gives them opportunity to work freehand, something which is difficult while working for commercial products. Secondly social advertising has been their ticket to fame. At the various international award functions Indian advertising agencies have made their presence felt mainly by riding on social advertising. But serious effort to fight for the issues has been missing. So it is recommended advertising agencies contribute by way of creative services at subsidised fees or no fees. Secondly the advertising agencies should ensure the issues they are advertising for, gets its due publicity not just by way of entry to award functions but by reaching to the intended audience. The advertising agencies should ensure social advertising is given professional treatment just as commercial advertising in terms of research, understanding of target audience, setting advertising objectives and decisions in relation to message tones. Appropriate media planning and scheduling based on understanding of media trends and target audience are as much needed in social advertising as in the case of commercial advertising. Conducting proper pre-testing to ensure the message has potentials to meet the pre determined goals and post testing to ascertain the fate of the advertising campaign is extremely vital. In brief social advertising must be treated on par with commercial advertising or perhaps be given more importance due to its noble cause.

10.2.4 In India social advertising is sponsored by various product manufacturers and service providers. Such social advertising serves dual purpose for the sponsoring organisations, they can contribute towards welfare of the society on one hand and ensure positive image for themselves on the other. As far as the positive image is concerned the motive is justified, but different advertisers latching on to the social idea to sell their wares has gathered momentum in recent times. Some advertisers have merged social idea with their products; some have taken the cause marketing route while some have used social advertising to break the clutter. Companies sponsoring social advertising with a genuine welfare motive are scarcely noticed. Rather than just using a social idea for advertising, the companies can get into more sustained efforts for public good by associating with NGOs / social organisations or even by starting their own social endeavour. Number of companies such as Wipro, Tata, Infosys, Reliance and National Thermal Power Corporation (NTPC) are setting good examples in India. ONGC and IOCL nave seriously engaged with NGOs on various causes and TCS runs a program, Adult Literacy Programme in association with central and state governments. Wipro's Azim Foundation and Infosys' Infosys Foundation are dedicated philanthropic wings of these companies which fulfils their social responsibility. Perhaps such efforts are expected from more and more companies where social advertising can be a part of their social commitment.

10.2.5 It is also recommended that celebrities contribute their services for social advertising. The celebrities are however expected to standby single or few social issues for which they genuinely care for. Their half-hearted support to every second social issue for enhancing their own image is not likely to yield any positive response. The celebrities are also recommended to play a responsible role in their personal and professional life since they are considered role models and their behaviour has influence on their followers. For e.g. a celebrity himself a smoker in public cannot preach others to quit smoking.

10.2.6 Film makers and producers have been addressing social issues through films and documentaries. Many films have been agents of social change in the past. The trend is seen even in recent times. Many Indian films and documentaries based on social issues have been recognised for their efforts at national and international film festivals. But the problem with such social movies is that they don't get the desired response as they don't reach their target audience. If companies and media support such endeavours in terms of sponsored screenings for schools and colleges or advertising to create awareness about them perhaps they will serve their purpose. So it is recommended, considering the significance of films as an advertising canvas, more film makers conduct research on social issues, make films on them and ensure that they reach the intended audience.

10.3 Specific Recommendations

10.3.1 The social advertisers are recommended to be cautious while using celebrities in social advertisements. It has to be noted celebrities can be effective in social advertising but their involvement has to be limited up to garnering initial attention or while propagating a new issue. While bringing up any considerable change among its public, social advertisements must use experts from relevant field. Though celebrities give the necessary hype to the social issues, the youth/subjects do not consider them as experts in such fields. The motive behind the celebrities supporting social causes was seen with a scanner and there was certain amount of suspicion or doubt about their motive. So to deal with this issue a celebrity as well as some experts from the relevant field can be used for best results. For e.g. celebrities can be used for appealing to youth to quit smoking. However while promoting this cause one of the issues may be how to handle the physical side effects of quitting and this can be addressed through advertisements featuring medical expert rather than celebrity.

10.3.2 Findings of the Study Two strongly recommend use of fear appeals. Fear is an emotional response to some actual or perceived threat or danger and fear appeals in advertising are included to increase the viewer's interest in an advertisement and enhance the persuasiveness of the advertisement. However fear appeals are successful in certain situations only and they can motivate the audience to take action in order to remove fear only when used judiciously. Therefore it is recommended that while using fear appeals proper research is conducted for determining appropriate degree of fear appeal, as too moderate or too intense fear appeal both can be ineffective.

10.3.3 The findings of Study Three that dealt with conduct of social advertising revealed that though television is an effective medium it suffers from problem of clutter. To tackle the problem of clutter one of the options available with private television channels and radio stations is that they can embed their serials or programmes with social messages, something what Doordarshan has been doing regularly. They can introduce such programmes where the panel of experts is available to give authentic issue related information along with help-lines where people can write or call up and get their queries sorted out. Similarly popular shows can also include social information in their programmes, especially if the audience's favourite characters can deliver social messages it can certainly make an impact. It could be called 'message placement,' the philanthropic corollary to product placements deals in which marketers pay to feature products in shows and movies. This practice is not new in foreign countries and officials who have used these methods say they had been effective in influencing public views and behaviour. There is a lot of research supporting the view that when a character from a popular show flaunts a social message it is much more effective than other advertising options such as pamphlets or posters. Many television channels in India are noticed doing this in recent times where the entire serial is woven around social issue/s. For e.g. channel Colors has a serial 'Baalika Vadhu' based on women issues in general and deals with child marriage in particular. Other channels like Star and Zee also address issues like dowry deaths, discrimination of girl child and female feticide through their serials. Many regional channels too address issues pertinent in their states through such shows. All these efforts can render several benefits. First the social issues can get the much needed publicity; it can initiate a public debate. Secondly such dedicated serials would not suffer from the problem of clutter and there would be unaffected flow of information. Lastly such shows can influence viewers even without the viewer's knowledge. However this form of social advertising to deliver best results requires a proper partnership between media and the social organisations working on the issue. Such partnership would ensure that necessary and accurate information passes through the shows. The writers of the show and the experts from the social organisations have to insert messages into the shows to influence the public attitude in such a manner that neither the entertainment value nor the accuracy of the information is compromised.

10.3.4 The findings of Study Four indicated that audio-video medium such as television is more effective than non-audio-video medium. Popularity of television among the subjects calls for more and more use of audio-video medium. But only using television might not be enough so additional visibility can be lend by posters and banners or other means of outdoor advertising. Similarly radio and cinema can provide additional reminder value. In short detail information can be projected on television and brief references can be made through other media options.

10.3.5 Study Five revealed that repetition plays an important role in the reach and success of social advertising. So it is very essential that social advertising messages are adequately repeated and that too on variety of media options.

Thus all parties connected with initiating, creating and propagating social advertising are expected to promote it with more sustained and dedicated efforts. It is recommended that sponsors like government and corporate allocate funds generously. Media can allot more and exclusive spaces and slots for social advertising. From advertising agencies not only creativity in making social advertisement but also professionalism in determining advertising objective, setting advertising budget, using message tones, media planning and use of appropriate pre and post advertising research techniques is highly recommended. Celebrities are expected to support social causes with commitment and film makers are recommended to bring social issues to fore and generate public awareness. Thus to ensure it produces positive results social advertising needs to be able to ignite a social debate and provide solution for general welfare. This will happen when the environment is conducive, which needs an active contribution from all quarters of the society such as policy makers, media, companies, social organisations and every one else who has the power to contribute in some way to the society.

10.1 Scope for Future Research

The present study was an attempt to evaluate the effectiveness of factors that affect or contribute to the success of social advertising. Various variables were evaluated in this research like celebrities, appeals, clutter, media used for social advertising and repetition. These variables contribute in a major way to the success or failure of social advertising. The present research was divided in five studies to investigate the role of these five variables individually and the research has satisfactorily proved that study of these factors is important for developing meaningful social advertisements.

The findings of the first study based on content related factor such as use of celebrities in social advertising revealed that celebrities in social advertising leads to enhanced recall. Celebrities are an important element of advertising and research in past has also indicated that they are influential on their target audience. But the present study concentrated on whether celebrities made a contribution or not when celebrity based social advertisements were compared to social advertisements without celebrities. However there is tremendous scope for research in this area where several aspects of celebrity in social advertising such as attributes on which to select celebrity, celebrity-audience match and issues that can be effectively addressed through celebrities can be further investigated.

The second study was based on use of fear appeals in social advertising. The findings indicated that social advertisements with fear appeals were more effective than social advertisements without fear appeals as far as the recall is concerned. For fear appeals to be effective in social advertising understanding of several other factors such as level of fear appeal, how fear operates and how different target audiences may respond to varying fear appeals is extremely crucial. But considering the scope of the study incorporating all these aspects of fear appeals was difficult and there is tremendous scope for future research in these areas. Apart from fear appeals, appeals based on humour, shock and sex can also be used in social advertising depending upon the cause in question. Effectiveness of such appeals other than fear offer scope for further research.

The third study dealt with the negative impact of clutter on the recall. The findings indicated that clutter affects the reception of the message. However the impact of clutter was studied only with reference to television. Research can be further conducted to investigate whether clutter affects other media such as radio, newspaper, magazine, films and Internet and if it does then to what extent. Similarly there is scope for research on ways and means that can reduce the impact of clutter.

The findings of the fourth study based on effectiveness of audio-video medium in comparison to non-audio-video medium indicated that television advertising was more influential in terms of recall. This study compared only two media namely television and posters, other media such as radio, cinema and newspaper that are popular with youth can be extensively studied for their effectiveness for advertising social messages. There is ample scope for research with respect to effectiveness of modern media options such as Internet and mobile phones in terms of impact and reach while targeting youth.

Fifth study determined the positive impact of repetition on the recall with particular reference to television advertising. Repetition proved to be an aid to memory. Research with reference to repetition can further investigate in to adequate number of repetitions required depending upon the nature of media for social advertising.

Lastly, the present study relied on a convenience sample of undergraduate students who are not necessarily representative of the broader population. Future research should clearly aim to ensure that a broader and more representative sample is included.

To conclude advertising is a fascinating and provocative phenomenon. At the outset it is used by many advertisers for many purposes with many different possible effects. The present study however concentrated on the social side of advertising, where in the intents of such advertising ranged from altering behaviour to affecting the way people think about a particular social or economic position. The study concentrated on identifying the factors that could aid in making social advertisements effective and capable enough to change or alter the audience's behaviour. Accordingly five such factors viz. celebrity, fear appeals, clutter, medium and repetition were extensively studied for their impact. The findings of these factors would certainly aid in creating and promoting social advertisements that would ultimately impact its target in the desired way. Second very important aspect of the present research is 'youth' since it constitutes an important segment of our society. India everyday resolves and fabricates multitudinous problems and a vital fraction constitutes the problems of the youth. The youth today faces innumerable challenges on personal, social and economic fronts at local and global level and these issues need to be rightly identified and addressed without delay. There is a dire need to create an environment conducive for their physical and mental well being and development. Media is an important source of information for youth. Mass media with sustained use of effective social advertising can create an environment in which good health as well as education is pursued and reinforced amongst the youth. Social advertising can be an entertaining and educative tool for addressing their issues.

Unfortunately, in spite of resurgence in recent years, social advertising has received significantly less theoretical and applied research in comparison to profit-oriented advertising. It is also noticed potentials of social advertising to entertain and educate is seriously undermined. Social advertising can be persuasive and can lead to favourable attitudinal and behavioural change provided created and promoted efficiently. Academicians and researchers can contribute immensely by way of conducting meaningful and comprehensive research. Such dedicated and persistent efforts will certainly aid in constructing influential and result-oriented social advertising that can accomplish the larger goal of social welfare.

And finally to end with a futuristic quotation from author Isaac Asimov[1]:

"We must sell the world through the persuasion techniques developed by advertology, on the necessity of reducing population, of conserving and recycling the earth's resources, of exploiting space for energy."

---

[1] Sandage C. H., Fryburger Vernon and Rotzoll Kim, Advertising Theory and Practice, All India Traveller Book Seller, Delhi, 1987, p. 5.

BIBLIOGRAPHY

Books

- **Ackoff R. L.**, *The Design of Research*, University of Chicago Press, Chicago and London, 1953.
- **Allport Gordon W.**, "Attitudes," in C. A. Murchison (ed.), *A Handbook of Social Psychology*, Clark University Press, Worcester, MA, 1935.
- **Andearson Alan R.**, *Marketing Social Change: Changing Behaviour to Promote Health, Social Development and the Environment*, San Francisco, Jossey-Bass, 1995.
- **Arens William F. and Schaefer David**, *Essentials of Contemporary Advertising*, McGraw Hill, Irwin, 2006.
- **Backman Jules**, *Advertising and Competition*, New York University Press, New York, 1967.
- **Batra Rajeev, Myers John G. and Aaker David A.**, *Advertising Management*, 5th ed., Prentice Hall India, New Delhi, 2004.
- **Bauer Raymond A. and Greyser Stephen A.**, *Advertising in America: The Consumer View,* Harvard Business School, Division of Research, Boston, 1968.
- **Belch G. and Belch M.**, *Advertising and Promotion, An Integrated Marketing Communications Perspective,* 6th ed., Tata McGraw-Hill Publishing Company Limited, New Delhi, India, 2003.
- **Bergh B. G. V. and Katz H.**, *Advertising Principles*, NTC Business Books, Lincolnwood, Illinois, USA, 1999.
- **Bhandarkar P. L. and Wilkinson T. S.**, *Methodology and Techniques of Social Research*, 16th ed., Himalaya Publishing House, Mumbai, 2000.

- **Biel Alexander L.**, *Brand Equity and Advertising*, Editors David A. Aaker and Alexander L. Biel, Hillsdale, New Jersey, 1993.
- **Bogart Leo**, *Strategy in Advertising*, 2nd ed., NTC Business Books, Lincolnwood, Illinois, 1990.
- **Book Albert C. and Cary Norman D.**, *The Television Commercial: Creativity and Craftsmanship*, Decker Communication, New York, 1970.
- **Borden Neil H. and Marshall Martin V.**, *Advertising Management, Text and Cases*, D. B. Taraporewalla, Bombay, India, 1971.
- **Bordon Neil H.**, *The Economic Effects of Advertising*, Richard D. Irwin Inc., Chicago, 1942.
- **Bovee Courtland L., Thill John V., Dovel George P. and Wood Marian B.**, *Advertising Excellence*, International Edition, McGraw-Hill, Inc., USA, 1995.
- **Chouhan Meenakshi**, *Advertising: The Social AD Challenge*, Anmol Publications, New Delhi, 2002.
- **Chrystal and Lipsey**, *Economies for Business and Management*, Oxford University Press.
- **Chunawala S. A. and Sethia K. C.**, *Foundations of Advertising Theory and Practice*, Himalaya Publishing House, Mumbai, 2006.
- **Clow Kenneth E. and Baack Donald**, *Integrated Advertising, Promotion and Marketing Communications*, Pearson Education Inc., 2002.
- **Cohen Dorothy**, *Advertising*, Scott Foresman and Company, USA, 1988.
- **Das D. K. Lal**, *Designs of Social Research*, Rawat Publications, Jaipur, 2005.
- **Davar Rustom S., Davar Sohrab R. and Davar Nusli R.**, *Salesmanship and Publicity*, 16th ed., Vikas Publishing House Pvt. Ltd., New Delhi, India, 2006.

- **Dunn Watson S. and Barban Arnold M.**, *Advertising its Role in Modern Marketing*, 5th ed., Holt Saunders International Editions, Japan, 1982.
- **Folkerts Jean and Lacy Stephen**, *The Media in Your Life*, 3rd ed., Pearson Education Inc., 2005.
- **Garbett Thomas F.**, *Corporate Advertising*, McGraw-Hill, New York, 1981.
- **Hart Chris**, *Doing a Literature Review*, Sage Publications Ltd., London, 1998.
- **Jefkins Frank**, *Advertising*, Revised by Daniel Yadin, 4th ed., Pearson Education, Harlow, England, 2000.
- **Jethwaney J. and Jain S.**, *Advertising Management*, Oxford University Press, New Delhi, 2006.
- **Jha S. M.**, *Social Marketing*, 1st ed., Himalaya Publishing House, Mumbai, 1999.
- **Kaatz Ron**, *Advertising and Marketing Checklists*, 2nd ed., Lincolnwood, NTC Business Books, 1992.
- **Kazmi S. H. H. and Batra Satish K.**, *Advertising and Sales Promotions*, 2nd ed., Excel Books, New Delhi, India, 2004.
- **Keller Kevin L.**, *Strategic Brand Management*, 2nd ed., Pearson Education Inc., 2007.
- **Kothari C. R.**, *Research Methodology, Methods and Techniques*, 2nd ed., New Age International Publishers, New Delhi, India, 2004.
- **Kotler Philip and Eduardo Roberto L.**, *Social Marketing: Strategies for Changing Public Behaviour*, The Free Press, New York, 1989.
- **Kotler Philip and Keller Kevin Lane**, *Marketing Management*, 12th ed., Pearson Education, Inc., Delhi, 2006.
- **Kotler Philip**, *Marketing for Nonprofit Organisations*, Prentice Hall Inc., New Jersey, USA, 1975.

- **Kotler Philip, Roberto Ned and Lee Nancy**, *Social Marketing, Improving the Quality of Life*, Sage Publications, California, 2002.
- **Kotler Philips**, *Marketing for Non-Profit Organisations*, 2nd ed., Prentice Hall of India Private Ltd., New Delhi, India, 1985.
- **Krugman H. E.**, "The Learning of Consumer Likes, Preferences and Choices," in F. M. Bass, C. W. King and E. A. Pessemier (eds.), *Applications of the Sciences in Marketing Management*. New York, Wiley, 1968.
- **Kundra Shipra**, *Introduction to Advertising and Public Relations*, 1st ed., Anmol Publications, New Delhi, 2005.
- **Lazarsfeld Paul F. and Merton Robert K.**, "Mass communication, Popular Taste and Organised Social Action," in *Mass Communications*, William Schramm, ed. Urbana, University of Illinois Press, 1949.
- **Leacock Stephen B.**, '*The Perfect Salesman*,' The Garden of Folly, 1924.
- **Loudon David L. and Bitta Albert J. Della**, *Consumer Behaviour*, 4th ed., Tata McGraw Hill, New Delhi, India, 2002.
- **Manendra Mohan**, *Advertising Management, Concepts and Cases*, 19th reprint, Tata McGraw-Hill Publishing Co. Ltd., New Delhi, India, 2004.
- **Marconi Joe**, *Marketing and Branding*, Tata McGraw Hill Edition.
- **Mcluhan Marshall**, *Understanding Media: The Extensions of Man*, McGraw Hill, New York, 1966.
- **Mukund A.**, *Celebrity Endorsement, Trends and Cases*, The ICFAI University Press, Hyderabad.
- **Nachmias D. and Nachmias C.**, *Research Methods in the Social Sciences*, New York, St. Martins Press, 1981.

- **Neelamegham S.**, *Marketing in India, Cases and Readings*, Vikas Publishing House Private Ltd., New Delhi, India, 2006.
- **Percy Larry, Rossiter John R. and Elliott Richard**, *Strategic Advertising Management*, 2001.
- **Pope Daniel**, *The Making of Modern Advertising*, Basic
- **Potter David**, *People of Plenty,* University of Chicago Press, Chicago, 1954.
- **Rathore B. S.**, *Advertising Management*, 1st ed., Himalaya Publishing House, Mumbai, 2003.
- **Ray Michael L.** et al., "Marketing Communications and the Hierarchy of Effects," in P. Clarke (ed.), *New Models for Communications Research*, Sage Publications, Beverly Hills, CA, 1973.
- **Rudolph H.**, *Attention and Interest Factors in Advertising,* Printer's Ink, New York, 1947.
- **Sandage C. H.**, "Using Advertising to Implement the Concept of Freedom of Speech," in *The Role of Advertising*, editors, C. H. Sandage and V. Fryburger, Homewood, Rich
- **Sandage C. H., Fryburger Vernon and Rotzoll Kim**, *Advertising Theory and Practice*, All India Travellers Book Seller, Delhi, 1987.
- **Sawyer Alan G.**, "The Effects of Repetitions: Conclusions and Suggestions About Experimental Laboratory Research," in G. David Hughes and Michael L. Ray (eds.), *Buyer/ Consumer Information Processing*, The University of North Carolina Press, Chapel Hill, 1974.
- **Schiffman Leon G. and Kanuk Leslie Lazar**, *Consumer Behaviour,* 6th ed., Prentice Hall of India Private Limited, New Delhi, India, 2000.

- **Sharma S. and Singh R.**, *Advertising Planning and Implementation*, Prentice Hall of India Private Ltd., New Delhi, India, 2006.
- **Sinclair John**, *Advertising Incorporated*, Croom Helm, London, 1987.
- **Stigler George J.**, *The Intellectual and the Market Place*, The Free Press, New York, 1963.
- **Surmanek Jim**, *Media Planning: A Practical Guide*, NTC Business Books, Lincolnwood, Illinois, 1986.
- **Thompson Walter J**, *Agency Business Pitch* (1925), quoted in Jackson Lears, *Fables of Abundance: A Cultural History of Advertising in Amercia*, BasicBooks, New York, 1994.
- **Wasem George**, *Marketing in Non-profit Organisation*, editor Patrick Montana, Amacom a Division of American Marketing Associations, 1978.
- **Wells William, Moriarty Sandra and Burnett John**, *Advertising, Principles and Practice*, 7th ed., Pearson Education Inc., 2006.
- **Wright J. S., Winter W. L. and Jr. Zeigler S. K.**, *Advertising*, 5th ed., Tata McGraw Hill Publishing, New Delhi, 1983.

Journals

- "Advertising Increasing in 'Non Commercial' uses," Advertising Age, April 30, 1980, pp. 34-38.
- **Alwitt Linda F. and Prabhakar Parul R.**, "Identifying Who Dislikes Television Advertising: Not by Demographics Alone," Journal of Advertising Research, Vol. 32, No. 5, 1992, pp. 30-42.
- **Atkin Charles and Block Martin**, "Effectiveness of Celebrity Endorsers," Journal of Advertising Research 23, February-March, 1983, pp. 57-61.

- **Berman Ronald**, "Advertising and Social Change," Advertising Age, April 30, 1980, p. 24.
- **Byrne A, Whitehead M. and Breen S.**, "The Naked Truth of Celebrity Endorsement," British Food Journal, 105 (4/5), 2003, pp. 288-296.
- **Cronin John J.**, "In-home Observations of Commercial Zapping Behaviour," Journal of Current Issues and Research in Advertising, Vol. 17, No. 2, Fall 1995, pp. 69-75.
- **Deb Pradip Kumar**, "Marketing Social Change and Community Development," Advertising Express, October 2008, The ICFAI University Press, pp. 25-27.
- **Erdogan B. Z., Baker M. J. and Tagg S.**, "Selecting Celebrity Endorsers: The Practitioner's Perspective," Journal of Advertising Research, 41, May-June 2001, pp. 39-48.
- **Fireworker R. B. and Friedman H. H.**, "The Effects of Endorsements on Product Evaluation," Decision Sciences, 8, 1977, pp. 576-583.
- **Fox Karen F. A. and Kotler Philip**, "The Marketing of Social Causes: The First 10 years," Journal of Marketing, Vol. 44, 1980, pp. 24-33.
- **Friedman H. H. and Friedman L.**, "Endorser Effectiveness by Product Type," Journal of Advertising Research, 19(5), 1979, pp. 63-71.
- **Hawkins Scott A. and Hoch Stephen J.**, "Low Involvement Learning: Memory Without Involvement," Journal of Consumer Research, 19, September 1990, pp. 160-171.
- **Heeter Carrie and Greenberg Bradley S.**, "Profiling the Zappers," Journal of Advertising Research, April/May 1985, pp. 9-15.

- **Henthorne Tony L., LaTour Michael S. and Natarajan Rajan**, "Fear Appeals in Print Advertising, An analysis of Arousal and Ad Response," Journal of Advertising, 22, No. 2, June 1983, pp. 59-69.
- **Holton Richard**, "How Advertising Achieved Respectability Among Economists, or Anyhow, They've Heard of It," Advertising Age, April 30, 1980, p. 56.
- **Janis I. and Feshbach S.**, "Effects of Fear-Arousing Communications," Journal of Abnormal and Social Psychology, 48, 1953, pp. 78-92.
- **K. Suresh**, "Celebrities and Public Service Advertising," Advertising Express, March 2009, pp. 31-34.
- **Kassarjian Harold H.**, "Applications of Consumer Behaviour to the Field of Advertising," Journal of Advertising, Vol. 3, No. 3(1974), p. 11.
- **Kirmani Amna and Wright Peter**, "Money Talks: Perceived Advertising Expense and Expected Product Quality," Journal of Consumer Research, 16, December 1989, pp. 344-53.
- **Kotler Philip and Zaltman Gerald**, "Social Marketing: An Approach to Planned Social Change," Journal of Marketing, Vol. 35, July 1971, pp. 3-12.
- **Krishna S. Jaya and Padmaja R.**, "Marketing Social Change," Marketing Mastermind, Vol. VIII, Issue 10, October 2008, pp. 45-49.
- **Krishnan Uma,** "Indian Advertisements, a Developmental History," Advertising Express, The ICFAI University Press, India, October 2008, pp. 33-35.
- **Krugman H. E.**, "The Impact of Television Advertising: Learning Without Involvement," Public Opinion Quarterly, 29, 1965, pp. 353.

- **Kunst-Wilson W. R. and Zajonc R. B.**, "Affective Discrimination of Stimuli That Can Not Be Recognised," Science, 207, February 1980, pp. 557-558.
- **Lacter Mark**, "Television Commercial Industry Fights Back," San Francisco Chronicle, February 11, 1983, p. 50.
- **Lex van Meurs**, "Zapp ! A Study on Switching Behaviour During Commercial Breaks," Journal of Advertising Research, 38 (1), (January/February 1998), pp. 43-53.
- **Madison Cathy**, "Researchers Work Advertising into an Emotional State," Adweek, November 5, 1990, p. 30.
- **McCracken Grant**, "Who Is the Celebrity Endorser? Cultural Foundations of the Endorsement Process," Journal of Consumer Research, 16 (3), 1989, pp. 310-321.
- **McGuire William J.**, "The Nature of Attitudes and Attitude Change," in Handbook of Social Psychology, 2nd ed., G. Lindzey and E. Aronson (eds.), Addison-Wesley, Cambridge, 1969.
- **McSherry John**, "The Current Scope of Channel Switching," Marketing and Media Decisions, June, 1985.
- **Mehta Abhilasha**, "Advertising Attitudes and Advertising Effectiveness," Journal of Advertising Research, 40 No. 3, May-June 2000, pp. 67-72.
- **Melton A. W.**, "The Situation with Respect to the Spacing of Repetitions and Memory," Journal of Verbal Learning and Verbal Behaviour, 9 (1970), pp. 596-606.
- **Michèle Dion**, "Is Fear Really Persuasive, The Case of Antismoking Advertisement for Young Adults," Communication Studies, Roskilde University, Spring 2005.
- **Mittal Banwari**, "Public Assessment of TV Advertising: Faint Praise and Harsh Criticism," Journal of Advertising Research, Vol. 34, No. 1, 1994, pp. 35-53.

- **Murphy Claire**, "Stars Brought Down to Earth in Television Ads Research," Marketing, January, 1998, p. 1.
- **Muruganantham G. and Dr. Kaliyamoorthy S.**, Indian Journal of Marketing, December 2006, pp. 20-24.
- **Nath Sirisha P.**, "Television and Its Impact on Children," Advertising Express, The ICFAI University Press, January 2008, pp. 52-58.
- **Ohanion Roobina**, "The Impact of Celebrity Spokespersons Perceived Image on Consumers' Intention to Purchase," Journal of Advertising Research, 31 (1), February-March 1991, pp. 46-54.
- **Olney T. J., Holbrook Morris and Batra Rajeev**, "Consumer Responses to Advertising: The Effects of Ad Content, Emotions and Attitude on Viewing Time," Journal of Consumer Research, March, 1991.
- **Pollay Richard W.**, "The Distorted Mirror: Reflections on the Unintended Consequences of Advertising," Journal of Marketing, 50, April 1986, pp. 18-36.
- **Rao Narsimha A. V.**, "Advertisements, Misrepresentations and Remedies," Advertising Express, The ICFAI University Press, India, August 2005, pp. 71-75.
- **Ray Michael L. and Wilkie William L.**, "Fear: The Potential of an Appeal Neglected by Marketing," Journal of Marketing, 32, January 1970, pp. 54-62.
- **Rosen T. John, Terry Nathaniel S. and Leventhal Howard**, "The Role of Esteem and Coping in Response to a Threat Communication," Journal of Research in Personality, 16 Spring, 1983, pp. 90-110.
- **Rotfeld Herbert J.**, "The Textbook Effect: Conventional Wisdom, Myth and Error in Marketing," Journal of Marketing, 64, April 2000, pp. 122-27.

✍ **Ruiter, Robert A. C., Abraham C. and Kok G.**, "Scary Warnings and Rational Precautions: A Review of the Psychology of Fear Appeals," Psychology and Health, Vol. 16, 2001, pp. 613-630.

✍ **Saiganesh S., Rajendhiran N and Asha P.**, "Likeability Matters in Commercials," Advertising Express, The ICFAI University Press, India, October 2008, pp. 39-41.

✍ **Scory Michael and Repka Shelley**, "The Description of Social, Cause-Related Marketing and Corporate Social Responsibility," Journal of the Canadian Institute of Marketing, Volume 7, Issue 2, Spring 2004, pp. 1-3.

✍ **Shankar Smita**, "Celebrity Endorsements: Is It the Only Survival Recipe for Marketers?," Indian Journal of Marketing, October 2006, pp. 3-5.

✍ **Stewart David W.**, "Measures, Methods and Models in Advertising Research," Journal of Advertising, 29, No. 3, 1989, pp. 54-60.

✍ **Strenthal Brian and Craig Samuel C.**, "Fear Appeals Revisited and Revised," Journal of Consumer Research, 1, December 1974, pp. 22-34.

✍ **Tanner John F., Hunt Jr., James B. and Eppright David R.**, "Protection Motivation Model: A Normative Mode of Fear Appeals," Journal of Marketing, 55, July 1991, pp. 36-45.

✍ **Till B. D.**, "Using Celebrity Endorsers Effectively: Lessons from Associative Learning." Journal of Product and Brand Management, 7(5), 1998, pp. 400-409.

✍ **Till Brian D. and Shimp Terence A.**, "Endorsers in Advertising: The Case of Negative Celebrity Information," Journal of Advertising Research, 27(1), Spring 1998, pp. 67-82.

✍ **Tripp C., Jensen T. D. and Carlson L.**, "The Effects of Multiple Product Endorsements by Celebrities on

Consumers' Attitudes and Intentions," Journal of Consumer Research, 20, March 1994, pp. 535-47.

- **Walsh Doris**, "Safe Sex in Advertising," American Demographics, April 1994.
- **Webb Peter H. and Ray Michael L.**, "Effects of TV Clutter," Journal of Advertising Research, 19, June 1979, pp. 7-12.
- **Webb Peter H.**, "Consumer Initial Processing in a Difficult Media Environment," Journal of Consumer Research, 6 (December 1979), pp. 225-236.
- **Weibe G. D.**, "Merchandising Commodities and Citizenship on Television," Public Opinion Quarterly, Vol. 1b, Oxford University Press, USA, (Winter, 1951-52), p. 679.
- **Zajonc R. B.**, "Feeling and Thinking: Preferences Need No Inferences," American Psychologist, 35, 1980, pp. 151-175.

Magazines

- "Over 94000 Join India Today Group's Movement Against Terror," India Today, December 13, 2008.
- Business Week, November 23, 1987, p. 38.
- **Subramanian Anusha**, "Changing Face of Social Advertising in India," Business Today, February 2007.

Newspapers

- "Aamir Khan to be Face of Incredible India," The Times of India, August 8, 2008.
- "Do Celebs Help a Cause?," The Times of India, April 20, 2006.
- "Moves That Tweak Attitudes," Financial Express, September 30, 2007.
- "Shahrukh May Campaign Against Smoking — **Health** Ministry Keen to Rope in Bollywood Star," Business Line, The Hindu, November 15, 2005.

- **Banerjee Rajeev and Irani Delshad**, "Bharat Nirman Vs. India Shinning," Brand Equity, The Economic Times, February 4, 2009.
- **Barnum P. T.**, "And in the Center Ring….," Pennsylvania Gazetter, May 1993.
- **Bosu Sujoy**, "Social Ads: The Way to a Consumer's Heart," The Times of India, August 13, 2001.
- **Guram Alice**, "Social Ads From India Make It To London Festival," Indian Express, November 15, 1998.
- **Jaisinghani Bella**, "The Hysteria of Activism," The Times of India, December 3, 2006.
- **Joshi Sangita**, "Face Value," The Hindu, April 24, 2003.
- **Malhotra Pervin**, "Ad Light on Problems That Concern Us," The Telegraph, Calcutta, India, October 11, 2007.
- **Mehra Priyanka**, "Ads With Social Pitch Pay More," Hindustan Times, Mint, June 4, 2007.
- **Mehra Priyanka**, "Riding on Discounted Rates, Govt Ads Rule TV," Hindustan Times, Mint, August 21, 2008.
- **Pande Bhanu and Sharma Amit**, "The Year of Mass Awareness, Assertion and Action," The Economic Times, December 25, 2008.
- **Paul Josy**, "Socially Active Advertising Idea on a High," The Economic Times, January 1, 2008.
- **Quraishi S. Y.**, "Cave of Flickering Shadows," The Indian Express, October 07, 2008.
- **Sen Shunu**, "In Society's Interest," Business Line's Catalyst, August 31, 2001.
- **Shahane Devayani**, "Social Advertising: Don't Condone It, CONDOM It," The Times of India, September 6, 2001.
- **Sharma Sanchita**, "Big B is Social Ad Superstar," Hindustan Times, New Delhi, January 03, 2008.

- **Turakhia Saurabh**, "Tata Tea Brews Up Big Bang Social Advertising Campaign," Hindustan Times, November 13, 2007.
- **Vyas Shuchi**, "Chief Endorsement Officer," Brand Equity, The Economic Times, February 21, 2007.

Reports

- "Doordarshan's Role in Socio-economic Development," Press Information Bureau, Government of India, Ministry of Information and Broadcasting, August 14, 2007.
- Cancer Patients Aid Association, Monthly Report, December 2000.
- DAVP Annual Report 2006-2007.

Websites

@ **www.afaqs.com**, Sumanto Chattopadhyay, "Some of the Most Outstanding Cannes Winners Were in the Social Categories : Cannes Special," June 23, 2003.

@ **www.agencyfaqs.com**, Joshi Devina, "What Drives Public Service Campaigns – Conscience, Money or Awards?," July 25, 2005.

@ **www.agencyfaqs.com**, Shatrujeet N., "Cannes 2003: Implications for India - Part II," July 01, 2003.

@ **www.agencyfaqs.com**, Shatrujeet N., "Cannes 2004: India's Showing Draws Mixed Response," June 28, 2004.

@ **www.agencyfaqs.com**. "Aaj Tak Bags Four RAPA awards."

@ **www.ddindia.gov.in**, "A Model to Fund Public Service Broadcasting."

@ **www.exchange4media.com**, Bedi Puneet Bahri, "Attack Aftermath: Media Houses Initiate Fightback Against Terror," December 04, 2008.

@ **www.indiantelevision.com**, Bhattacharyya Anushree, "Campaigning Against Terror," December 26, 2008.

@ **www.infochangeindia.org.**

@ **www.intentblog.com**, Rahul Bose, May 02, 2006.

@ **www.jaagore.com.**

@ **www.rediff.com**, "New Face of Social Advertising," November 29, 2005.

@ **www.startv.com**, Heroes Project, Star Care.

@ **www.un.org**, "United Nations Public Information Department, Global Public Relations Association to Honour Publicity Campaign on Condom Use for Safe Sex, Family Planning," Press Release, Note No. 6096, August 20, 2007.

@ **www.wikipedia.org.**

@ **www.yuva.nic.in**, "Threat to Youth From AIDS in India.'

@ **www.zeetelevision.com**

INDEX